WHAT HAPPENED TO NETAJI?

Anuj Dhar

Vitastaa

Let Knowledge Spread

Published by
Renu Kaul Verma
Vitastaa Publishing Pvt Ltd
2/15, Ansari Road, Daryaganj
New Delhi - 110 002
info@vitastapublishing.com

ISBN 978-93-82711-88-9
© Anuj Dhar
First Edition 2016
4th Reprint 2021
MRP ₹425

Cover designed by Priyanshu Banerjee
Typeset by Vit Press
Printed by Vikas Computer and Printers

Contents

Acknowledgements

I would like to thank my publisher Renu Kaul Verma, my editor Papri Sri Raman for her competent editing and Labanya and Ram Kumar, Vitastaa's production team.

Prologue

A bombshell of sorts exploded on India's political landscape in April 2015. Stories about Subhas Chandra Bose began appearing across the media— print, electronic and digital. All major national channels in their prime time shows beamed heated discussions which invariably centered around the fate of Netaji. There was considerable prime time focus on the role of the Congress party and the country's first Prime Minister, Jawaharlal Nehru.

Nothing like this had ever happened in the last seventy years.

Those who followed the stories closely knew that this media onslaught started with a cover story in India's No 1 magazine *India Today*.

The magazine reported that certain declassified files in New Delhi's National Archives showed how the government of Jawaharlal Nehru had spied on the nephews of Netaji—brothers Amiya Nath Bose and Sisir Bose—for nearly two decades. The sophisticated manner in which this snooping was carried out made Richard 'Tricky Dick' Nixon's attempts to put his political opponents under surveillance look amateurish.

However, the real import of the Bose family spying scandal was aptly captured by senior journalist and BJP national spokesperson M J Akbar, who said that there could be 'only one reasonable explanation for this long surveillance'.

'The government was not sure whether Bose was dead, and thought that if he were alive he would be in some form of communication with his family in Calcutta.'

The *India Today* exposition was followed by further revelations in *Mumbai Mirror* and *DNA*. 'India's first government, led by Nehru and Patel, not only authorised snooping on the extended family of Subhas Chandra Bose well after Independence, but "on many other ex-Indian National Army veterans", including prominent Mumbaikars who served as union and state ministers', wrote Shekhar Krishnan in the *Mumbai Mirror*.

'The internet and Google were unheard of. Edward Snowden was yet to be born. India as a free country was barely two years old and extremely poor. Yet the Jawaharlal Nehru government was running a sophisticated interception mechanism that targeted the kin of Subhas Chandra Bose', wrote Sai Manish in the *DNA*.

Caught unaware by the shocking disclosures, both top political parties of India, the Bharatiya Janata Party and the Congress, groped for proper words. On 10 April, a rattled Congress party issued a statement alleging that 'a systematic and sinister propaganda of selective leaks and half-truths has been unleashed by the current BJP government to malign national icons'.

The front page story in *The Times of India* on 12 April 2015 enlarged the ambit of the controversy by reporting that there was a signed note demonstrating that Nehru had himself sought to track Amiya Nath's movements in Japan. What was worse, months after Independence in 1947, information pertaining to Bose was shared by the 'free' Indian government with the British intelligence.

This writer was identified in the *Times* story as the source of the information. Earlier, in a story in *The Mail Today* of the *India Today* group, it was mentioned that I had 'first spotted the files at the National Archives'.

Participating in the Newshour by Arnab Goswami, India's most watched news programme on No 1 channel *Times Now*, I voluntarily owned up my catalytic role in the entire controversy.

Meanwhile, the Congress continued to float conspiracy theories—something that the party has been really good at.

Congress spokesperson Sanjay Jha went on to repeat on *Times Now* that the documents represented 'selective leaks made by the Bharatiya Janata Party'.

This was followed by a statement issued on 13 April by senior Congress leader and former minister Anand Sharma, who repeated the Congress line that the Narendra Modi government was indulging in 'motivated news plants, based on selective and mischievous leaks...with the sole aim of diverting the attention of people from miserable performance, betrayal of mandate and failed promises'.

The truth was nothing like that. The coming into the public domain of the snooping files was a triumph of the Right to Information Act enacted by the previous Congress regime, and the long-lasting spirited efforts put in by a group of Netaji admirers comprising this writer and friends. It was we who had prepared the conducive ground and then dropped this bombshell. Had it not been for the tragic earthquake in Nepal, which all of sudden diverted the media focus from the Netaji-related issues, rumblings set off by this megapolitical explosion would have brought down decades-long institutional opposition to resolving the Netaji mystery—arguably modern India's longest-running controversy.

More than ten years ago, Sayantan Dasgupta, Sreejith Panickar, Chandrachur Ghose, Vishal Sharma and I had got together on an internet chat room and decided to do something. Our focus was to do something about the controversy surrounding Netaji's fate, and also something which would keep his memories alive. From New Delhi, Sayantan Dasgupta suggested that something needed to be done on the ground by forming a group. From Thiruvananthapuram, Sreejith Panicker came up with its name—Mission Netaji.

In the fullness of time, Mission Netaji came to include many more—Abhishek Singh, Saurabh Garai, Saibal Majumdar, Koushik Banerjee (all in Kolkata), Adheer Som (Lucknow), Jayanta Dutta Majumdar (Hong Kong), Anindya Ghosh (Australia), Diptasya Jash (Singapore), Abhishek Bose (United States) and Anirban Mukhopadhya (United Kingdom), to name some.

By 2005, I had already done a book on the Netaji mystery. But despite some scattered praises, I had become disillusioned for not having succeeded in creating enough interest about it, which was a prerequisite to resolve the controversy.

Chandrchur Ghose, whose grandfather had known and worked with Netaji, joined us while he was living in the UK. When he moved to New Delhi, our brainstorming sessions began formulating an action plan to carry forward our work.

The turning point came in May 2006, with the Congress-led government dismissing the report of the Justice Mukherjee Commission of Inquiry without giving any reason in the Action Taken Report tabled in Parliament. Overturning the official view upheld by most historians and two previous panels set up during Congress regimes, Manoj Kumar Mukherjee, a former Supreme Court judge, had concluded that the story of Netaji's death in an air crash was actually a smokescreen deliberately set up to obfuscate the trail of his escape towards Soviet Russia.

Prompted by Chandrachur's idea, we decided to take recourse to the then newly-enacted Right to Information Act.

So, barely a month after the rejection of the Mukherjee Commission report by then Home Minister Shivraj Patil, who had upheld reports of previous inquiries set up during the Congress era, we filed an RTI application in Sayantan's name. We sought from the Ministry of Home Affairs the 'authenticated copies of documents used as exhibits by the Shah Nawaz Khan and GD Khosla panels', set up during the days of Nehru and Indira Gandhi, under public pressure.

Put in other words, the ministry's bluff was called. The Special Officer on Duty, who handled our RTI request, wasted no time in telling us that it could not be 'acceded to' for reasons covered by section 8(1) of the RTI Act. This was the section empowering the government not to part with security-classified information.

After receiving this point-blank refusal, we complained to the Central Information Commission (CIC). Information Commissioner AN Tiwari was the adjudicator. In the first hearing, the ministry officials asserted that they did not know of any such exhibits; because unlike the Mukherjee report, the previous two had not appended any such lists. Obviously, Shah Nawaz and GD Khosla were not on the same page as MK Mukherjee over transparency.

Anyhow, round one went to the MHA officials. Noting that 'the matter was quite old and the institutional memory was quite blurred', Tiwari directed us to seek specific documents. It was a tough task, considering that no details of the exhibits were available anywhere in any archive or library.

But I had my sources. So, before the next hearing, we were able to give the ministry's memory a booster. A copy of a classified record, listing out 202 documents used as exhibits by the Khosla Commission, was furnished along with a revised application seeking release of all these documents. 'Where did you get this list from?' the ministry officials protested at the start of the next hearing. It was of no use; the tables had been turned on them. Tiwari

Page 4 - Sketch drawn by Mr. K. Saksi of Taihoku Airport - 1945 Tokyo on 15.4.1971.

Re-interrogation of Capt. Habib-ur-Rehman C&DIC(I) B-1269

Page 6 - Statement dated 30.11.1964 containing photograph of Mongolian parliamentary delegation - submitted by Shri Nikunja Bihari Haolder.

Page 1 - Historical Potsdam Agreement.   3

ITEM 8 - Extract from German Military   8 Intelligence (photostat copy)

- U.S.A. - Office of the strategic   14 service Washington - Bose Journey to the FAR EAST.

Page 115 - Military HQ papers Far East   15 Memorandum by the Director of Intelligence dealing with the statement by Mr. Gandhi 'Bose Legend'

Page 117 - Diaries of Supreme Allied   19 & 33 Commander South East Asia in W.O. Class No. 1972 - (Mountbatten)

Document obtained in public interest

directed the ministry to release the 202 documents specified by us. He wondered why the government was keeping the Netaji-related records secret in the first place. 'Why don't you send them to the National Archives?' he asked. He got the answer by the year end.

A 'secret' letter from the Home Secretary, a friend of his, stated that the 'matter had been considered carefully at the highest level in the Ministry'. Some records related to Netaji's fate were deemed to be 'sensitive in nature', the letter said. The disclosure of some of them, in the Home Secretary's estimate, was most likely to 'lead to a serious law and order problem in the country, especially in West Bengal'.

This was too much for Tiwari to bear. He transferred the matter, to be heard by the full Bench of the Commission in an extraordinary session. On 5 June 2007, the full Bench of the CIC, comprising Chief Information Commissioner Wajahat Habibullah and Information Commissioners OP Kejariwal, Padma Balasubramanian, MM Ansari and AN Tiwari—who succeeded Habibullah as the chief—hammered home that the matter was of 'wide public concern and, therefore, of national importance'.

The Ministry officials agreed because there was no running away from it. They admitted, to the utter shock of the Information Commissioners, that apart from the records sought by us, the Home Ministry had in its possession Netaji-related records 'running into 70,000 pages'. The officials repeated that some of these documents were 'top secret in nature and may lead to chaos in the country if disclosed'.

There were heated exchanges before the Commission. From our side, Chandrachur, Sayantan, I and Vishal Sharma, Mission Netaji's youngest member at that time, countered the arguments given by the officials. The Commission took our side. In its decision favouring us, it directed the MHA to release 202 records to us and even recommended that all those

70,000 pages in the Home Ministry's custody should be sent to the National Archives. 'By doing so, the MHA would not only be discharging its legal duties and rendering an essential service to a public cause, it may finally help resolve an unsolved mystery of independent India', the Commission's landmark decision read.

As conceded by the MHA officials before the Commission—that 'the decision concerning disclosure has to be taken at the highest level'— in late September-November 2007, Home Minister Shivraj Patil took the matter of the 202 records to the Cabinet Committee on Political Affairs. The CCPA decided in favour of the release because it was felt, as reported in *Hindustan Times*, 'the worst that the Congress-led coalition government may have to face was a controversy that would die a natural death'.

But despite this highest-level decision, out of 202 only 91 exhibits were eventually released by the MHA to us. One paper—a note by Prime Minister Jawaharlal Nehru—remained classified. There was no word about the rest 110—including Home, Foreign Ministry records/files, letters from previous Home Ministers, High Commissioners, the government of Taiwan and Intelligence Bureau Director; a report on the INA treasure, said to have been lost along with Bose and a memo from the then Director of Military Intelligence about Mahatma Gandhi's view on the matter.

The matter was further pursued rather vigorously by Chandrachur, by way of another RTI request. Eventually, after six years of tug of war, he finally managed to compel the ministry to declassify a chunk from their 70,000-page cache. And these pages, roughly 10,000, were then declassified and sent to the National Archives. The still-secret PMO file No 915/11/C/2/2009-Pol deals with the transfer of these records.

The records eventually reached the archives in 2012 and in November 2014, were opened to researchers. I visited the National Archive in December. I spotted among the released documents, the photocopies of two West Bengal Intelligence Branch files on Netaji's nephews, Amiya Nath Bose and Sisir Bose. It was evident that these copies had reached the archive due to an oversight, as the original files, along with many others remained locked up in a secret locker in Kolkata at that time.

As I flipped through the files, the Watergate scandal of the US came to mind. What I was seeing was far worse than that. Without wasting much time, I wrote about what I had discovered in my online column in *Swarajya* and then on the *Daily O*, which belonged to the *India Today* group. This was how the top editors at the magazine came to know about the files. Sandeep Unnithan, Deputy Editor of the magazine and ace journalist with lot of experience in covering matters related to security and intelligence, contacted me. He went on to do a detailed, insightful cover story, which imploded the Netaji issue like never before.

And so, today, we are witnessing a never-before surge in interest in the Netaji mystery. More and more Indians—especially the young, in all nooks and corners of the world—are giving vent to their strong yearning for the truth. Since April 2015, I have personally sensed it across India and the United Kingdom, where NRIs and PIOs at Cambridge and London Business School (picture) heard my talks with rapt attention.

In the centre of the eye of this political storm in the making is our Prime Minister. Narendra Modi finds himself bound to the promise the BJP made to the people of India prior to elections—that once the party is in power, the Netaji mystery would be unveiled. The BJP came to make that promise in the first place due to the efforts of Mission Netaji, backed by the family of Subhas Chandra Bose.

On 9 May, Prime Minister Modi met members of the Bose family, led by family spokesperson Chandra Kumar Bose, in Kolkata and made heart-warming statements that had never been made by any Prime Minister before. Chandra Kumar Bose, accompanied by his wife Usha, also presented the PM with the copy of this writer's bestselling book *India's Biggest Cover-up* (2012) describing it as the best-ever book on the Netaji mystery.

The Prime Minister told Chandra Bose that it was 'the country's responsibility to resolve the mystery around Netaji's disappearance'.

But even after such encouraging words, no action was taken by the PMO to release the files. And, after a lull, on 12 September 2015 came this big story:

Mamata pips Modi on secret Netaji files, to declassify 64

'Want People To Know Truth About Our Icon'

TIMES NEWS NETWORK

Kolkata: In the most significant step yet in unravelling the Netaji mystery, chief minister Mamata Banerjee on Friday announced that the Bengal government would make public all its files on Subhas Chandra Bose. A masterstroke, it will put pressure on PM Narendra Modi to come good on his promise to declassify secret files held by the Centre.

"We want people to know about the Netaji incident. He is our national icon. What the Centre will do is their matter. For our part, we have decided to place all files that are with the state government in public domain," the CM said at the secretariat on Friday, adding that 64 files are being declassified.

Nine of these were with the State Intelligence Bureau. Nothing is known about the other 55. Mamata said they surfaced during a search by the home secretary and chief secretary earlier this year. The status report of Justice Mukherjee Commission had referred to these files earlier. All 64 files will be placed for public viewing at the Police Museum near Rajabazar in north Kolkata.

The first batch of Netaji files to be digitized were those from the period 1937 to 1947, the CM said. There are several files from 1948 to 1968, including intelligence reports on surveillance over Netaji's kin. Contents from two of these files became public this April, trig-

BONANZA FOR RESEARCHERS

➤ 64 files to be declassified, 9 of these with **State Intelligence Bureau**. No clarity on the remaining 55

➤ Some of the files are from 1937 to 1947 and others from 1948 to 1968

➤ Some of the files contain details of **snooping on Netaji kin** and an ascetic called **Shaulmari**

➤ Baba, and correspondence between PM **Nehru** and Bengal CM **BC Roy** on the fate of the ashes at Tokyo's Renkoji temple

➤ All 64 files will be placed for public viewing at the **Police Museum near Rajabazar** in north Kolkata

gering a sensation and giving credence to the belief that Netaji was alive till then.

Mamata's announcement created a stir on Friday afternoon. Members of the Bose family and activists campaigning for declassification of Netaji files congratulated Mamata for "showing the way" while Modi continues to dither on opening up the 130-odd files lying with the PMO, and home and external affairs ministries. "This is a huge development, a big victory for everyone who has been fighting for the truth on Netaji and de-

> This is a huge development, a big victory for everyone who has been fighting for the truth on Netaji and demanding declassification.. We can now include Mamata in our team and put pressure on Modi to make public the files that are with the Centre
>
> **Chitra Bose** | NETAJI'S NIECE

manding declassification. We can now include Mamata in our team and put pressure on Modi to make public the files that are with the Centre," said Netaji's niece and Sarat Bose's daughter Chitra.

Rajeev Sarkar, chief functionary officer of NGO India's Smile that has been fighting a legal battle on declassification of the files, remarked: "If the Bengal government can do it, why can't the Modi government? This is a dynamic step by Mamata."

▶ '**Kin should scan files**', P 4

The Times of India

Mindful that the declassification demand was picking up steam, and perhaps worried that the Modi government was rumoured to be contemplating releasing the Bose files before next elections in Bengal, West Bengal Chief Minister Mamata Banerjee surprised everyone by her momentous decision. 'We know Netaji's date of birth but we have no idea about his demise. People deserve to know about his last days', she said.

For the record, this writer had in November 2013 first filed an RTI application with the Bengal government, seeking details of the classified Netaji files.

GOVERNMENT OF WEST BENGAL
HOME DEPARTMENT, RTI CELL,
'NABANNA', 4th FLOOR, HRBC BUILDINGS,
325, SARAT CHATTERJEE ROAD, HOWRAH-711102.

From : Shri C.C.Guha, IAS
       SPIO & Joint Secretary.

To   : 1. Shri L.K.Das,
          Assistant Secretary,
          General Establishment Branch, Home Department.
       2. Shri A.Samanta,
          Assistant Secretary, Secret Cell, Internal Security Branch,
          Home Department.
       3. Shri B.Pandit,
          Assistant Secretary, Police Branch, Home Department.

No.681-H (RTI)/1A-362/13   Dated, Howrah the 17th day of June, 2014.

Subject: Information sought for by Shri Anuj Dhar.

In continuation of this department's Memo No.1973 (3)-H (RTI) dated-25/11/2013 the undersigned is sending herewith a copy of the reminder petition dated-03/06/2014 received from Shri Anuj Dhar and is again requesting him to send the information as requested vide this department's letter no.1973 (3)-H (RTI) dated-25/11/2013 to this department's at the earliest for onward transmission of the same to the applicant.

On 17 September, Mamata gave a massive boost to the declassification demand by releasing 64 classified files. Their reading convinced the chief minister that Bose had perhaps not died in 1945 and the earlier snooping reports were correct.

Speaking in short, measured sentences, Mamata requested the central government to release its lot of secret files. 'In 70 years, the mystery of Netaji's disappearance has not been solved. It is unfortunate. How long you can keep it under secrecy', she said.

The sensational disclosure received massive public attention, reflected in yet another round of unprecedented media coverage. The Bose family began getting calls from the PMO. Within two days, Prime Minister Narendra Modi announced that he was going to meet the delegation led by the family members in October.

As we await and gear up for what might eventually lead to India's moment of truth, for a prerequisite, this new book takes my readers on an insightful tour of the various fascinating aspects of the Netaji mystery. It contains retrospectives that were not possible earlier. Presented for your consideration, here is the most incisive and definitive account of what really happened to Subhas Chandra Bose.

Having brought about a paradigm shift in how today's India sees the Netaji mystery, I wanted to make available a reader-friendly, concise and no-holds-barred account covering all arcane aspects of the mystery, from a present-day perspective. The underlying idea behind coming up with *What*

Happened to Netaji? is that once the people of India have been made aware of the facts, they will want to see their government take steps that the previous regimes avoided for political reasons, in the absence of a public outcry—the consideration that overrides everything else in a democracy.

Today, the options running for the question, 'What happened to Netaji?' are limited to just three. One, as the official version goes, he was killed following an air crash in Taipei three days after his benefactor, Japan, decided to surrender to the Allies. Two, he did not die in Taipei because he was in the USSR after August 1945. Three, he was possibly in India in the guise of a holy man and lived up to 1985 (at about age eighty-eight).

After surveying all the theories with a fine tooth comb, I am endeavouring to give you clear insights based on sound reasoning. For the ease of comprehension, the narrative in the subsequent chapters has been spruced up with the images of relevant documents, some still classified, and all major claims have been sourced credibly. As you read, you see images of relevant documents and the source details to enable you to judge the veracity of the narrative. It is not for nothing that a recent High Court judgment determined my journalistic enquiry into the Netaji issue 'to be genuine and based on relevant material'.

What Happened to Netaji? is a look-back at the Netaji mystery from today's perspective. It is not a historical account of a matter from a bygone era; it's an expose of a political scandal as it unfolded through the decades, peaking in ours. One really doesn't have to be a Netaji admirer to be intrigued by the mindboggling details that this case entails. Anyone who fancies mysteries, politics, history and skullduggery associated with state secrets-related matters would find this account engrossing.

I have never claimed to have found answers to all the questions. But the numerous that I have answered in this book would have you believe that truth is indeed stranger than fiction.

One

LATE CITY EDITION

Hindusthan Standard

VOL. VIII, NO. 326   CALCUTTA —FRIDAY, AUGUST 24, 1945, BHADRA 7, 1352 B. S.   PRICE TWO ANNAS

MR. SUBHAS CHANDRA BOSE DEAD

SUCCUMBS TO INJURY FROM AIR CRASH

ANNOUNCEMENT BY JAP NEWS AGENCY

LONDON, AUG. 23.—The death of Mr. Subhas Chandra Bose is announced today by the Japanese News Agency.

The Agency added that Mr. Bose died in a Japanese hospital from injuries received in an air crash.

The Agency further said : "Mr. Bose, head of the Provisional Government of Azad Hind, left Singapore on August 16 by air for Tokyo for talks with the Japanese Government. He was seriously injured when his plane crashed at Taihoku airfield at 2 p.m. on Aug. 18. He was given treatment in hospital in Japan, where he died at midnight.

"Lt.-Gen. Tsunamoto Shidi was instantaneously killed, and Col. Habibur Rahaman, Mr. Bose's adjutant, and four other Japanese officers were injured in the crash."

Reuter adds that last 1931. He was elected Mayor of reports of Mr. Bose's activities from Japanese sources.

Leaders' Sorrow

VISIT TO EUROPE

NEHRU CAUTIONS BRITAIN

CONCERN OVER INDIAN NATIONAL ARMY

"IT WOULD BE TRAGEDY IF THEIR PRECIOUS LIVES PERISH"

MURREE, AUG. 22.—"The war is over but the problems created by it still remain and the present Government is incapable of solving them," said Pandit Jawaharlal Nehru speaking at a reception arranged in his honour.

He instanced the problem of resettling the two million Indian soldiers and said : "Though the present Government now and then shows sympathy with them it cannot solve their difficulties."

Pandit Nehru referring to those Indians who had joined the Indian National Army to fight the British, said : "It would be a supreme tragedy if these officers and men and their precious lives were liquidated by way of punishment by the British."

Late News

Russians Capture Manchukuo Ruler

The news of Subhas Chandra Bose's death fell like the blow of a hammer on 23 August 1945. Newspapers such as *The Hindu* reported that Netaji had 'left Singapore on 16 August by air for Tokyo for talks with the Japanese government. He was seriously injured when his plane crashed at Taihoku airfield at 14.00 hours on 18 August'.

Even by the standards of the pre-'breaking news' era, the story had taken rather long to travel. If he had not 'died' on 18 August 1945, Netaji would surely have been apprehended by the colonial British, baying for his blood for daring to do all that he did. The Japanese Imperial Army-Indian National Army alliance had been routed by General William Slim's Fourteenth Army, with a little help from American B-29 bombers and the menacing monsoon. Bose's struggle was all but up by early 1945, and the volatile world scenario only foretold more trouble for the INA leader.

Nuked twice over (6 and 9 August), Japan had no option but to surrender to the Anglo-American forces. Subhas was informed in advance that 15 August would be the day of capitulation. 'So, that is that!' he thought aloud, pondering his options. Those surrounding him in his darkest hour were amazed by his stylish sangfroid, as if he had seen it all coming.

'The worst they can do is to put me against the wall and shoot me. I am prepared for it', he said at a meeting later on. Speaking presciently, he told his close aides in Singapore that 'tremendous sacrifices made by the soldiers of the Azad Hind Fauj and civilian population will not go in vain'.

Bose's attempts to anticipate the future were successful at times. In July 1941, after Nazi Germany attacked Soviet Russia, a journalist arrived to see him in a Berlin hotel. Finding Bose sitting in a lotus posture, like a yogi in front of a world map, Giselher Wirsing waited silently until the Indian leader opened his eyes and remarked tersely *'Das kahn nicht gut gehen'*. This cannot go well. It didn't.

By the time Bose arrived in Japan, the tide of the war had turned against the Axis. Months before the war came to an end, he could see it coming. He also foresaw the onset of the Cold War between the Anglo-Americans and the Russians. A born-fighter that he was, Netaji weighed the options before him. His close aide Colonel Pritam Singh said that 'surrendering would not serve any useful purpose'.

At 9.30 am on 16 August 1945 Bose left Singapore for Bangkok, the seat of the Azad Hind Government (Provisional Government of Free India), so as to confer with Hachiya Teruo, Minister-Designate to the PGI and Lt General Saburo Isoda, chief of Hikari Kikan—the Japanese military organisation liaising with the PGI.

In a Bangkok bungalow a secret meeting took place between Bose, his ADC Colonel Habibur Rahman, INA Chief of Staff Major General JK Bhonsle, Hachiya Teruo, Isoda and his deputy, Colonel Kagawa. According to Rahman's version:

> Teruo and Isoda informed Bose that no orders had been received from the Japanese government regarding the INA surrender, and therefore, they were not in a position to advise them on the proposal of a separate surrender by the INA.

Hachiya Teruo proposed and Bose agreed that they should now contact Field Marshal Count Terauchi Hisaichi, commander of the Japanese forces in South East Asia.

After the meeting was over, Bose, according to the account given by his Confidential Secretary Major Bhaskaran Menon, went on an overdrive to finish unfinished INA business as if he wouldn't have another day for it. He did not sleep a wink, kept Bhaskaran on his toes dictating one after another frantic messages—one of which was going to haunt Bhaskaran for the rest of his life:

I am writing all this to you on the eve of a long journey by air, and who knows an accident may not overtake me .

Around noon on 17 August, two planes landed at a deserted aerodrome in Saigon (Ho Chi Minh City). The one that arrived first was Bose's personal 12-seater with the INA insignia painted on it. The passengers were Bose's aides SA Ayer, Pritam Singh, Gulzara Singh, Debnath Das, Abid Hassan and others.

As he deplaned, the camera captured Netaji for the last time, historically speaking.

At Saigon, General Isoda confabulated with Lt Colonel Tada Minoru, a staff officer from Terauchi Hisaichi's HQ. At noon, Bose was advised to leave his own plane there and board another, all alone. He appeared to have no issue with it, but his aides protested. 'Sir, please, for heaven's sake, insist on the Japanese giving you one more seat.' Bose went back to the Japanese and returned in no time. 'We are getting one more seat', he said. He glanced over all those present and told Habibur Rahman, 'You will come with me'.

Picture from *Challenges to the Empire—A study of Netaji* by SC Maikap

On 17 August evening, Bose and his aides returned to the aerodrome. On the taxi strip was a Mitsubishi Ki-21 bomber.

Its door clunked open and out came a Japanese general. Looking remarkably young for his almost fifty years, Lt General Tsunamasa Shidei, staff officer of Terauchi Hisaichi's HQ and just appointed Deputy Chief of Staff (Intelligence) of the Quantung Army, greeted his guest. The bomber was carrying him to Manchuria where the Quantung Army was preparing to surrender to the Red Army. Shidei happened to be an expert on Russia.

Netaji, dressed in the familiar garb most of us remember him in—khaki bush shirt, trousers and cap—bid his aides goodbye and got in quickly, followed by Rahman. This was the last time his aides would see of him.

That Netaji and Rahman left Saigon on the evening of 17 August is not in dispute. What happened next is. Around 7pm, the bomber landed in Tourane, now Da Nang, on the south Vietnamese coast. Bose and the others spent the night there, according to the official version the 'eyewitnesses' came up with later on. The next day, 18 August, around 2 pm the bomber touched down at the lone landing strip at Matsuyama aerodrome in Taihoku, Formosa—today's Taipei, the capital of Taiwan.

Considering that the bomber was carrying, as it was given out, a recognised head of a state and a senior general, friend of the local army commander, top officials should have been there to receive Netaji and Shidei. Strangely, no one turned up.

After half an hour, the bomber was speeding up on the runaway. Its nosewheel lifted off the ground gently. Gaining altitude, it circled the aerodrome and was still going up when a terrifying boom jolted it. With a wailing sound it began to nosedive instantly. Falling at the rate of 100 feet per second, the bomber impacted the ground at nearly 300 kmph, skidded forward for several feet before hitting a pile of rubble.

The impact proved deadly for Shidei and the pilots. The general was flung forward. He hit the starboard even as a fuel tank collided and exploded over his head. One of the pilots had the joystick gruesomely pierced through his face. Many passengers survived with relatively little or no injuries. Lt Colonel Shiro Nonogaki was thrown out by the impact; Major Taro Kono broke through the honeycombed celluloid top; Lt Colonel Tadeo Sakai, Major Ihaho Takahashi and Captain Keikichi Arai jumped out of the wreck that had now caught fire. One of the survivors ran around the burning wreck, hysterically shouting, 'Chandra Bose, Shidei, come out!'

Inside, Rahman—his forehead ruptured and right knee bruised—saw Bose, dazed, blood on his forehead too, looking lost and confused. '*Aage se nikliye, Netaji!*' he shouted. Bose staggered to the front to find the entrance door blocked by a firewall. It was touch and go. He covered his face with his hands and jumped out.

Rahman followed. When he got on the other side, he saw Bose wrapped in flames. Drenched in gasoline, his clothes were rapidly turning him into a human fireball. He was floundering, trying to take off his clothes. Gathering his wits, Rahman tore off Bose's burning clothes with his bare hands, unmindful of the singing his hands received as a result.

But it was all in vain. Bose had suffered third-degree burns by now. Carbonised skin hung off him in shreds. Soon he was taken to a local army hospital nearby. Despite the efforts of the young army doctor in charge, Dr Tenayoshi Yoshimi, he passed away late in the evening.

On 19 August afternoon, Rahman desired that the body should be taken to Singapore. The Japanese regretted their inability to do so as there was no plane available in Taipei to carry the coffin. Embalming was also ruled out as preservatives were out of stock. Now the body had to be cremated in Taipei itself.

A photographer arrived and the lid of the coffin was removed. A shot of the body covered in the shroud was taken. Rahman disallowed taking of a photograph with the shroud removed. Though the face could be recognised by him, it was disfigured.

At the crematorium, the body was taken out of the coffin, laid on a sliding tray and pushed inside the incinerator. Its metallic door was then shut and bolted from the outside. For about half-an-hour, Rahman stayed there as fire began to consume the body. Then he left, and returned to the crematorium the next day. The sliding tray was pulled out. Following a Buddhist custom, the bones were picked up with chop-sticks and placed in a wooden urn. The urn was placed next to another urn, which Rahman was told contained Shidei's ashes.

Inexplicably, the local Japanese top brass, including Shidei's batchmate Lt General Haruki Isayama, chief of staff of the Japanese forces in Formosa, had made themselves scarce throughout this period. Not one of them turned up anywhere—aerodrome, hospital or crematorium. They just gave directions and let junior officials handle the extraordinary situation.

None of Netaji's other aides elsewhere were kept in the loop about the mishap. Two days later, Lt Colonel Tada Minoru took SA Ayer aside on 20 August and told him about the crash. 'I must see Netaji's body with my own eyes…. Do not tell me afterwards that Netaji's body has been disposed of', said Ayer, demanding to see 'conclusive proofs'. The others were taken to Hanoi on 19 August and given the impression that they were following Bose to his destination. A week later in Hanoi, a senior Japanese military intelligence officer mumbled something startling to Debnath Das and Pritam Singh:

'Don't believe the plane crash as a real crash.'

The urn containing Bose's remains was taken to Japan by Rahman on 5 September 1945. Two days later, at the entrance to the Imperial Military Headquarters, a small box containing the urn was unceremoniously handed over to Ayer by a Japanese military officer. Two more boxes, said to be containing 'gold bars and diamonds', were handed over to Munga Ramamurti, a local Indian leader.

This was the beginning of free India's first ever scam—the loot of the INA treasure. Ramamurti, and his brother J Murti, became rich overnight. According to a Japanese media report, the Murti brothers 'bought two sedans and were seen riding about in them, seemingly leading quite a luxurious life' at a time when even affluent Japanese were reeling under the hardships

brought about by the World War in which their country had suffered defeat.
Ayer's name also started doing the rounds, for keeping his 'share'.

By their own account, Ayer and Ramamurti took the 'ashes' to the Renkoji
Temple in suburban Tokyo, where a kind-hearted priest, Kyoei Mochizuki,
agreed to keep them temporarily. Under the impression that the ashes were
of Bose, whom he admired, Mochizuki would later write to Prime Minister
Jawaharlal Nehru that he 'was asked to keep the ashes by people who were
strangers to me, including Indians of whom I have never heard since that time'.

Meanwhile, five days after Bose had reportedly died and just after the
Quantung Army formally surrendered to the Russians in Manchuria, the
Japanese announced the news of Bose and Shidei's death through their
official agency *Domei*. This announcement was based on a release jointly
drafted by Ayer, the Azad Hind Government's information minister, and a
Japanese official, most likely Tada Minoru.

The inexplicable delay in relaying the news and its timing led to eyebrows being
raised in India. It would seem to Bose's British foes that 'death' had apparently saved
him from being handed over to them. Doubts were instantly raised in official circles.
'"Bose dead" story not believed in London', said a report in the *Hindustan Times*.
'Today's Japanese reports of the death of Subhas Chandra Bose are taken with a grain
of salt in circles close to Far Eastern official quarters. ...Opinion expressed is that...
the timing is too good to be entirely fortuitous....'

A person no less than Field Marshal Archibald Wavell, the Viceroy of
India, noted in his diary:

> I wonder if the Japanese announcement of Subhas Chandra Bose's death
> in an air-crash is true. I suspect it very much. It is just what should be given
> out, if he meant to go underground.

The popular perception that the Bose mystery somehow sprouted from his
home state Bengal is a myth. The Bose mystery couldn't have been a creation
of some Indian mind, as Indians in those days were too simple-minded to
even imagine that a man could make good his escape under the cover of a
make-believe air crash. The nomenclature 'Bose mystery', itself was coined by
a British military officer later, when inquiries into the
matter were launched. And the first person to claim
to have seen Subhas after his 'death' was certainly not
someone hailing from Midnapur. It was an American
journalist, who had been embedded with the US Army
during the war.

Alfred Wagg, associated with the *Chicago Tribune*,
dramatically interrupted a press meet of Nehru on 29
August 1945 to announce that he had seen Bose near
Saigon, a few days after his reported death.

SUBHAS SAID TO BE ALIVE 30.8.45

SEEN IN SAIGON
PANDIT NEHRU EXPLAINS ATTITUDE

NEW DELHI, AUG. 29—An American journalist asked for clarification of Pandit Nehru's 'attitude' to Subhas Chandra Bose who, he said, was not probably dead but alive in Saigon. He said that Bose should be treated as a war criminal because his men fought and killed many Americans and he extorted money from the poor in Burma and Malaya.

Our New Delhi correspondent added: The American correspondent asserted that Subhas was "alive and seen four days ago in Saigon". Pandit Nehru felt surprised and said it was the first time he heard the suggestion that Bose was alive.

On 1 September, London's *Sunday Observer* picked up Wagg's claim and added that the Japanese report was 'not believed in British and American military circles'. Wagg would repeat his claim to top Indian leaders, Gandhi downwards. A 14 September military intelligence report from the British South East Asia Command noted that 'political circles' were 'greatly interested in the recent news item which alleged that Bose had been seen alive in Saigon after the aircraft accident'.

To shatter yet another myth, the 'chief promoter' of the Bose mystery wasn't some Nehru-baiting Bengali politician but Mahatma Gandhi himself. 'If someone shows me ashes, even then I will not believe that Subhas is not alive', he told jailed INA men in December. His January 1946 statement made headlines the world over. *The New York Times* on 6 January reported Gandhi 'as declaring in a speech that he believed Subhas Chandra Bose was still alive and awaiting a propitious time to reappear'. On 30 March 1946, the *Harijan* newspaper announced that 'there was strong evidence to counteract the feeling that Subhas Bose was dead'.

In Calcutta, Subhas's family swung from despair to hope. Sarat, his elder brother and closest associate in life, shook off his debilitating sense of devastation. He undertook a tour of Europe and learnt from reliable sources that the Allies had heaped discredit on the Taipei crash. 'The story of the plane crash connected with his death is a myth', he briefed the *United Press* in July 1946.

Was it really? As it happened, the matter was inquired into in great detail by several military and intelligence officers of the British Raj under the aegis of the Combined Section (CS) at the Military Intelligence Directorate in the GHQ, India. The CS was headed by Intelligence Bureau (IB) Deputy Director McK Wright. Working under him were several officers, including IB Assistant Director Phillip Finney and his colleague Bakshi Badrinath, both of whom had been keeping their eyes on Bose for long.

The investigators realised at the very start that the only real 'evidence', as it were, of Bose's death was whatever the Japanese and Rahman had to say. There was no dead body, not even a picture of it. The Japanese had destroyed all records of Bose's last movements, but had left 'in their proper place' secret telegrams exchanged between Isoda's Hikari Kikan and the Southern Army in Saigon discussing the crash. An obvious deduction made by British intelligence sleuths was that they 'must have been purposely left where the British would find them'.

First to go into the field, Finney rounded up several people who had seen Bose in the days preceding the crash. What Japanese interpreter Kinji Watanabe told Finney about the secret meeting between Bose, Rahman,

Bhonsle, Isoda and others was diametrically opposite to what had been claimed. Watanabe startled Finney by telling him that he heard Isoda and others discussing 'how to get Mr Bose to his destination'.

It was generally understood that he was to get to the Russians, probably to Manchuria....With regard to Bose's going to Russia, it was an understood thing in the embassy and in the Hikari Kikan.

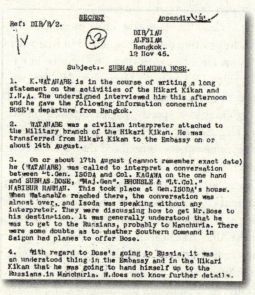

National Archives, New Delhi

Finney reported back that when Bose left Bangkok, he 'took a formal farewell of everybody', taking 'with him four iron boxes of gold', and indicated that he was 'not likely to come back to this part of the world'. A very unlikely behaviour, if he was indeed going to Tokyo and was to have come back and surrendered, as Rahman was still claiming.

The officers began to connect the dots in their reports:
- At the time Bose arrived in Saigon, General Isoda was also there, and this fact may be significant if there was any plan on the part of the Hikari Kikan to allow Bose to escape, and to publish a false story regarding his death. This would have been the ideal place for Isoda to put into operation any such plan.
- It is also suspicious that Bose had to change planes at Saigon and go on in another plane, with one of his staff officers. It would appear more likely that a person of Bose's importance, even though he may have been discredited, would still be allowed to travel in his own special aircraft.

• Assuming that the whole affair is a gigantic deception by the Japanese, it is necessary to consider for what reason they would require Bose to be alive, though officially dead.

Did Japan stand to gain anything by sending Bose to Russia? Most remarkable were Bose's own words in an IB report based on interpreter Watanabe's recollections:

> I earnestly request Tokyo to act as 'go-between' and let me approach Soviet Russia. Once I have been given an interview with the Russian Ambassador, I have perfect confidence in my success in persuading Russia to help our independence movement, and at the same time I am sure that I can do something to improve the relations between Japan and Russia, and it might serve to decrease the menace Japan is feeling on the Manchurian side. I trust if I succeed it will result in killing two birds with one stone. And if my trial proves unsuccessful, I shall only lose my face, that's all. I am nothing but head of a Revolutionary Government ....

After questioning Rahman in February 1946, Badrinath advised McK Wright to get JK Bhonsle 'specially interrogated...to discover from him the truth regarding the meeting in Bangkok'. Carried out by the India branch of the Combined Services Detailed Interrogation Centre (CSDIC), the interrogation revealed that while 'not anxious to provide further information' on his previous stand that Bose had 'left for Tokyo' on 17 August, Bhonsle eventually conceded that the Bangkok meeting was about 'how to get Bose to his destination'.

> It was Bose's intention to try to find his way into Russia. Bose was certain that once the Russians agreed to take him, they would give him all the necessary protection. He also thought that in the event of an Anglo-American split with Russia, which he definitely foresaw, he might be of some service to the Russians and thus further the cause of his own country .

National Archives, New Delhi

Bhonsle added that even 'if Bose's exact plans were known by his trusted henchmen, none of the latter would ever reveal them now'.

As if to prove him right, lengthy interrogations failed to get much out of Rahman. He continued to insist that during the Bangkok meeting 'the main subject under discussion was the separate surrender' of the INA. The CSDIC deduced that even if Rahman 'was in the know of Bose's plans, he would not disclose them'. Its chief, Colonel GD Anderson, was told: 'His manner is not very convincing. He talks in a secretive way, even if no one is about'.

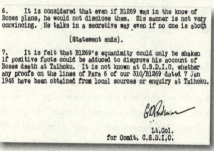

6.   It is considered that even if B1269 was in the know of Boses plans, he would not disclose them. His manner is not very convincing. He talks in a secretive way even if no one is about

(Statement ends).

7.   It is felt that B1269's equanimity could only be shaken if positive facts could be adduced to disprove his account of Boses death at Taihoku. It is not known at C.S.D.I.C. whether any proofs on the lines of Para 6 of our 310/B1269 dated 7 Jan 1946 have been obtained from local sources or enquiry at Taihoku.

Lt.Col.
for Comdt. C.S.D.I.C.

National Archives, New Delhi

The last known round of interrogation was run on Rahman in April 1946, after the Intelligence Bureau sent a lengthy questionnaire.

The outcome was much the same. 'Throughout the protracted questioning, resentment was visible on Rahman's face and he made no bones about it'.

It was around this time that Sir Norman Smith, the IB Director, visited London and 'mentioned the receipt from various places in India of information to the effect that Subhas Bose was alive in Russia'. Some circumstantial evidence was forthcoming and consequently Smith was 'not more than 90% sure that Subhas is dead'. He was made aware of and recognised the possibility that the Russians were themselves 'circulating the story for reasons of their own'.

But that possibility had been precluded by the officers in India. Finney and others sat down for a meeting on 9 April 1946, some eight months after Netaji had been reported dead, to ponder over intelligence pooled from several independent sources in the last few months. Helping the discussion was a three-page note from the Combined Section, summarising the case so far. It noted at the very start that it was 'clear that Bose and his staff were trying to make a getaway to Russia' and that 'Habibur Rahman, Pritam Singh, Gulzara Singh and Hasan have all…appear to have lied, or withheld their knowledge, about the reasons for the journey which was being made'.

Intelligence inputs received from Congressmen revealed that Gandhi's claim about Bose being alive was not based on his 'inner voice' as he had said, but 'a secret information which he has received'.

Most important was the information coming from outside the country:

In December, a report said that the Governor of the Afghan province of Khost had been informed by the Russian Ambassador in Kabul that there were many Congress refugees in Moscow, and Bose was included in their number. There is little reason for such persons to bring Bose into fabricated stories. The view that Russian officials are disclosing, or alleging, that Bose is in Moscow is supplied in a report received from Tehran. This states that Moradoff, the Russian Vice Consul-General, disclosed in March that Bose was in Russia .

By May, the doubts had grown so much that the Americans were approached for help. Badrinath met Lt Colonel Hannessy, head of Military Intelligence in Bombay, who then saw US Consule General William Donovan. Hannessy told the Consule that 'the hold which Bose had over the Indian imagination was tremendous, and that if he should return to this country, trouble would result which...would be extremely difficult to quell'.

Donovan obliged Hannessy by writing to the State Department. 'Positive proof of some kind that Bose is dead would be most interesting.' The State Department conferred with the War Department in the Pentagon and reverted to the Consulate in June 1946:

> A search of our files in the Intelligence Division reveals that there is no direct evidence that Subhas Chandra Bose was killed in an airplane crash at Taihoko [sic], Formosa, despite the public statements of the Japanese to that effect .

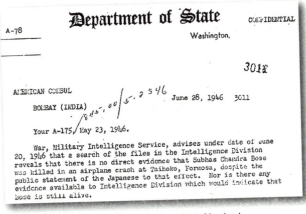

National Archives at College Park, Maryland

Unable to find any direct evidence of Bose's death and concerned over the reports that he could be in Soviet Russia, the governments of India and the UK remained non-committal about his death in the 1940s. The Japanese 'eyewitnesses' were questioned again towards the end of the decade at the behest of the Allied authorities. 'Government is not in a position to make any authoritative statement on the subject', then Home Member (Minister)

Sardar Vallabhbhai Patel said as he dodged a question in October 1946. While surveying the activities of the personnel at the Indian Mission in Berne, the MI6 recorded in December 1948 that Counsellor AC Nambiar, an aide of Netaji in Germany and a long-time friend of Nehru, believed 'Subhas Bose to be alive and to be in Russia'.

Two years earlier, as the Partition madness overtook the subcontinent—one casualty of which was Rahman, who crossed over to Pakistan—Gandhi wished that his 'other son was here!'

'Harilal?' asked a Congressman who had witnessed the Mahatma rebuking Nehru and Patel for failing to contain the communal violence.

'Not him. Subhas, I meant!'

'But he's dead!'

'Not dead. He's in Russia!' Gandhi said.

As the new decade dawned, the whispers about Bose being in Soviet Russia grew loud enough to be heard by the American intelligence agencies. In November 1950, a highly-placed CIA agent in India reported to the agency that 'it is now currently rumored in the Delhi area that "Netaji", which is Bose's nickname, is alive and is in Siberia, where he is waiting for a chance to make a big comeback'.

Two

Given such a backdrop, one would have expected the government of free India to launch an official inquiry into Subhas Bose's death in the year 1947 itself. But nothing of that sort happened. The government did not tell the people about the findings of the intelligence inquiries, discouraged all talks of the Russian angle and, in fact, began supporting the air crash theory with Prime Minister Jawaharlal Nehru taking the lead in the whole build-up.

The first man to demand clarity and transparency was Hari Vishnu Kamath, former Forward Bloc general secretary and the second Indian after Bose to have quit the ICS to serve the people. Kamath often clashed with the Prime Minister, who was somehow dead sure that his one-time friend had died in Taiwan. 'I have no doubt in my mind—I did not have it then and I have no doubt today—of the fact of Netaji Subhas Chandra Bose's death....There can be no inquiry about that', he told Kamath in Parliament in March 1952.

Pandit Nehru's outright refusal to inquire into the matter made the legislators in the West Bengal Assembly explode with rage on 6 August that year. Atindra Nath Bose, a former revolutionary, said he could not understand New Delhi's intransigence. The demand for inquiry, he said, was an 'echo of the national desire which is surging in the heart of Bengal'. Dubbing the Taipei death theory a fabrication 'circulated by Netaji Subhas Chandra

Bose himself to hoodwink his enemies', Atindra Nath asserted that Bose had flown 'to an unknown destination in the USSR'. He fulminated that the only people who believed in Bose's death were 'his erstwhile colleagues who cannot bear to hear his name'.

> Is there any free government in any part of this world which can get rid of their national hero in such a disgraceful, in such an unsympathetic and unseemly fashion? Could you imagine a more wretched instance of such jealousy, meanness and ingratitude?

The Bengal Assembly resolution, requesting the government to 'take all necessary steps for ascertaining the real facts about the alleged death' of Bose, was handled without much alarm by the Ministry of External Affairs (MEA). 'The State government wishes to know what actions we are taking in this matter', read a noting by the then Foreign Secretary, in a still-secret file. Below the Foreign Secretary's note, there appeared a hastily scribbled directive from the PM himself:

> The state government should be informed that we have taken all steps that was possible for us and we are satisfied that the reports of Shri Subhas Bose's death is correct. Nothing more can be done now.

Pandit Nehru would go on to stubbornly dismiss every demand for the inquiry. His February 1953 note left no scope for any discussion on the matter.

> PRIME MINISTER'S SECRETARIAT
>
> I have read Kamath's letter. I believe we are answering a question on this subject in Parliament.
>
> 2.   I am quite clear in my own mind that all the enquiries we could make have been made and the result is a conviction that Shri Subhas Chandra Bose died as has been stated. There is an abundance of evidence on this, which I consider convincing. In the circumstances, I see absolutely no justification for appointing a Commission to make further enquiries.

Record obtained under the Right to Information

Former Bengal minister and lawyer Niharendu Dutt-Mazumdar mooted the idea of a 'special fact-finding commission' in a January 1954 letter to Nehru. The Prime Minister's 21 January response was that of a man hassled:

> I really do not understand what more the Government of India can possibly do about finding facts in regards to Netaji Subhas Chandra Bose. We have done everything possible within our ken and got all the facts that were available. I have no doubt in my mind about them.

In July the same year, Berhampore Municipality Commissioners making a demand for a 'thorough enquiry...to dispel misgivings' were given the same curt rejoinder by the PM's Private Secretary: 'All the enquiries that the Government of India could make have been made, and result is conviction that Shri Bose died in the fatal air crash. No further enquiries in the matter are considered necessary.'

The basis for these assertions was the finding of a hush-hush inquiry conducted by SA Ayer. The moment he saw Nehru in India after the end of the war, Ayer, in his own words, 'bowed to him' and 'touched the ground', signaling the shift in loyalties. He was given a plump government job and in 1951 sent to Japan on a secret mission that had the MEA's tacit backing, with all the cost borne by his generous friend Munga Ramamurti.

Ayer arrived in Tokyo, to a hostile reception by the Indian mission there. Ever since the war had ended, the Indian mission had been getting reports that Ramamurti and Ayer had made off with the INA treasure. The Head of the Indian Liaison Mission, KK Chettur, forewarned New Delhi: 'I hope you are not seeking Ayer's assistance with regard to the disposal of Netaji Subhas Bose's ashes.'

> The fact that both Ramamurti and Ayer were alleged to have had something to do with the mysterious disappearance of the gold and jewellery collected by Netaji should, I think, have deterred us from encouraging him in his visit to this country or in giving his visit an official backing.

Chettur had not been told that Ayer was on a government-backed mission to inquire into Bose's death and trace the INA treasure. Chettur, arguably India's first whistleblower, would go on to give New Delhi damming details about the loot of the treasure by Ayer and Murti, in cahoots with Colonel JG Figges, Military Attaché at the British Embassy. Nehru would ignore it all, but accept without batting an eyelid Ayer's report supporting the air crash theory.

While he toed the official line, Ayer could not help but bring on record—for Nehru's eyes only—some details going against it.

7. I may add that we have since been able to secure on a personal and private basis a confidential report from the Japanese Foreign Ministry on the question of Netaji's "treasure". It appears that Netaji had with him in Saigon substantial quantities of gold ornaments and precious stones, but that he was allowed to carry only two suitcases on the ill-fated flight. These two suitcases must have carried very much more than has now been handed over to us and.even if allowances are made for the loss of part of the "treasure" when the 'plane crashed, it seems obvious that what was retrieved was substantially very much more than is in our possession. What is still more important is that the bulk of the treasure was left in Saigon and it is significant from information that is available that on the 26th January 1945, Netaji's collection weighed more than himself. In this context you will notice that Iyer came to Tokyo subsequently from Saigon and that his statement at that time was that: "The gold is intact as I brought it from Saigon. The cash is balance after changing Piastre into Yen and meeting my expenses during my stay in Japan since August 22, 1945". 'There is a party here who has seen the boxes in Iyer's room and who was also told by Iyer of the contents of these two boxes. What happened to these boxes subsequently is a mystery as all that we have now got from Iyer is 300 grams of gold and about 260 Rupees worth of cash. You will, no doubt, draw your own conclusions from all this, but to me it would appear uncommonly as if Iyer, apprehensive of the early conclusion of the Peace Treaty, came to Tokyo to divide the loot and to salve his and Murty's conscience by the handing over of a small quantity to the Government in the hope that by doing so he would also succeed in drawing a red herring across the trail. How far he has been successful, time will show.

Yours sincerely,

(K.K. CHETTUR)

S. Dutt, Esq., I.C.S.,
Secretary, Commonwealth Relations,
Ministry of External Affairs,
NEW DELHI.

Chettur's Top Secret report of 20 October 1951

As directed by the PM, Ayer wrote his report datelined 24 September 1951, Churchgate, Bombay, loaded with his own assumption that 'I am convinced beyond the shadow of a doubt that the report of the crash is hundred per cent correct'.

Nehru was mighty impressed with the former *Reuters'* and *Associated Press* Correspondent's investigation. On 1 March 1952, he sent a personal letter to the West Bengal Chief Minister and Bose's old political rival, Dr BC Roy, saying he had 'no reason to doubt the correctness of the report'. His conviction was on full public display when he informed the nation about Ayer's findings. In the Lok Sabha on 5 March, Nehru read out aloud the conclusion reached by Ayer: 'I [Ayer] have not the faintest doubt in my mind that the ashes that are enshrined in the Renkoji temple are Netaji's.'

What Nehru did not tell Parliament was that the report tabled was actually the sanitised version of the original. Expunged from it was the portion where Ayer had referred to a secret, high-level Japanese plan to 'drop Netaji and General Shidei at Dairen' in Manchuira.

> The intention was that General Shidei would look after Netaji in Dairen as long he remained there. Then Netaji would disappear with a view to crossing over to the Russian-held territory, and thereafter the Japanese would announce to the world that Netaji had disappeared.

If this was not outrageous enough, the PM had gone on to completely hide from the nation an explanatory handwritten note by Ayer on the plan, as narrated by Colonel Tada Minoru, who had helped work out Bose's last known movements.

Tada Minoru's perspective on the events of August 1945 was of paramount importance. It was he who had told Ayer of Bose's death. He was the one to brief the HQ in Tokyo. His inputs had formed the crux of the official *Domei* news agency story that Bose died while on his way to Tokyo. Minoru's surfacing, along with Isoda, just before Bose's 'death' had made intelligence sleuths suspicious. One report suggested that the duo could have turned up to execute a 'deception plan'. The British tried to lay their hands on Tada Minoru but he slipped away, never to be caught.

And now, six years after the end of the war, Tada Minoru was talking to Ayer. What he told him was conveyed to Nehru in that handwritten note. Minoru told Ayer that all the Japanese manoeuvrings in August 1945 were directed at sending Netaji to the Russians. Ayer's note read:

> Soon Netaji & party (including myself) landed at the Saigon airport from two planes from Bangkok at about 10 am on 17.8.45. Colonel Tada flew to Dalat, contacted Field Marshal Terauchi, Commander-in-Chief, Southern

Command (starting from Burma to China and Manchuria) and conveyed Netaji's request for facilities to fly to Russian-occupied territory in Manchuria, to enable him ultimately to reach Moscow. Netaji had been making this request to Tokyo ever since March or April 1945, and had been perusing it since the collapse of Germany....

Field Marshal took the responsibility on his own shoulders and without referring the question to the Imperial (Military) Headquarters in Tokyo, told Colonel Tada to tell Netaji that all facilities would be given to him to reach Russia-held territory.

Count Terauchi had great respect and affection for Netaji and wished to let Netaji have his wish and do whatever he liked on his own responsibility, whatever the consequences might be. A plane was leaving for Diren and to Tokyo. General Shidei, who had been ordered to proceed forthwith to Diren to take charge as Vice-Chief of Staff, was going by that plane. Netaji could take the only seat they could spare and General Shidei would look after Netaji up to Diren. Thereafter, Netaji would fall back on his own resources to contact the Russians.... Count Terauchi had told Colonel Tada that if Tokyo asked him about Terauchi's decision to help Netaji to reach Russia-held territory, Colonel Tada was to tell Tokyo that Terauchi had done so on his own responsibility.

Terauchi [in picture] couldn't care less about Tokyo's reaction. Terminally ill in August 1945, this 65-year-old son of a former prime minister, who had earlier saved Rash Behari Bose from the British dragnet, knew that death would get him before Allied 'justice'. He passed away in 1946 while in custody. Tada Minoru died young—sometime after he met Ayer.

Wikimedia Commons

Three

Nineteen fifty-five was a crucial year in the Bose mystery chronology. The controversy returned to the headlines not only in India but also in Japan. It all started with Subhas's admirers and INA veterans meeting in Calcutta. Fed up with the Nehru government's unwillingness to have the mystery inquired into officially, they proposed a public-funded enquiry committee.

If it had come into being, this civil society-backed unofficial committee would have had for its head Justice Radha Binod Pal, the only Asian judge at the Tokyo war crimes trials. Pal's pro-Japan judgment had won him the eternal admiration of the Japanese. That's why his Kolkata-based elderly son Prasanta was paid a special visit by Japanese Prime Minister Shinzo Abe in 2007. A year earlier, considering the esteem in which Justice Pal is held in Japan even today, Prime Minister Manmohan Singh was constrained to praise him in the Japanese parliament.

The fear of this very Radha Binod Pal as head of an unofficial enquiry into Bose's fate made Nehru take a quick decision. It was well-known that Justice Pal had himself heard from reliable Japanese and American sources that the Taipei crash was 'possibly a myth'.

'The whole thing demands a thorough investigation. Statements by individuals made here and there will not convince me as to the truth of the story given out', he had written to Japan-based freedom fighter, AM Nair, in 1953. It so happened that one of the men who attended the Calcutta meeting was picked up by Nehru to head the first official inquiry committee. His glorious past and robust appearance, set off by a handlebar moustache, made Shah Nawaz Khan come across as a formidable choice for ascertaining the facts. But looks were deceptive. He may have been an INA hero once, but Shah Nawaz was now, and for all times to come, a loyal Congress party man.

On 13 October 1955 Prime Minister Nehru wrote in a secret file that he had decided to set up a team of three people to inquire into the matter. The team would comprise one representative each from the government, the INA and the Bose family. A subsequent note by the PM said: 'The inquiry should be carried out without too much fuss or publicity.'

But this was not to be. Even as word about the demands for an inquiry reached Japan, the government there upped the ante. On 17 September, the Japanese government offered to send the Renkoji temple ashes to India even as the temple priest suddenly decided to hold another memorial service on 18 September. Local Indians let out their pent-up frustration. 'Alive or murdered? Indians seek the truth about Chandra Bose', screamed a *Nippon Times* headline on 18 September 1955.

Two days later, the same paper reported what clearly was an officially-backed attempt to stifle the mindless charges of murder. News agency *Domei*, now called *Kyodo*, organised an extraordinary press conference, where it paraded three former army officers who vouched for Bose's death: Lt General Haruki Isayama, Dr Taneyoshi Yoshimi and Lt Colonel Morio Takakura in Tokyo. According to the newspaper, *Kyodo*

> produced the men after cries went up from the Indian community here this month, insisting that Japanese authorities tear aside the veil of secrecy that has surrounded the death of their leader for the past decade and give an account of the missing treasure. ...Many still insist he is alive. Others believe he is dead but think he was murdered for the treasure.

Takakura, who was posted at the political affairs section of the Imperial Japanese Army HQ in Tokyo in 1945, revealed that he had 'personally delivered Bose's ashes and a fortune in gold and jewels' to Ramamurti. 'The fortune belonging to the Bose movement has since vanished.' Takakura said that Ramamurti had been threatening him to 'keep silent about the treasure', and he had done so 'out of fear of war crimes prosecution'.

To counter the conspiracy theory about Bose's 'murder', these officers were compelled to jettison the original *Domei* line—that he had died while on his way to Tokyo. The Japanese finally accepted what the British intelligence had uncovered in 1945:

> According to the former army men quoted by *Kyodo*, Bose was being transported from Singapore to Russia to escape prosecution by the Allies. Lt General Shidei, a Russia expert who was being transferred to the Manchurian theatre, was to see that Bose got to the Soviets.

In December 1955, Nehru announced the setting up of the Netaji Inquiry Committee under the chairmanship of Shah Nawaz Khan. The other two members on this panel were the Bengal government nominee SN Maitra and Suresh Chandra Bose, eldest surviving brother of Subhas who wasn't into politics.

The PM actually wanted to nominate Amiya Nath Bose, son of Sarat Bose, but he was unwilling and Shah Nawaz did not want him on the panel. In hindsight, London-educated barrister Amiya would have been a far greater 'nuisance' to the government than his sexagenarian, mild-mannered uncle turned out to be.

Secret records reveal that from the start, the unseen hand of the Ministry of External Affairs worked the Shah Nawaz Committee from behind like a puppet. A letter of 18 October discloses the names of two prominent string pullers: Joint Secretary TN Kaul in New Delhi and First Secretary AK Dar, who was to be attached to the committee 'for help and guidance' in Japan.

Dar met the Director, Asian Affairs Division, at the Japanese Foreign Ministry, who told him the Indian government's proposal to inquire into Bose's death was 'acceptable to the Government of Japan in the terms in which the proposal was made by the Indian Ambassador to the Foreign Minister [of Japan]', at the specific instruction of Prime Minister Nehru.

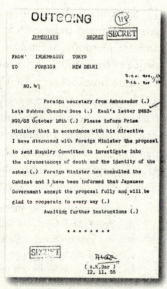

Dar's 12 November 1955 telegram confirming Japanese nod for inquiry

Dar's subsequent note for New Delhi throws further light on 'the terms' and the implied meaning:

> Mr Nakagawa added that the Government of Japan hopes there would be no departure from the main objective in view, and extraneous inquiries and aside researches would not be made.

And to ensure that there was 'no departure from the main objective in view', the terms of reference for the inquiry committee came preloaded with the assumption that Bose had died following an air crash.

Shah Nawaz's original draft of the committee's basic terms of reference—'to inquire into the departure of Netaji Subhas Chandra Bose from Bangkok on or about 16th August and the subsequent events leading to his disappearance'—had been okayed by unsuspecting Deputy Secretary AJ Kidwai. 'This appears to be a sufficiently elastic formulation and the word "disappearance" is more appropriate than the word "death", which we have used so far', he noted. Not for Kaul. 'I would suggest "alleged death" instead of "disappearance"', he countered. The final text approved by Foreign Secretary Dutt made the aircraft accident a foregone conclusion. The dotted lines were drawn.

True to the spirit that no 'extraneous inquiries and aside researches' should be made, Shah Nawaz conducted an inquiry which came to be labelled as his 'command performance' for Nehru. How he did it was rather simple: He just cherry picked the 'right' pieces of evidence from a jumble of contradictory statements. That's why several slips showed in his 'made-to-order' report. Sample a few quotes from it:

- Different witnesses have given the time of halt at Taihoku airfield from half-an-hour to two hours.
- Witnesses inside the plane gave different estimates of the heights....
- According to Colonel Habibur Rahman, the plane split in the front portion, while Captain Nakamura, alias Yamamoto, is positive that the plane was intact and the body was not broken....the statement of Lt Colonel Nonogaki [is] that the two split parts went in different directions on the ground.
- There is some doubt about the fate of the two pilots and some of the crew who were initially trapped inside the plane. Captain Nakamura alias Yamamoto definitely says that Pilot Takizawa and Co-pilot Ayoagi perished along with General Shidei, and he helped to bury their entrails and put their ashes in three boxes… The two doctors, Yoshimi and Tsuruta, definitely say that they had treated Co-pilot Ayoagi who died later in the hospital.
- Dr Yoshimi stated that…blood transfusion to the extent of 400 cc was given. …A more serious discrepancy is the statement of Dr Tsuruta, who attended on Netaji, that no blood transfusion was given.
- Colonel Habibur Rahman has said that Netaji had a cut on his head, four inches long, which was bleeding. This is a discrepancy.
- There is some discrepancy between the witnesses as to who were in the same ward with Netaji.

- The evidence of the fellow injured persons does not help to establish the correct hour. ...So, the time of death cannot be established with accuracy; it could be any time between 8 pm and midnight on the 18th August 1945.

- General Isayama...says that neither he nor General Ando went either to the hospital to pay respects to Netaji's body, or attended any funeral ceremony. ...In justification, he has said that they kept away so as not to give prominence to the fact that an important person like Netaji was fleeing to Tokyo. That explanation does not appear very convincing when he himself said a week later, he went and received Dr Ba Maw, the Prime Minister of Burma, and General Tanaka, Chief of the General Staff, Burma Army, who were on their way to Tokyo.

- One would have at least expected a formal inquiry into the air crash, which is more or less a routine matter. More so, as the plane carried distinguished persons like Netaji Subhas Chandra Bose and Lt Gen Shidei. But no such enquiry was held.

- For reasons not very clear, the Japanese authorities maintained a great deal of secrecy....

Suresh Bose would go on to provide further insight into Shah Nawaz's modus operandi. He alleged that Shah Nawaz considered SA Ayer's book, *Unto him a witness*—which had been vetted by the government prior to its publication—as an 'authoritative book', and put questions to some witnesses from relevant portions of that book, and at times allowed a few of them to peruse the book during their examination.

> Whenever any witness made a statement that did not fit in with his opinion, he [Shah Nawaz] would make a suggestion to him as to whether he remembered it definitely, as the incident had taken place about eleven years ago, or would put other questions or suggestions to him to confuse him and to make him modify his answer or change his definite statement to a vague one.

Actually, sparks began flying from day one of the committee's work on 1 April 1956. Witness No 1 was Bose's friend and Forward Bloc leader Muthuramalingam Thevar, who made some unbelievable claims. Elucidating them later before reporters, Thevar asserted that he had met Subhas Bose in China recently and that 'he would furnish conclusive proof' in support of his claim, if the inquiry committee was reconstituted. He called the committee 'an eyewash'.

> 'Dr Radha Binod Pal should be invited to function as the chairman. The government must make it known categorically to the public whether Netaji's name is still in the list of war criminals and if not, when it was removed and how?'

Other than Suresh Bose, no one took these seemingly bizarre claims seriously. In a letter to the PM on 2 April, Suresh Bose proposed that 'Pal be requested and persuaded to join the committee and lead it'. The next morning he ran into Nehru and took the opportunity to reiterate this demand and raised the war criminal issue.

By evening, Nehru's response had been recorded officially:

> Our effort should be to get as many facts as possible about Netaji Subhas Chandra Bose's last days—the disappearance or death or whatever it was. Apart from direct evidence which we have thus far received and which may further be obtained, it seems to me almost inconceivable that Netaji should be alive. Over ten years have passed since the aircraft accident. Even if he had escaped then, I cannot conceive how he could possibly remain silent during all these years when it was very easy for him to communicate in various ways with India....

> ...the question of War Criminal does not arise and we are not going to ask the USA or any other country as to whether Netaji is in the list of their War Criminals. Possibly, their answer would be that they believed he was dead. Anyhow, we do not propose to do anything in the matter.

The PM further wrote that Radha Binod Pal's appointment to the committee 'was not suitable because of the part he had played in the war criminals' trial'.

> He is, of course, a very eminent criminal jurist and is well-known in Japan and elsewhere. But, in the circumstances, his functioning in this committee might not be liked by some foreign countries like the USA....

Digging deeper into secret files reveals that Nehru was imagining things. The part Pal played in the Tokyo trial—where many of the people facing 'war crime' charges had aided the Indian freedom struggle— actually made him the best person for the job. The Japanese had come to regard him as a moral giant. A decade after the end of the war, the Americans couldn't have any issue with any inquiry in Japan over Netaji's death following an accidental air crash.

In a personal/secret letter to the PM on 8 February 1956, India's Ambassador to Japan, BR Sen, had in fact rooted for the judge, saying he could 'see no objection whatever from this end', as Pal enjoyed 'a great reputation in Japan for his dissenting note as a Member of the War Crimes Tribunal'.

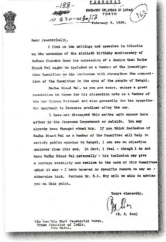

Document obtained in public interest

Nehru saw Sen's letter and dictated his terse stand. He would brook no argument:

PRIME MINISTER'S SECRETARIAT

I have already spoken to you about this matter. I do not think that Radha Binod Pal will be suitable.

(J. Nehru)
21-2-1956.

Document obtained in public interest

Eventually, Suresh Bose decided to leave the committee to write a separate report. The last meeting he had with Shah Nawaz as a member of the Netaji Inquiry Committee was on 16 July 1956. Shah Nawaz frowned and asked him to vacate the committee's office. 'Spoilsport' Suresh was now at the receiving end of the government officers' tantrums. As per his account, he was humiliated, compelled to leave Delhi and 'not a single piece of important and relevant paper or exhibit from the record' was provided to him for writing his report.

On 29 July, Suresh Bose received a communication from Shah Nawaz, demanding that he should submit his dissenting report in two days. He saw the government's hand behind the pressure tactics. A few days later, Shah Nawaz's predetermined findings were leaked out to a Calcutta newspaper. Suresh immediately sent a letter to Shah Nawaz, with a copy to the Prime Minister. The PM replied that the leak

> was some kind of an intelligent guess by 'some reporter or some clerk in our office here. Obviously, the chairman of the enquiry committee had nothing to do with it'.

Suresh Bose reacted angrily.

> When the chairman [Shah Nawaz] curtly turned down my request for relevant papers, I suspected that without inspiration from higher ups, he would not have had the audacity to decline the legitimate request of his colleague. My opinion has now been confirmed.

Nehru did not respond to this scathing attack, which amounted to accusing him of trying to obstruct justice. A controversy at this stage had to be avoided. A little later, Bengal Chief Minister, Dr BC Roy started backchannel manoeuvres. Those were rainy days for Dwijendra Bose, son of Satish Chandra Bose, the eldest among the Bose siblings. The Chief Minister spoke to him over the phone.

'Hello! Dwijendra, I am in search of you. Why are you afraid of seeing me? Come to my office, my dear!'

The discussion continued in the Chief Minister's office.

'What are you doing in this business, earning a thousand here or a thousand there? How will you keep your family prestige with this paltry income? I will give you business.'

Dwijendra wasn't averse to the idea. 'You are a friend of the family. Rather you were—in the '30s and in the '20s. If you are in love with the family again, I am here, you may give me business. I will take it.'

'You get the report of Shah Nawaz signed by Suresh, and I will give you whatever business you want', Roy proposed.

'Not at that cost! I will never ask my uncle. And for argument's sake, why would he listen to me?' Dwijendra resented proposition.

Roy then had Suresh Bose come over to Writers' Building. As he entered his chamber, Roy confronted him. 'Subhas is dead. How come you are stating to the contrary?'

'Who told you that Subhas is dead?' Suresh shot back.

Roy recounted the statements of some witnesses and Suresh discounted them, citing the findings of intelligence agencies. Thereafter, Roy asked Suresh if he would like to be a Governor. This led to a fresh exchange of heated words.

On 3 August 1956, Shah Nawaz handed over his report to the PM. Ghost written by Shankar Maitra, it had six neatly-narrated chapters interspersed with images of the plane wreck, shrouded body of 'Bose', a bandaged Habibur Rahman, Renkoji temple and the ash container placed next to a picture of Bose. Testimonies of six of the seven survivors of the reported air crash, doctors and other witnesses, were used to conclude that 'Bose met his death in an air crash, and that the ashes now at Renkoji temple, Tokyo, are his ashes'.

It added: 'The evidence given by witnesses before us as to Netaji's death is corroborated by the findings of British and American intelligence organisations...and the conclusions of an unofficial enquiry conducted a year later by an Indian journalist [Harin Shah].'

Afterwards, a copy of the report was sent to BC Roy. The accompanying letter by Foreign Secretary Subimal Dutt levelled the charge that Suresh Bose—grandfather of current West Bengal Finance Minister Amit Mitra—was using Subhas's name to further business interests in Japan.

On 11 September, a reassured Nehru placed the committee's report before Parliament. He said that 'the evidence put forth in the report was adequate, and no reasonable person who read it could come to any other conclusion. If a person had an unreasonable mind, it was difficult to reason with him'.

The report alleged that as late as 30 June 1956, Suresh Bose had agreed with and hence signed on a note which said that 'there had been an air crash...in which Netaji met his death'. Appending a copy of the note, the report took a swipe that 'since then, for reasons of his own, Shri Bose has taken a different view and has not signed the report'.

This was the government's side of the story, not the truth. Suresh Bose's signature had been fraudulently obtained to create an impression that he agreed with the views of other committee members. As secret records demonstrate, Suresh's views before June 30 were by no stretch of imagination supportive of the air crash theory. The Intelligence Bureau and Ministry of External Affairs had spied on him to know where he stood. One of the persons used for snooping happened to be someone Suresh blindly admired, because of his past association with Subhas. On 5 May 1956, a secret letter was sent to Nehru by turncoat Anand Mohan Sahay, India's Consul-General in Hanoi at that time. While Sahay's aim was to badmouth and discredit Suresh, his letter lent a testimony to Suresh Bose's firm belief in his brother's not dying in any air crash.

> It was very clear from his talks with me that he has gone with the preconceived ideas and is making all possible efforts to discredit the work of the Committee itself. I doubt if he is going to sign the joint report. He may, perhaps, submit a separate report based on his own fantastic ideas....He is bent on proving that Netaji is alive...

Any doubts about the government ignoring Sahay's high-value intelligence or not understanding its import must be removed, because Nehru saw this letter and asked TN Kaul to reply to Sahay on his behalf:

'We are aware of this problem and can only hope that the gentleman concerned will express a fair, unbiased and impartial opinion on the subject', Kaul pontificated to Sahay on 26 May.

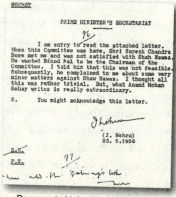

Document obtained in public interest

Expressing his opinion fairly and squarely, Suresh Bose published his *Dissentient Report,* in which he stated that the evidence he had come across as a member of the committee proved that Subhas had escaped to the USSR. The report detailed that…

- Netaji's plan of going to Russia via Manchuria, after his failure in his armed struggle against the Anglo-Americans in South East Asia, was not a cursory suggestion, but was a carefully-thought-of well-matured plan, which, as a matter of fact, was the only alternative left to him, as he did not want to surrender himself to the Anglo-Americans and thereby be instrumental in not only finishing himself, but also bringing to an end his only cherished goal in life, viz. the independence of his mother country.

- It would have been an act of extreme meanness and downright treachery on the part of the Japanese government to have handed over Netaji, their erstwhile friend and collaborator, to the Anglo-Americans and of this they were incapable as a self-respecting and a cultured nation. The only other alternative, therefore, was to broadcast his death after he had left, and continue to support it with manufactured and tutored evidence.... They could not very well say that Netaji had escaped from their territory to an unknown destination, as they would have been accused of aiding and abetting the flight of a man who, in the eyes of the Anglo-Americans, was a war criminal.

- The conduct of the Japanese, in offering only one seat to Netaji, could reasonably be surmised to be the outcome of their and Netaji's agreed plan of removing him as secretly as possible and with the minimum of publicity, so that their conduct would not be exposed to the Anglo-Americans to whom they had surrendered.... They were taking a great risk and it involved great danger to themselves, if their plan was found out by their victors.

- If Netaji had received injuries and burns, as a result of that plane crash and had been treated in a hospital and he had actually died there, and if his dead body had been cremated, the Japanese government, for warding off any accusation of calumny or treachery that may have been leveled against them, if not for anything else, would have decidedly taken pains to maintain correct and detailed photographic records of the true incident for the satisfaction of the Indian people...As Netaji did not die, his dead body was not available for being photographed.

- Colonel Rahman was selected by Netaji from the last six of his trusted and loyal followers.... It, therefore, naturally follows that Netaji considered him to be his most reliable follower, in whom he could repose his trust, confidence and secrets, who would not disclose them under all trials and tribulations, who would implicitly obey all his commands and instructions and who would ever remain loyal to him.

- [The other] witnesses are citizens of Japan, whose patriotism is probably unique in the world. They have made statements to different authorities at different times, supporting the aforesaid plan of their government. As such, I consider it an impossibility for them to go beyond their previously recorded statements and thereby disgrace themselves as well as their government, who, after all, had done a magnanimous act by giving succour to their friend and ally, 'Mr Chandra Bose'.

Suresh Bose concluded his report with a call for transparency, something inconceivable in those days. He asked people not to accept either his or Shah Nawaz's report and instead

> make a demand to our government to place at their disposal the whole evidence that was made available to the committee and...form their own opinion after a careful perusal and consideration of the same, and, if the general opinion be that the aircraft accident did not take place and that Netaji Subhas Chandra Bose did not die, as alleged, to demand an impeachment of all those who have taken part in this nefarious game.

Shah Nawaz's inquiry became particularly controversial over his not making on-the-spot investigation in Taipei. In his defence, Shah Nawaz would go on to claim that

> the matter was discussed amongst the members of the committee and it was decided not to go there. It was not under any pressure from our government.... It was decided that no useful purpose would be served by going there after such a long time.

Secret files are full of records giving the lie to this. The fact is that Shah Nawaz himself was very keen to visit Taipei to ascertain facts, before the government came in his way. On 18 April 1956, the Foreign Secretary turned down Shah Nawaz's request with the following reasoning:

> As you are aware, we have no diplomatic relations with the Formosan government, nor do we recognise them. It is unlikely that they will give any facilities to our enquiry committee appointed by the Government of India in this matter. It is even possible that they would put obstacles in the way of the committee, and create difficulties and complications which would hinder rather than help the work of the committee. In these circumstances, we do not think it would be practical or advisable for the committee to go to Formosa.

The 'we' in the 'we do not think' was actually the 'PM'. A self-explanatory letter [see image] was dispatched by the diplomatic bag to Ambassador BR Sen in Tokyo by TN Kaul the same day.

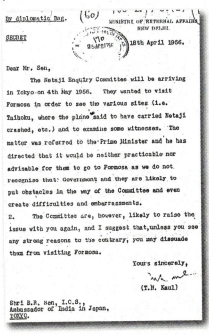

By diplomatic Bag.   (60)

MINISTRY OF EXTERNAL AFFAIRS
NEW DELHI.

SECRET   18th April 1956.

Dear Mr. Sen,

The Netaji Enquiry Committee will be arriving in Tokyo on 4th May 1956. They wanted to visit Formosa in order to see the various sites (i.e. Taihoku, where the plane said to have carried Netaji crashed, etc.) and to examine some witnesses. The matter was referred to the Prime Minister and he has directed that it would be neither practicable nor advisable for them to go to Formosa as we do not recognise that Government and they are likely to put obstacles in the way of the Committee and even create difficulties and embarrassments.

2.   The Committee are, however, likely to raise the issue with you again, and I suggest that, unless you see any strong reasons to the contrary, you may dissuade them from visiting Formosa.

Yours sincerely,

(T.N. Kaul)

Shri B.R. Sen, I.C.S.,
Ambassador of India in Japan,
TOKYO.

As anticipated by Kaul, Shah Nawaz wrote to Ambassador Sen on 18 May that the committee feels 'that it would be very desirable to pay a visit to Formosa' so as to 'examine Formosan witnesses and to visit the alleged place of occurrence'. He exuded confidence that the Japanese Foreign Ministry 'would be willing to use their good offices with the Taiwan authorities', if approached by the Indian government.

'My view [is that] the committee should be permitted to approach the Japanese government for their good offices in the matter, even if the embassy keeps out of it', Ambassador Sen informed New Delhi, with the request that the matter be placed before the PM for a decision.

The return telegram repeated the government's firm stand not to allow the Taiwan visit:

> Matter has been placed before Prime Minister....We have considered the matter again and are not in favour of the committee visiting Formosa. Japanese good offices may enable committee to land there, but it is unlikely that the Formosan government will give any facilities. In fact, they may put obstacles and suggest degrading conditions. Apart from this, politically, this will be very embarrassing for us and might lead to complicating the situation.

This was a clear case of New Delhi acting mala fide. Afterwards, when the government sought British help to get some evidence from Taipei, the Taiwanese responded in the most considerate way possible—nothing like what the Nehru government had charged that they would.

The committee did not wait for the British feedback and submitted its report to the PM. Just a week later, the British/Taiwanese report reached New Delhi. It revealed that there was no proper proof of Bose's death.

Post-1956, the career graph of Shah Nawaz and SN Maitra went up. Maitra flew out on a plump diplomatic assignment. And from that time till his death in 1983, Shah Nawaz remained a minister or head of some government entity. Throughout, he also had to endure barbs from INA compatriots and Subhas's near and dear ones for his 'betrayal'. *Kya bhaijaan, deputy ministership ke liye aapne Netaji ko maar diyya!* (Brother, you killed Netaji for a deputy ministership!) Suresh Bose's daughter Shiela Sengupta, now in her 90s, taunted him once.

One INA man would claim that Shah Nawaz's conscious pricked him towards the end of his life. Colonel AB Singh recalled how once, over a dinner, Shah Nawaz became tearful and admitted that he had 'made the blunder of my life as chairman of the Netaji Inquiry Committee'—whatever that meant.

Prime Minister Nehru continued to flip flop on the issue till he passed away in 1964. While holding up the Shah Nawaz report publicly, he nevertheless kept up his ante for any rumour or claim about Bose's fate or his continued existence.

For the Bose family, there was no closure obviously. Six years after the Shah Nawaz report had been accepted, Suresh Bose managed to extract from the Prime Minister something that partially upheld his view. Irked by Nehru's 7 May 1962 statement in the Lok Sabha that 'the basic conclusions reached by the committee have never been seriously questioned', he dared him to furnish 'proof' of his brother's death. The PM had to concede in his reply that the proof was not 'precise and direct', but merely circumstantial.

No.704–PMH/62

प्रधान मंत्री भवन
PRIME MINISTERS HOUSE
NEW DELHI

May 13, 1962.

Dear Shri Suresh Bose,

I have your letter of the 12th May. You ask me to send you proof of the death of Netaji Subhas Chandra Bose. I cannot send you any precise and direct proof. But all the circumstantial evidence that has been produced and which has been referred to in the Enquiry Committee's report has convinced us of the fact that Netaji has died. In addition to this, the lapse of time now and the extreme probability of his being alive secretly somewhere when he would be welcomed in India with great joy and affection, adds to that circumstantial evidence.

Yours sincerely,

Jawaharlal Nehru

Courtesy: Shiela Sengupta

Four

Four years after the Government had accepted Shah Nawaz's report, a most unusual thing happened. It began to be propagated that a holy man in Shaulmari pocket of the Cooch Behar district of Bengal was Subhas Bose himself.

Swami Saradanand smoked imported cigarettes and conversed in Bangla and English. Getting an access to him was tough as the ashram administration insisted on tardy bureaucratic procedures. Rumours spread thick and fast, and by 1961 the 'Shaulmari Sadhu' was the talk of the entire state.

The way the Bengal government reacted to this scenario was baffling. Secret Bengal government files show that the entire state police and intelligence apparatus was rattled by the claim, no matter how preposterous it appeared on the face of it.

Completely ignoring the fact that Subhas was officially dead, the state government machinery went into an overdrive to find out who Saradanand really was. As early as in 1961 police had laid a secret siege of the Shaulmari ashram, but it took some time before the rumours could be scotched. The ashram itself clarified more than once that 'the founder of Shaulmari ashram is not Netaji Subhas Chandra Bose, nor had he any relationship with Shri Netaji'. And yet, there was no end to the controversy fueled by all sorts of people—rumour-mongers and publicity seekers included.

```
SPECIAL DECLARATION.

From: Shaulmari Ashram.
      Dist. Coochbehar
      P.O. Falakata.

    It is hereby emphatically announced that the Founder
of Shaulmari Ashram is not Netaji Shri Subhash Chandra
Bose nor had He any relationship with Shri Netaji'
    One of the team members,Sri Haripada Bose, who had
cherished own ideas before he joined the Ashram and who
inspite of every effort made to change them still persisted
in the misguided belief that , "The Founder of the Ashram
is None But Netaji".
```

The police obtained Saradanand's handwriting sample and ran it through a CID expert who could spot differences between it and Bose's handwriting, even though the samples were not sufficient to draw a conclusive inference.

In April 1962, the state government muddied the waters further by publicly declaring that 'so far as the government is concerned, it has had no approach to Srimat Saradanandji and therefore it is not in a position to make any statement' regarding his identity.

Meanwhile, numerous intelligence reports were received in Calcutta and New Delhi. Interestingly, one of the young IPS officers trying to clear the air was Nirupam Som, grandson of one of Subhas's sisters and a would-be Police Commissioner of Kolkata. Som found the claims of one of the propagators, Satya Gupta, as 'incoherent' and 'childish'.

On 26 April, the IGP of West Bengal was informed through a secret report that one of the visitors to Shaulmari was, of all the people, Shah Nawaz Khan himself.

By 1963, the matter was being discussed at the national level. Atal Bihari Vajpayee asked Nehru in the Rajya Sabha on 22 August 'whether any inquiry has been made?' The PM replied that 'inquiries we have made and the Government of West Bengal have made have conclusively established that Swami Saradanand is not Netaji Subhas Chandra Bose, and he himself denies it absolutely'.

One such inquiry had been carried out by Rajya Sabha MP Surendra Mohan Ghose after Prime Minister Nehru personally directed him to do so. Ghose went to Shaulmari ashram on 11 September 1962 and met Saradanand face to face.

'Can anybody mistake me for Netaji?' Saradanand asked. Ghose replied: 'Not he who saw Netaji alive and knew him.' Saradanand nodded and said he was 'not the son of Janaki Nath Bose'.

On 4 October Ghose informed Nehru that...

> This man is not Subhash Bose. I wonder, how he could be confused with Subhash by people who knew him. One thing, I find that some people are bent upon to make a political Capital out of this Sadhu's presence there. It would have been much better for the Sadhu himself to disclose his antecedents. However, I have no doubt in my mind that this Sadhu has nothing to do with Subhash Bose.
>
>   With kindest regards,
>
>   Yours sincerely,
>
>   S. M. Ghose
> Shri Jawahar Lal Nehru,   (S.M.GHOSE)
>   Prime Minister of India
> Prime Minister's House,
> NEW DELHI-1

Record obtained under the Right to Information

But who really was the Shaulmari Sadhu? A still-secret record of the West Bengal government has the possible answer. Ashok Chakrabarti, Superintendent of Police, Cooch Behar made a trip to his ashram in December 1961 to uncover Saradanand's real identity. 'I have got some secret information about the identity of the sadhu', Chakrabarti wrote in a memo to PK Basu, Deputy Inspector General of Police, Intelligence Branch. He added that one source

> has been able to identify the sadhu as Shri Jatin Chakrabartti of Vigna, Meher near Comilla, Victoria College and was a member of the revolutionary party. He was charged for the murder of Mr Davis, District Magistrate, Comilla and since the [time of the] murder has been absconding. He was clearly related with Anushilan Party and was a chain smoker.

If this was the truth of Shaulmari, what lay behind the intrigue to publicise him as Subhas Bose? A revolting view soon emerged that the Shaulmari Sadhu had been propped up at the government's behest to befuddle the public, take their attention away from the Bose mystery, to discredit it even.

When Subhas's nephew and freedom fighter Dwijendra Nath Bose visited Shaulmari ashram, to his utter shock, he saw the then Director, Intelligence Bureau (DIB) BN Mullik snooping around in person. 'The people who propagate that these sadhus are Netajis are all financed by the government', Dwijen would go on to allege.

Journalistic investigation by young Barun Sengupta, founder of the Bangla daily *Bartaman Patrika*, threw up many such imponderables. 'I was told by so many intelligence officers working in the eastern region of the country that it is Mr Mullik who looks after all these things....'

The crux of Sengupta's inquiry was that the IB knew 'fully well...about many saints and monks masquerading as Netaji' and that it was constantly on a lookout for the 'dead' Bose.

> Whenever there is a rumour or a story, the central intelligence and the state intelligence go and investigate it. They also come to us [journalists] for further enlightenment and to know whether we have any information.

And then, just as the Shaulmari episode subsided, up came Samar Guha.

The former freedom fighter and chemistry professor set out the main agenda of his public life—recognition for Netaji and settlement of the mystery—with his maiden speech in the Lok Sabha on 3 April 1967. He made an issue of the absence of Bose's portrait in the Central Hall of Parliament. He charged that 'it was not an omission but...a deliberate and calculated act on the part of the Congress government to minimise the position of Netaji and relegate him to secondary leadership in the history of national freedom'.

Samar Guha

For all his good intentions and sincere efforts, Professor Guha actually behaved oddly at times. His arguments, while valid, sounded like he was caught up in a time warp. For some strange reason he always referred to Subhas Bose in the present tense.

'I know that many people feel that I am crazy', he yelled out to the jeering MPs in the Parliament once. 'I am a gullible person, and I easily believe any kind of rumour about Netaji being alive.' LK Advani, as Deputy Prime Minister of India, remembered Guha as someone who 'was always talking and writing about Netaji' during the Emergency days when he, Vajpayee and Guha were lodged in the same jail.

With the Indira Gandhi government unwilling to consider his demand for probing the mystery afresh, Guha shored up support from friends like Atal Bihari Vajpayee and formed a 'national committee'. As a PMO note subsequently recorded, '44 MPs addressed a letter to the Prime Minister on August 7 [in 1968], requesting for the appointment of a fresh inquiry commission, consisting of retired Supreme Court judges and

eminent public men, on the plea
that a fresh probe [the Jivanlal Kapur
Commission] was being conducted
in regard to the assassination of
Mahatma Gandhi'.

Poring over secret files further
shows that the government was, as
usual, not too keen on any inquiry.
In a dismissive note for the Cabinet,

> COPY NO._____   S E C R E T
>
> MINISTRY OF HOME AFFAIRS
>
> Note for the Cabinet
>
> Subject:- Disappearance of Netaji Subhas
>   Chandra Bose in 1945.
>
> In April 1956, in response to the public
> demand, Government of India appointed an Enquiry
> Committee to ascertain the circumstances concerning
> Netaji's departure from Bangkok on 16.8.1945 and his
> alleged death in an air-crash. The Committee

Home Secretary LP Singh reasoned that 'unless fresh evidence or new facts
were brought to light, a further inquiry was not warranted'.

That the government view was prejudiced became all the more evident
from another PMO note of 1969. Joint Secretary VP Marwaha repeated the
discarded Japanese line, ignoring the Russian angle. The note said, Subhas
'was picked up in a Japanese Air Force bomber for being carried to Tokyo'.

> Any decision to order a re-inquiry would go against government's repeated
> stand in the time of three Prime Ministers, turning down such a demand. It
> will also have the demerit of raising an altogether new excitement over this
> issue which is believed to be dead except by some followers of Netaji like Samar
> Guha, with whom it is obviously an obsession. In the circumstances, it might
> not therefore be considered desirable to set up a fresh commission of inquiry
> into Netaji's death.

Further, in a minute taken by the Cabinet Secretary on 5 September,
Prime Minister Indira Gandhi herself opined that she favoured explaining
the official position to the agitated MPs. 'I doubt if many will support Shri
Samar Guha once the position is made clear to them.'

The opposite happened when the Home Minister tried to clarify. Mulka
Govinda Reddy, SN Dwivedi, Balraj Madhok, SM Joshi, Amiya Nath Bose,
Bakar Ali Mirza, KL Gupta, Tridib Chaudhuri, Era Sozhiyan, Shashi Bhushan
and future Lok Sabha Speaker Rabi Ray did not agree with the government's
stand in a meeting on 5 December 1969. Speaking for everyone, Amiya Nath
Bose, then an MP, said that 'there were certain materials in the custody of
the Government of India which were not placed before the Shah Nawaz
Committee' and, therefore, 'it should be treated, not so much as a question of
fresh evidence, but as the need for a fresh inquiry into the evidence available'.

The last straw came with ministers opining in a Cabinet meeting that
the 'Government should not have given the impression that it was against a
fresh inquiry, when millions of people were interested in knowing what had
happened to Netaji' and the refusal to inquire into the matter was creating
an 'impression among some people that there was something to hide'.

Consequently, in July 1970, orders were issued for the formation of a one-man commission. Former Chief Justice of the Punjab High Court, GD Khosla, took over as chairman. There was something about Justice Khosla that should have set off alarm bells. For a start, he was friends with Nehru.

Also, Khosla had a history of spewing venom at those whom he thought had rubbed him the wrong way. Denied a ceremonial sendoff on his retirement in 1961, Khosla gave vent to his frustration by writing a snide newspaper article attacking Advocate General of Punjab SM Sikri, and his wife. Sikri asked Khosla to make amends but he refused.

Left with no option and heeding the advice of then Attorney General of India, MC Setalvad, Sikri then filed a criminal complaint against Khosla. The former judge reacted by escaping to London. Eventually, he had to apologise publicly and the criminal complaint was withdrawn by Sikri in the larger interest of the judiciary. Today, we remember him as Justice Sarv Mittra Sikri, the 13th Chief Justice of India.

To cap it all, Khosla had endured a public slight from Bose in London in the early 1920s, when both were there for the ICS exams. Young Khosla happened to be passing by when Bose was telling fellow Indians about his decision to quit the 'heaven-born service'. Khosla went on to write in his autobiography that Bose gave him 'a withering look of contempt' as Khosla said that he did not see anything unpatriotic in Indians substituting Englishmen in the service. Writing in *The Tribune* in 2001, historian VN Datta commented that this experience 'was bound to rankle in Khosla's heart'.

And rankle hard it did. Throughout the course of his inquiry, suave Khosla put up a veneer of impartiality but did the opposite. For instance, he saw to it that British-era intelligence reports did not reach lawyers representing different parties; howlers made by Japanese witnesses were ignored; doctored documents were used to support the official line; his own inquiry in Taiwan was sabotaged.

The last instance took place against the backdrop of eminent MPs Mulka Govinda Reddy and Prakash Vir Shastri telling the commission on oath that during their visit to Taiwan they had been told by the authorities there that 'at no time Netaji Subhas Chandra Bose appears to have been involved in any air crash in Taipei' and that the Taiwan government would 'be ever ready to cooperate with the Government of India' on this matter.

In May 1972, however, Khosla was informed that he would not be allowed to visit Taipei like the Shah Nawaz Committee because India did not have diplomatic relations with Taiwan. This forced an intervention by Samar Guha and the other lawmakers. A joint letter to Prime Minister Indira Gandhi signed by twenty-six of them—Atal Bihari Vajpayee's name appearing on top—demanded that the commission 'should be given facilities to visit Taiwan'.

It was pointed out that 'many Indian government officials visit Formosa every year, even though India has no diplomatic relations with the island'.

When the government still did not concede to their demands, Guha had to play hardball. In a private meeting with Indira Gandhi, he threatened to take the lid off India's intelligence links with Taiwan:

> I told Indira Gandhi that during the 1965 Indo-Pak war, the Indian government procured weapons and intelligence from Israel through the Taiwan government, and India also has trade relations with Taiwan through the Hong Kong route. I was able to collect this secret information from a representative of the Taiwan government.

It worked, for the time being, and in July 1973, GD Khosla landed at the spectacular Taipei Songshan Airport which had come up on the site of the old Matsuyama aerodrome. Waiting for Khosla here were Samar Guha and Sunil Krishna Gupta, a lawyer representing the Forward Bloc. Guha beseeched Khosla to contact the Taiwanese authorities only to be informed that the Ministry of External Affairs had already told the judge not to. 'Why have you come over here, then? Why did you not tell us this in Delhi?' Guha shouted.

'Why have you come to Taipei after twenty-seven years?' people asked Guha and Gupta. Somehow, they obtained permission from the Taiwanese authorities to inspect the out of bounds, unused old airstrip from where the Japanese bomber had allegedly taken off and crashed. But persuading Khosla to go there proved trickier. After he reached there, Khosla acted up. He wouldn't get off his car and when he did, he began gazing at the sky, his arms crossed on his chest, a clear sign of negative body language.

Sunil Gupta (left), Samar Guha (in specs) and Justice Khosla (in black suit) in Taipei

Guha tried to draw his attention to the apparent mismatch between the topography of the area and the one seen in the pictures of plane debris furnished by the Japanese to prove Netaji's death.

Netaji Inquiry Commission report, 1956

The pictures showed the debris strewn near a hill, whereas according to the survivors, and a sketch confidentially provided by the Japanese foreign office to its Indian counterpart, the plane had crashed just next to the runaway.

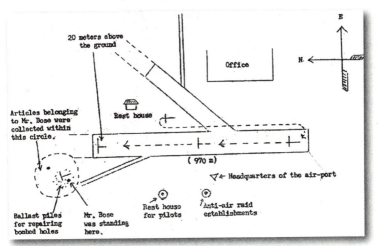

The hills, as Guha and others saw, were miles away even from the runaway. Apparently the Japanese had fobbed off to the Allies pictures of debris of some other plane. His adrenal running fast, Guha turned to GD Khosla. 'Look at the pictures! Look at the hills in the background! They don't match! These pictures were planted!'

'What am I to do with these pictures?' Khosla became blazing mad. 'I have nothing to do with them.' Turning away, he barged into his car. He was treating the pictures as 'inadmissible in evidence' because of the legal technicality that Habibur Rahman had not appeared before him to testify 'to what they depict'.

By now, the High Commission of India in Islamabad had been informed by the Pakistan Foreign Ministry that Rahman, then a senior Pakistan official, had 'nothing to add to what he had already said in his evidence before the Shah Nawaz Committee' and was 'of the opinion that no purpose would be served by his going to New Delhi or by the visit of the Inquiry Commission to Pakistan'.

Returning home, Guha went to Indira Gandhi to complain about Khosla's conduct. Sunil Gupta quietly slipped away to somewhere in Uttar Pradesh to brief a holy man. While he would not appear in public, this mysterious

Indira Gandhi with GD Khosla

person was keeping an eye on the commission's work. Sitting behind a curtain, he told Gupta that 'Khosla's pen was Indira's pen' and this was another 'command performance' in the making.

Gupta was only one of many doubling as the eyes and ears of the unseen holy man. Another was a frail-looking Pabitra Mohan Roy. Nothing on his genial, bespectacled facet told of his daredevil past in the service of the nation. An Anushilan Samity revolutionary to begin with, Roy had followed Netaji to SE Asia, deserting his wife and young children for the cause of India's freedom.

Riding on a Japanese submarine, Roy returned to India in 1944 as an INA secret service operative. But his mission was doomed by betrayal. A fast-track trial under the Enemy Agents Ordinance against Pabitra, fellow spy Americk Singh Gill and Haridas Mitra, who had dared to shelter them, commenced in May and by June end their execution orders were out. The sentence was eventually commuted as Mahatma Gandhi was approached for intervention by Haridas's wife Amita, niece of Subhas Chandra Bose.

Pabitra's first meeting with the holy man had taken place on a spooky night in 1962 in a run-down structure in a deserted Shiva temple complex somewhere in Uttar Pradesh. A black curtain blocked the holy man's view, but not his stentorian voice. As that booming voice addressed Roy as *my intelligence officer*, cherished memories of someone presumed dead for seventeen years flickered in his mind's eye.

In 1971, this holy man—who'd given himself a strange sobriquet, Dead Man—had been greatly displeased with the government's decision to accede to the UN 'convention on the non-applicability of statutory limitations to war crimes'. The convention had ensured that persons accused of war crimes during the World War II would 'not escape prosecution merely because no legal case is brought against them within a specified period after the commission of the crime'. The parties to the convention agreed 'to adopt domestic measures for the extradition of persons responsible for these crimes'.

The matter was even raised before Khosla by Niharendu Dutt-Majumdar, representing Suresh Bose and other family members as a lawyer.

> I am wondering what was the special urgency or occasion for India at this time to make such a ratification and what was India's special interest in this matter, unless India has somebody in view.

'I don't know anything. Why they have done so, I don't know', Indira Gandhi told Samar Guha, pretending not to know about her own government's directive to Khosla regarding Taiwan. Exasperated, Guha blasted the government in Parliament a few days later. 'If the Ministry of External Affairs had not issued any instruction, perhaps the Netaji mystery would have been finally resolved.... When I met Taiwan leaders, they never raised any diplomatic or political issue. ...I say they were eager to give all the necessary help to us', he said.

In response, then External Affairs Minister Swaran Singh touched Guha's raw nerve. He complained to the Speaker about Guha's 'agitated manner'.

'You do not feel agitated?' Guha asked him angrily.

'This posture, as if he really is the only person in this country who has reverence for Netaji Subhas Bose is, if I may say so, completely misplaced', the Minister retorted.

'This attempt to monopolise the conscience of the nation is, if I may say so, much too pretentious', he rubbed in.

Guha flew off the handle: 'For all those twenty-seven years, what did you do? Did you care to hold an inquiry? Did you care to visit the alleged place of occurrence of the plane crash?'

He asked: 'Is the government going to place the text of the suggestion (to Khosla) on the table of the House?'

'No, (Mr Speaker) Sir, I have no intention', said Singh flatly, turning down the request. Backing Guha's demand, Atal Bihari Vajpayee and Madhu Limaye argued that 'the Minister had no right to deprive the members of information, if no public interest or national security was involved'. The Minister said it was 'not customary' for him to produce the directive in original.

So, the government did not produce the copy of the instruction and with that the last hitch was gone.

In September 1973, lawyers representing different parties began arguing their cases before the commission. 'What to speak of your Lordship, even a fool will not believe in these stories', said Gobinda Mukhoty of the national committee about the discrepancies and contradictions marring the Japanese eyewitnesses' testimonies.

For instance, Tadashi Ando, the military officer in charge of media in Taipei when the plane carrying Bose and Shidei allegedly crashed, told the commission on 30 March 1971 that when he heard about the mishap, he felt greatly concerned for the general, his 'teacher in the military academy'. So, shouldn't he have rushed to the airport to look for Shidei? Ando told the commission that he 'went to the airport immediately and was told that General Shidei was already dead. Subhas Chandra Bose was taken to the army hospital and those who had suffered minor injuries were taken to other hospitals'.

Khosla asked Ando if he saw the general's body and his strange response was: 'I did not see directly the body of General Shidei.'

'Did you see any other dead bodies?' was Khosla's next question. 'I did not see the bodies, although I knew that they were dead.'

'Did you go to the hospital where Netaji Bose was lying?' Khosla asked him pointedly. 'I did not go. I presume Staff Officer Shibuya knows everything about this accident.'

In fact, the testimonies about Shidei's fate—more than that of Bose—as coming from the witnesses before Khosla, and also Shah Nawaz, were so utterly lacking in details and yet so full of discrepancies that they clearly appeared to be invented, rather than being a genuine recollection of what they had gone through. Eyewitness accounts of a complex occurrence are bound to differ in minor details, but once in a lifetime happenings—especially tragedies—are hard to expunge from one's memory.

No one who was unfortunate enough to have witnessed the carnage in Delhi in November 1984 would ever forget those grisly scenes. It would be hard for anyone to ever forget where one was when the hijacked airplane rammed into one of the towers in New York on 11 September 2001, or when the news about terrorists rampaging Mumbai on 26/11 broke.

One expected clear recollections from the men who used to be military/air force men and were senior business executives by the time Khosla examined them. And yet, GD Khosla had to tell Major Taro Kono to give 'evidence from your memory and not from the book' because many Japanese witnesses were seen checking their notes while giving evidence. According to one account, they had done so even before the Shah Nawaz Committee.

Kono said that the moment the plane impacted the ground, a petrol tank fell on General Shidei and he died on the spot. Nakamura insisted that along with the pilots, the general too perished in the flames. But Captain Keikichi Arai's recollection was that he was taken to hospital, where he expired.

Actually no one knew when, how, by whom and in what condition the General's body was extricated from the wreck. In hospital no one saw his body or even heard about it. The cremation was a big mystery.

Shiro Nonogaki, ex-colonel and president of Japan Furnace Material Company at the time of his appearance before the Khosla Commission, testified on 7 April 1971 that he was 'in charge of the plane', having been specially 'appointed by General Shidei'—his teacher in the army academy.

When the plane crashed, Nonogaki was supposed to have run around the burning wreck, screaming 'Chandra Bose, Shidei, come out!'

And then, like Tadashi Ando, Nonogaki too forgot about General Shidei.

```
Shri Trikha: You did not go back to the place of occurrence
    to find out about Gen. Shidei?
Col. Nonogaki: No, I did not go.
Shri Trikha: You thought that Gen. Shidei's life was not of
    much importance?
Col. Nonogaki: It was not that I did not consider his life
    important.
Shri Trikha: But you took no steps to find out about Gen.
    Shidei?
Col. Nonogaki: No.
```

Record of Nonogaki's examination before Khosla commission
obtained under the Right to Information

Shri Trikha: You did not go to attend the cremation?

Colonel Nonogaki: No.

Shri Trikha: You had no injuries on you and General Shidei was your superior. Did you not consider it necessary to attend the cremation?

Colonel Nonogaki: It may be worthwhile, but I did not go to the cremation.

Shri Trikha: So you do not personally know whether the cremation of General Shidei was done?

Colonel Nonogaki: No.

Lt Colonel Masanari Shibuya was attached to the army HQ in Taipei and he was, in Tadashi Ando's words, 'in charge of looking after Netaji' after the crash. Shibuya told the commission that after he received the telephone call from the airport battalion HQ, he 'reported that information to General [Rikichi] Ando, commander-in-chief of the army in Taiwan' and later visited the airport and 'saw the wreckage of the plane'.

In the course of examination by GD Khosla and Balraj Trikha, Shibuya conceded that he had, in fact, seen no wreckage and that his superiors showed little interest even though there had been a major mishap involving an ally, and the Vice Chief of staff of an army which was still on the battlefronts. General Ando gave Shibuya 'no instructions' and Isayama was not too much concerned about either Bose or his batchmate Shidei. Shibuya said he went to the hospital soon after the crash following an instruction from Isayama.

But Isayama's evidence to the Shah Nawaz Committee was that 'he learnt of the accident when he went to his office the next morning'. Shibuya himself forgot what he had told the committee:

Khosla: Are you quite sure that when you reached the hospital, Mr Bose was alive and you heard only the next day that he had died?

Shibuya: It is certain that Mr Bose was still alive when I reached the hospital, and I heard that Mr Bose died on the following day.

Khosla: You gave evidence before the Shah Nawaz Committee also?

Shibuya: Yes.

Khosla: In your statement it is written that when you reached the hospital, Mr Bose was dead and you never saw him alive. Which is the correct statement?

Shibuya: When I reached the hospital Mr Bose was still alive, that is certain.

Khosla: So your previous statement is not correct?

Shibuya: Perhaps the previous statement may be incorrect if you so ask me.

Half-way through his examination, a confused Shibuya told the commission that 'if there are any differences between my present statement and previous statement, please take my previous statement as correct and treat my today's statement as incorrect'.

As the examination proceeded, Shibuya's responses raised more questions than they answered.

Trikha: What is the system in the army? When a plane crashes, is it not your duty to inquire into the matter?

Shibuya: During the war time, there were no specific inquiries about air crashes unless that was of specific importance.

Trikha: But here you said that a very special person was travelling. So is it not a special reason to make an inquiry into the matter?

Shibuya: The Japanese Army Headquarters in Taiwan had nothing to do with this accident because the aeroplane was just to pass the area. It was not in the jurisdiction of the Taiwan Army Headquarters.

Trikha: But you have just now deposed that if there is any special reason then the inquiry is made. My question was that since a very special person was travelling on the plane, was it not the duty of an officer to make an inquiry?

Shibuya: Decision of the Army Headquarters at that time was not to touch this case.

Dr Yoshimi, who 'appeared to be a most convincing witness of truth' to Khosla, was examined at his residence at Miyazaki. But his statements wouldn't tally with his own before Shah Nawaz.

Shri Chakravarti: You have already told that he was seriously burnt. Was his heart also burnt?

Dr Yoshimi: His heart was not burnt.

Shri Chakravarti: What were the places burnt seriously?

Dr Yoshimi: He was burnt all over the body. So it cannot be said which part was more serious.

Shri Chakravarti: But, doctor, if heart is burnt can a patient survive?

Dr Yoshimi: He cannot survive.

Shri Chakravarti: But when Mr Bose was brought into the hospital, he was fully conscious and he had a talk with you through an interpreter?

Dr Yoshimi: Yes.

Shri Chakravarti: So the statement you gave before the Shah Nawaz Committee was mistaken. You have stated: 'I found that he was severely burnt all over his body and all of it had taken on a grayish colour like ash. Even his heart had burnt.'

Dr Yoshimi: It should be chest and not heart. That is a mistake....

Shri Chakravarti: How much blood you extracted from the body of Mr Bose?

Dr Yoshimi: I did not take out any blood.

Shri Chakravarti: When a patient is burnt, his blood becomes thicker?

Dr Yoshimi: Yes.

Shri Chakravarti: Unless the blood is let out, new blood cannot be transfused. Is it so?

Dr Yoshimi: Blood transfusion can be made without extracting blood.

Shri Chakravarti: Mr Bose's burns were of the third degree?

Dr Yoshimi: The general burning all over his body was of the third degree.

Shri Chakravarti: So, what you deposed before the Shah Nawaz Committee is not correct: You have stated: 'In case of severe burns of the third degree, the blood gets thicker and there is high pressure of the heart. In order to relieve this pressure, usually blood is let out and new blood is given in its place. In the case of Mr Bose, I let out approximately 200 cc of his blood and transfused 400 cc of blood into him.' But today you have said that no blood was let out and blood can be transfused without extracting blood even in the case of third degree burns.

Dr Yoshimi: As I said before, blood transfusion was not done by me.

Shri Chakravarti: Then this statement is wrong?

Dr Yoshimi: If it is said so, that is wrong.

```
Shri Chakravarty: Mr. Bose breathed his last at 12 midnight
            and after arranging for his body you left at 1 A.M.?
Dr. Yoshimi: Yes.
Shri Chakravarty: The statement made by you before the
            Shah Nawaz Committee that "it was shortly after 8 P.M.
            that Mr. Bose breathed his last. I tried to give
            artificial respiration to him, but it was of no use"
            is not correct?
Dr. Yoshimi: I think it is incorrect.
Shri Chakravarty: And today's statement is correct?
Dr. Yoshimi: Yes.
```

Khosla proceeding record shows Dr Yoshimi fumbling on the time of Bose's death

It was quite unlikely that the witnesses' previous statements were recorded incorrectly. Khosla would himself write in his report in some other context that 'a perusal of the file of the previous committee shows that almost all statements were…sent to the respective witnesses, who studied them at leisure, made corrections, signed them and then returned them to the committee'.

In late 1973, Justice Khosla began dictating his report in his chamber in New Delhi's Shastri Bhawan. He broke the rules to spice it up and made fullest use of his superb writing skills. By June 1974, the report was handed over to Home Minister Uma Shankar Dikshit. To Dikshit's delight, the report had listed out twenty-five findings favourable to the establishment. Not only was the air crash theory upheld, it was also claimed that:

- There is not the slightest evidence of any attempt by Nehru to suppress the truth about Bose at any stage.
- There is no evidence of any attempt by the present government to withhold evidence or place impediments in the way of this commission.
- Mahatma Gandhi's expression amounts to nothing more than wishful thinking or a symbolic tribute to Bose.
- Dr Yoshimi struck me as an eminently respectable individual whose status in life and whose professional pride would prevent him from committing perjury….
- Suresh Chandra Bose was willing to be used as a tool by persons, who for reasons of their own, wanted to proclaim their disbelief of the crash story, and who continued to assert that Netaji was alive and constituted a challenge and a hazard to Nehru's political position in the country.
- The argument relating to Bose being accused of war crimes is, therefore, nothing but the purest conjecture, put forward not as an argument but as a piece of rhetoric and casuistry to cloud the issue and to distract attention from the real points for determination.

The Government backing him to the hilt, Khosla went on to vilify Subhas Bose and his benefactor Japan, forgetting that he was a judge in free India, not some WWII propagandist:

- Bose's proposal that the INA men should lead the charge into India was 'the proposal of a zealous but impractical patriot'.
- Their 'respect for Bose began and ended with his usefulness to them'. 'Despite the outward respect and honour with which the Japanese treated him, he [Bose] was looked upon as a puppet, a tool which could be discarded and ignored, when deemed no longer useful'.

- The 'true attitude of the Japanese' towards Indians was best summarised by the quote', what is the harm in being puppets? You should be proud to be puppets of the Japanese'.

- 'Bose entering India with Japanese assistance could only mean one thing, viz. India would become a colony or a suzerainty of Japan.'

Even as Khosla's report was made public by the government in September 1974, the former judge released two books—one based on his report and the other a hagiographical biography of Prime Minister Indira Gandhi. If a judge were to engage in such misdemeanours in our times, he'd be roasted by the media and political parties and his report trashed without a word of it being read.

Back then, Bose's nephew Dwijendra took Khosla to court. In a re-run of the defamation suit filed by Justice Sikri, for more than a year Khosla was literally on the run. Finally, on 1 April 1978, this former retired high court chief justice accepted his come-uppance in a magistrate's court in Kolkata. He tendered an unqualified apology in which he accepted that Subhas Bose was 'the liberator of our Motherland'.

No proper discussion could ever take place in Parliament over Khosla's report as the Emergency was imposed in 1975. When the Janata Party was in power in 1977, Samar Guha hit back with a vengeance. He adduced fresh evidence against the crash theory and exposed the dubious ways of Justice Khosla. On 28 August 1978, Prime Minister Morarji Desai had to concede that the conclusions reached by GD Khosla and Shah Nawaz Khan were not 'decisive'.

At that stage, Guha got carried away. He announced in the Lok Sabha 'in the name of God' that 'Netaji is alive'.

> Naturally, my friends will ask the question, why are you not divulging his whereabouts? I am too eager, too impatient to let the country know what I know, but then I have not the freedom yet to disclose what I know. ...But this much I can say, Netaji is nowhere under duress. He is a free man. I again pray to God along with all of you, so that Netaji keeps well and we get him back in our midst as early as possible.

Guha was laughed down, obviously. But he repeated the same claim the next year, even producing a picture which, according to him, showed Netaji in a temple in India. The picture was an out and out fake and all of Guha's good work was lost. The then general secretary of the West Bengal Congress party, Subrata Mukherjee, currently with the Trinamool Congress, demonstrated that Subhas's 'head' was morphed on to a picture of Sarat Bose.

Towards the end of his life, Guha would rue how he had fallen victim to a ploy devised by his political opponents, who knew of his belief in the holy man as Netaji. The picture was fake, but the holy man, who would not let anyone capture him on camera, was for real. Soon after the breaking of the picture controversy of 1979—when Netaji at 82 would have been a year younger to incumbent Prime Minister Desai—the holy man severed links with many of his followers in Bengal. For months he remained incommunicado, and he would never ever allow Guha to contact him again. A few months later, Pabitra Mohan Roy mustered courage to reach out to him. In a detailed letter written in Bangla, he provided a blow-by-blow account of the photo controversy, apologised for not being able to stop Guha in time, begged for forgiveness, and reaffirmed his allegiance to the holy man:

> I wish to say something—your own words—You are my intelligence officer-without fear or favour must act. Now allow me to begin in a similar way. Keeping in mind Ma Kali-Deshmata-Bangajanani-Bharatmata [Mother Bengal-Mother India] and your feet, I wanted to tell you that just like in the past, I still have the same **unflinching faith and love-trust; unwavering obedience; total dedication** and **loyalty** towards you....

[Translated from Bangla. Highlighted words appear in English in the letter]

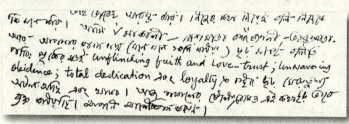

Courtesy: Ashok Tandon

Five

If only the circumstances were more favourable, 1986 would be a turning point in Indian history. For the first time, a court of law suggested in January that there should be a new inquiry into Subhas Bose's fate. In February, another court order almost uncovered the secrets of the holy man Pabitra Mohan Roy, Sunil Krishna Gupta, Samar Guha and others believed was Subhas Chandra Bose in disguise.

Through his writ petition in the Rajasthan High Court in 1985, Nand Lal Sharma prayed for a judicial inquiry 'to know about the whereabouts of Netaji' and get him released, 'if he is still confined as a war criminal in any country'.

The court directed the government to file its response 'within one month'. On 8 May 1985, the government counsel sought time and the case was fixed for hearing in July. Meanwhile, Justice SN Bhargava, who was hearing the petition, was moved to another Bench, 'and the case was not listed before any other Bench in spite of application for early hearing' by Sharma.

Justice Bhargava returned to the Jaipur Bench after some time to find that 'no reply was filed by either the State of Rajasthan or the Union of India'. The government counsel submitted that he had received no instructions from New Delhi. He repeated the same in November 1985 when the Rajiv Gandhi administration just clammed up.

Those days were not particularly known for judicial activism, and the courts were lenient. Dare the government ignore a court directive like this today!

Finally, the case was taken up for arguments in December 1985. Nand Lal Sharma was heard *ex-parte* as the government was still mum. In his 18 January 1986 order, Justice Bhargava chided the government for not caring 'to file any reply of the writ petition and produce relevant material before this court'. He felt that 'either because the Union of India is indifferent to this question... or the Government of India itself is not satisfied with the reports of the two commissions and, therefore, does not want to contest the writ petition'.

The court directed Sharma to make his case before the government. The government was given six months 'to examine the whole matter afresh with open mind...before coming to a prima facie decision as to whether a fresh commission is necessary or not'.

A 1987 memo from the Join Secretary (Coordination Division) in a secret file tells us that no action was taken even after this by the government because the petitioner, Sharma, was 'no longer in this world', having passed away in July 1986. In the intervening one-and-a-half years, all that the government did was to touch base with him telephonically.

That was the Rajiv Gandhi government for you! Propagandist fillers on state-controlled TV and adulatory print adverts issued by the ministries not too long ago would have young people believe things were perfect in those days.

What happened in the other instance was quite intriguing. In September 1985, the reported death of an unseen holy man in Faizabad created a stir across Uttar Pradesh for he was identified as Subhas Bose by his local followers. Known to his followers as *Bhagwanji,* but called by others *Gumnami Baba,* he had earlier lived in Basti and Ayodhya, before arriving in Faizabad in the dead of night in 1983. The claim  that he was Bose was first picked up and highlighted by Ashok Tandon, editor of Hindi daily *Naye Log.*

Then followed the investigation by the *Northern India Patrika* team of Nirmal Nibedon, VN Arora and Sayed Kauser Hussain. Their reports pushed the people of UP into a vortex of emotion. And the instant reaction of the state government was to float a conspiracy theory—that the Janata Party and the BJP were behind the public outcry.

The truth was that the public discontentment was spontaneous, with every section of the society, including local Congress leaders, pitching in. The BJP never showed much interest in the matter.

Alarmed by reports that the authorities were contemplating auctioning some belongings the holy man had left behind, activists MA Haleem and Vishwa Bandhav Tewari approached the District Magistrate of Faizabad on 30 January 1986. Their letter, marked CC to the Foreign Secretary in New Delhi and a disinterested state Chief Minister, called for an inquiry.

> An important English daily of Uttar Pradesh, *Northern India Patrika*, has after months of inquiry and investigations come to the conclusion that the saint was none else than Subhas Chandra Bose. The most important evidence which the paper has cited is based on the records, documents and materials found in his residence, of which an inventory was prepared cursorily by a police officer of a lower rank.... We, therefore, submit to you that the documents and other materials found in the said house should remain sealed and preserved for the purpose of inquiry, and the guards posted there should continue to remain there in the national interest. We would like to be informed of the steps you propose to take in the matter.

The District Magistrate did not revert to the two. On 25 February 1986, the issue reverberated in the state Legislative Assembly. Krishanpal Singh and Nityanand Swami (would be Chief Minister of Uttaranchal) raised the matter. Jagdambika Pal of Congress (now a BJP Member of Parliament), in all fairness, called for a probe, even though he saw no Bose link. Speaking for the government, Finance Minister Baldev Singh Arya stated that an inquiry had revealed that Bhagwanji was not Subhas Bose. The members wanted to see the inquiry report, but the Minister refused to oblige them.

That was an obvious thing to do because the inquiry of the state police was an eyewash. Even so, the police report—now available thanks to the Right to Information—could not dismiss the Bose link altogether as it failed to identify who this man really was, if not Bose. It ran into just three pages, with another one carrying one concluding sentence, drawn by the then SSP of Faizabad.

Should an inquiry be conducted like this? Examples of a proper inquiry include the recent Sohrabuddin Sheikh and Ishrat Jahan fake-encounter cases. We know what all the CBI did to fix the responsibility for the gangster's extra-judicial killing. The investigative agency caught hold of existing and retired senior cops, extracted information from them and filed a chargesheet running into thousands of pages before the Supreme Court. The CBI also told the court that it would like the case to be moved 'out of Gujarat as a fair trial wasn't possible in a hostile atmosphere'.

In the Ishrat Jahan case, the Gujarat High Court on 1 December 2011 directed that the investigation be handed over to the CBI, 'because it could not trust either the special investigation team or the state police to do a credible job'. The CBI's 1,500 page chargesheet before an Ahmedabad

Court in July 2013 charged the Gujarat government and the Intelligence Bureau with the fake encounter of Ishrat and three alleged Lashkar-e-Taiba operatives. Leaving aside political aspects, so far as 'politically sensitive' cases go, this is the right model of inquiry. A three-page long rudimentary report can hardly do justice to any serious matter under investigation.

And we do know how the police functions in our country when it comes to cases that are either politically sensitive or in the eye of a media storm. Don't we? A 2013 *Times of India* story read that the Delhi Police, after a thorough inquiry, was not able to find any evidence linking any politicians to the cash-for-votes scam. Now which cop would have dared to find any?

The 1985 police inquiry was based on the inputs of some junior cops who questioned a few *Bhagwanji* followers, seeking from them 'any solid evidence to suggest that this person was, in fact, Netaji'. Some of those questioned did not know much, others were afraid and some others were evasive. The report says that 'a police party was sent to Calcutta to talk to Dr Pabitra Mohan Roy and other associates of "Neta Ji" but none of them were able to give any information about this matter and, in fact, they appeared to be reticent about providing any information to the police'.

Pabitra Mohan Roy had actually said a little earlier, when Bhagwanji's passing away was reported to him, that 'the country would burn' if he opened his mouth. In 1986, local media published the transcript of Pabitra Mohan Roy's police examination. It appeared that he was being untruthful and concealing something.

According to the police report, when they scoured through Bhagwanji's room in September 1985,

> a large number of belongings and literature associated with the 'Indian National Army' in general and Sri Subhas Chandra Bose in particular came to light. There were a large number of family photographs, reports of enquiry commission related to the death of 'Neta Ji', etc. It also transpired that a special ceremony used to be held in the room of 'Bhagwanji' on every 23rd January, which incidentally is the birthday of Sri Subhas Chandra Bose and on this date no person from Faizabad was allowed to visit him. But some persons from Calcutta used to come and stay with him for that day.

Not intrigued by all this, the SSP concluded that 'on inquiry it could not be ascertained as to who was the deceased man', which in plain English means that police found no clear clue about Bhagwanji's identity. What the Minister had said in the Assembly was untrue.

Things changed when Lalita Bose, daughter of Suresh Bose, rushed in from New Delhi. Her arrival in 1986 put paid to the conspiracy theory that the BJP and others were causing the commotion as Lalita was a member of the Congress party at that time.

Lalita Bose made her own enquiries. Breaking down occasionally, she admitted to many in Faizabad that Bhagwanji/Gumnami Baba appeared to be her missing uncle. She would tell the *Hindustan Times* that Bhagwanji was of the same age, size and colour as Netaji. His accent was Bengali. His notes on books in English and Bengali looked like the writing of Netaji.

After failing to stir the state government into doing anything, Lalita Bose, Haleem and Vishwa Bandhav Tewari moved the Lucknow Bench of the Allahabad High Court. Sayed Kauser Hussain, the *Northern India Patrika* news editor, was the real force behind the move.

Through their lawyer Robin Mitra, the petitioners lamented that despite widespread public interest, the District Magistrate was merely 'sitting tight over the matter'. They stated how perfunctorily the police had made an inventory of the items left by Bhagwanji. To pre-empt the state government's plan to auction Bhagwanji's belongings, they argued that 'the petitioner No 1 [Lalita Bose], being the niece of Netaji Subhas Chandra Bose, has a right to the property, if the nameless saint is found to be Netaji'.

They even suggested that the belongings should be sent to the National Archives. The court's intervention was sought as there was 'no other alternative remedy available' due to 'the callous inaction of the opposite parties', including the Chief Minister (Vir Bahadur Singh of the Congress), who had been 'absolutely unreasonable'.

Making up for the executive's inaction, Justices SS Ahmad and GB Singh announced an interim relief. The opposite parties were called upon to file a counter affidavit 'within six weeks'. (It would take thirteen years before the government responded). The main request was agreed to. The Faizabad DM was ordered to oversee the preparation of an elaborate inventory, giving details of and about the items, correspondence, books, etc, found in Bhagwanji's rented room at bungalow 'Ram Bhawan' in the Civil Lines area of the city.

The High Court order should have made the Bhagwanji episode national-level news. But it did not happen. One reason for which was that it was overshadowed by a bigger development, engineered allegedly by the Rajiv Gandhi government. In January 1986, an appeal was filed at the district court in Faizabad to unlock the Ram Janambhoomi-Babri

Ram Bhawan in Faizabad

Masjid complex. This was akin to lighting a powder keg. The petitioner was not a party to the dispute and yet the judge, in 'utter disregard for procedure' and in 'undue haste' allowed the prayer promptly.

Six

Faizabad holy man Bhagwanji's fascinating tale goes back to the year 1956, when he arrived in Lucknow from Nepal, accompanied by one Mahadeo Prasad Misra. A Sanskrit teacher, Misra would die in 1970 without seeing Bhagwanji's face. The holy man would remain holed up in a room behind a curtain. His ruse was that he was deep into a *sadhna* (spiritual quest) which forbade his appearance in public. Anyone going to the other side would find a somewhat big-built, fair man with his face covered, often with a monkey cap.

He would not speak, preferring to communicate by writing on a slate. If he ever wrote anything on paper, he ensured it remained with him or was destroyed.

When he ventured out, it would be mostly at night with his face wrapped up like an Egyptian mummy. Perhaps that was just as well because he regarded himself as a ghost who walked. *I am just a will o' the wisp...It is born, does its work, runs around, stays still for a while, vanishes from one place and then shows up at another. It manifests itself but cannot be caught. I am just not here. I have no existence. My name has been crossed out from the human register,* he said once philosophically.

While in Lucknow, Mahadeo
was joined by his widowed daughter
Saraswati Devi [father-daughter
seen in picture] and her infant
son Rajkumar. Both were to serve
Bhagwanji as attendants till the end.
From his younger days, Rajkumar
got to see Bhagwanji face-to-face
and his mother from 1980 onwards,
when the old man broke his leg
and couldn't move around without

Saraswati with father Mahadeo Misra

assistance. Saraswati died in 2001; Rajkumar continues to eke out a living
for his family in Basti.

One person who remained in contact with Bhagwanji right from 1955 to
1985 was Surendra Singh Chaudhury, the former king of Itawa. Perhaps no
one knew about Bhagwanji's early years and his secrets as well as he did. One
day, the two checked into a famous optician's shop in Lucknow's Ameena
Bagh area because Bhagwanji desperately needed a new pair of glasses. While
trying out a round-rimmed one, Bhagwanji, clean shaven like a Buddhist
monk, removed his headgear and looked into a mirror. In an instant, his
shaved bald pate and familiar visage had stunned another customer.

'Netaji!' he blurted out. The next moment, two young men were
prostrating in front of him, causing both Bhagwanji and Surendra Singh
Chaudhury to flee. 'This is why I now keep this moustache and beard', the
holy man summed up the moral of the story a few years later to Pabitra Roy.

When he was still in Lucknow, Bhagwanji was said to have a special
friend— Sampurnanand, the then Chief Minister of Uttar Pradesh. The
Sampurnanand papers kept at the National Archives in New Delhi only
testify to his close association with Subhas Bose in the 1920s and his interest
in the paranormal, a pet subject with Bhagwanji too.

Through Sampurnanand perhaps, renowned Sanskrit scholar,
philosopher and tantra expert Gopinath Kaviraj came in contact with
Bhagwanji. A follower's diary recorded in Bangla a conversation between
Bhagwanji and Sampurnanand.

'Do you know Tripathi?' the CM asked. Bhagwanji replied that he had
heard his name. Sampurnand rejoined: 'Tripathi's guru, Gopinath Kaviraj,
has told him about you.' The allusion was to a UP state minister and would-
be Central Minister Kamalapati Tripathi, a believer in tantric rituals. It is
said he made Indira Gandhi interested in the occult.

One can only conjecture what really made Sampurnanand broach the question of Subhas's fate with Clement Attlee, when the former British Prime Minister visited Lucknow in October 1956. This came to light in 1985, when a retired IB field operative, Dharmendra Gaur, made an astounding claim that Earl Attlee, the man who cleared independence for India, was subjected to bugging by the Intelligence Bureau.

Gaur said, he heard the former British PM telling an inquisitive Sampurnanand that Bose had escaped to the USSR via Manchuria. The tape of the bugged conversation was sent to the head office.

Again, there's no way to prove late Dharmendra Gaur's account. But there's no doubting the fact that Attlee did display extraordinary candour at that time. When he arrived in Calcutta during the same trip, Attlee discussed the Indian freedom struggle over dinner with his host. He told acting Governor PB Chakrabarty, Chief Justice of the Calcutta High Court, that his setting India free had little to do with Mahatma Gandhi's peaceful persuasion. The actual reasons cited by him included Bose's violent push.

Justice Chakrabarty confided in RC Majumdar, the historian, what Attlee had told him and later recounted it in a letter.

Majumdar was the first man to indirectly refer to Bhagwanji. He did so during his deposition before the Khosla Commission. How he came to know of Bhagwanji's existence is a long story. It is set in a year which was a watershed for the Bhagwanji and the Bose mystery saga.

Wherever Bhagwanji stayed, his unusual ways aroused suspicions and so he changed residences every now and then. In Lucknow, he stayed in at least two places, before taking refuge in a run-down structure next to a deserted Shiva temple in Naimisharanya, now Neemsar. Then he was in Basti, Faizabad and Ayodhya, where he changed addresses at least four times before heading to Faizabad again.

A small-time lawyer in Basti, whose sheepish look concealed his astuteness, was never at peace after coming to know the big secret of the unfriendly neighbourhood holy man. Durga Prasad Pandey spent months in summoning courage before writing Bhagwanji a letter in English as he knew it.

'An old and very religious ex-revenue officer, late Sri Jawala Misra, Vakil, Basti, told me as to your identity while breathing his last, keeping full confidence in me to maintain the secrecy of this vital secret.'

'Truth can't be pressed in, it abruptly comes out. You had been an ex-ICS officer…January 23 was celebrated as your birthday.'

Pandey's imploring met with this response:

I am a bonafide dashnami sanyasi and you will know that a man under the holy orders incurs death according to the civil laws and a sanyasi is dead to his former life….

As an afterthought, Bhagwanji added:

In passing, you shall find cogent answers to all your hypotheses, queries, thoughts…both as expressed in your letter, and which remain unexpressed in your heart. Peruse with your heart calmly, quietly, lovingly. Every word, phrase, sentence and their constructions are pointers for you, they are pregnant with possibilities. Seek and thou shall find.

One of the locals in Naimisharanya who was mesmerized by Bhagwanji's chanting of Sanskrit hymns with flawless pronunciation and a booming voice was the temple priest's relative Srikant Sharma. Two decades earlier, Srikant had seen Subhas Bose during his tour of the United Province. When he did get to talk to Bhagwanji, his curiosity was further aroused. In the near future, Srikant was going to get luckier.

In 1962, Professor Atul Sen—a freedom fighter who had been acquainted with the top leaders of his times, Gandhi, Nehru, Bose included—fainted while touring some remote area in Naimisharanya. He was brought to the temple complex where he conversed with Bhagwanji. On his return to Calcutta, Sen told his friend RC Majumdar, the historian, that he had spoken to 'Subhas Bose'.

Confused, Majumdar would go on to write in 1966 that while the holy man did not appear before Sen (whom he did not mention by name), he told him many past episodes which were not likely to be known to others. He recounted that this 'highly-educated and respected gentleman really believed that the person with whom he had conversed was Netaji'.

Ignoring Bhagwanji's caution, Professor Sen wrote a letter to Prime Minister Nehru on 28 August 1962. It now lies in one PMO file:

Dear Jawaharlal Ji,

I take the liberty of addressing these few lines to you in the matter of the widely-prevalent belief that Netaji Subhas Chandra Bose is not dead. Mine is not mere belief but actual knowledge that Netaji is alive and is engaged in spiritual practice somewhere in India. Not the Sadhu of Shoulmari, Cooch-Behar, in West Bengal about whom some Calcutta politicians are making a fuss at this moment. I deliberately make the location a little vague because from the talks I had with him for months together not very long ago, I could understand that he is yet regarded as

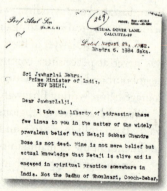

Record obtained under the
Right to Information

Enemy No 1 of the Allied Powers and that there is a secret protocol that binds the Government of India to deliver him to allied 'justice' if found alive.

If you can persuade yourself to assure me that his information is not correct or even if it is correct, your government shall resist any action by any of the said powers against the Great Patriot, I may try to persuade him to return to open life.

Nehru's response was somewhat odd. One, he shouldn't have taken kindly to Sen's claim that Bose was alive in view of his own long-standing belief that he had died in 1945. Two, the bit about a secret protocol was so patently absurd that it warranted a contemptuous dismissal. Since Nehru had a marvelous intellectual capacity to personally dictate cogent responses to the numerous letters he received from all over the country each day, it cannot be assumed that he did not apply his mind while responding to Sen's posers.

Dear Professor Sen,

Your letter of August 28th.

I have never heard of any secret protocol about Netaji Subhas Chandra Bose. Certainly the Government of India have not bound themselves to any such thing. Even if any country asks the Government of India to hand him over, it is not going to be agreed to.

Yours sincerely,

Jawaharlal Nehru

But a reading of his 31 August reply gives one the impression that he was *open* to the idea of Bose's remaining alive, though he denied, somewhat apologetically, any knowledge of the alleged secret protocol.

Sen would never get to be in touch with Bhagwanji again, but word about his meeting 'Netaji' reached veterans of the secretive revolutionary group Anushilan Samity. Pabitra Mohan Roy, one of them, met Sen and decided to check his claims.

After considerable efforts, in December 1962 Roy managed to get an audience with Bhagwanji at Naimisharanya and he too became convinced that the man was Netaji. Overcome with emotions, the *Dead Man* began opening his heart and secrets to him.

You cannot even understand under what awfully abnormal mental stress, bodily pain and circumstantial handicaps I am living here.

Pabitra wanted to stay with him to serve him better but Bhagwanji declined:

I do not for the present want to take you away from your family's tender circle. Please remember my humble self to your good wife. I wish she could feed me with ilisher jhol bhaat,' Dhaccai parota, aloor dom and kalia.

And then came Dead Man's most vital order. No one was to know he was at Naimisharanya:

From this moment you must not mention me and 'N' to any one, whatsoever and whoever. When you shall meet in the future, you must not even by the slightest indication give out that you contacted me at 'N'. You shall sacrifice your head but keep your lips sealed. Only when you shall be ordered in clear verbal tones 'Your seals are off now', then you can. Similarly, tell others of this present phase. Let no one come to me. If anyone asks about—turn a complete blank. Keep a true and factual scrutiny of persons and parties.

Pabitra was given a surreal lowdown on Bhagwanji's 'post-death' activities. *The ghost of the dead* had been *floating in and floating out* of India, appearing in different places like Erebus, the Greek god of darkness.

When your Dead Man was in Berlin, a great German doctor-scientist became very very friendly—affectionate and attached. …And in the course of his talks, he said that in his lab he found that Radar beam particles do not bounce back if they strike '…', and the doctor felt astonished. That doctor could not inform any of the government agencies or other scientists. He was a bombing raid casualty.

…In one secret place, your Dead Man tested about the truth of that German scientist's findings, and, he found it to be 100% fact. Particles of beams, directed at a point blank range, on 'something' did not bounce back…. Even now, the scientists of the Great Powers are feverishly trying to find out some means to avoid Radar detection.

For Mother Bengal's sake and for the sake of my entire trust in you, do not get startled or perturbed, he comforted Pabitra, bewildered by the disclosures.

In his first letter to Pabitra in English, whose copy Pabitra was allowed to make in his own handwriting, Bhagwanji discussed his long-standing mystic inclination, citing episodes from his life:

To understand a man you have to understand the bedrock on which he stands and he works. My most beloved mother was a direct disciple of Paramhansa Dev. By every suck of her breast, through every kiss of hers, by the channels of her caresses, touches, tender looks and words, the Tattwa-Shakties of the Divine Mother flowed in and filled me.

My father gave unto me thoroughness and strength in service to others and fighting activeness. My Governor, first tutor-guardian, gave me missionary sacrificing zeal and all fighting, all overcoming stamina. Collectively this I got through heredity, birth, infancy and childhood. This is my bedrock.

…Essentially I have been and shall ever be alone. I inherited Mysticism from Mother, Paramhansa and Vivekananda. Throughout I have been constant. Even during the most hectic times the deepest hours of the night afforded me of time for that.

Details that he would offer later on made it clear that he claimed to be Subhas Bose:

From my childhood I began hearing and perusing scriptures. As I grew up my mystic hunger also grew. I went through all scriptures and philosophies again and again. In my college and University years I used to seek out, hunt the so-called great seers and wise men of our days and I questioned them on mysticism. None satisfied me.

I even left everything once in search of a true mystic satguru and searched far and wide in the country and high and low in the Himalayas. None could satisfy me. It was bitter winter. I remembered my own mother, my darling adored mother, and came back to her lap and feet. [Originally in English]

Master moshai's influence on my life was the greatest. Do you know why? It was Beni Babu who turned my life around. ...And if there was a bosom friend, it was Hemanta. [Translated from Bangla]

First you all knew me as the son of Rai Bahadur so and so, son of so and so mother, etc. Then you knew that he entered politics against his will because of Deshbandhu's magic. Besides a few have got to know that he does sadhana secretly. Some have also got to know that some tantric practitioners meet him at certain places in other countries under different situations to advise him. Then he went abroad, became the Supreme Commander and then died or disappeared. Suddenly you knew he is alive, that he did not die. Even now many people see him alive. [Translated from Bangla]

It was never a secret that a young Subhas Bose had run away from his home on a spiritual quest; or that Beni Madhav Das was his school teacher and Hemanta Sarkar his childhood friend; or that Deshbandhu Chittaranjan Das was the one who had initiated him into politics. Just because someone rhapsodised all that did not mean he was Subhas. Anyone could have lifted these details from already-published books.

But wouldn't Pabitra see through it all? And what about those who came after him? These people had known Subhas for decades, not for just two-three years, as most INA compatriots did. Before he became 'Netaji', Subhas Bose was a top Congress leader and the uncrowned king of Bengal's revolutionaries.

As Hindu godmen go, Bhagwanji was clearly out of the ordinary. In the sense that any Indian holy man who could speak and write in English like him would have either found salvation in Europe or America or had the hippies flocking in droves to hear him speak. He could have easily gotten out of his life of anonymity, misery and self-imposed solitary confinement—he described it as a 'vexatious dog-life'—but he wouldn't. He did not even allow the number of his close disciples to go beyond a dozen at any given time. He just simply hid himself away, as if he was a fugitive of some sort.

In the confines of his room, Bhagwanji would occasionally puff away on his pipe or roll a cigar in his mouth. He'd have bread and butter for breakfast and he savoured the best of Western literature—William Shakespeare, Charles Dickens and PG Wodehouse being his favourites. Actually, his room housed an entire library. It included voluminous *Encyclopaedia Britannica*, volumes I to X of Will and Ariel Durant's magnum opus *The Story of Civilization*, the complete collected works of Rabindranath Tagore and

Sarat Chandra Chattopadhya and many more. Books dealing with recent history, such as *Between the lines* and *India: Critical Years* by Kuldip Nayar, *Himalayan Blunder* by Brigadier John Dalvi, *India's China War* by Neville Maxwell, carried his outpourings as comments on the margins.

'A man always wrong', Bhagwanji commented on Morarji Desai. He praised Brigadier Dalvi, who had been taken a PoW during the 1962 war: 'God bless you for your nobility and honesty. He saved you from death and brought you back to your people.'

In fact, he tarred his copy of Brigadier Dalvi's once-banned book with angry scribbles.

'Oh God, What blunders from HQ & ND', 'Oh, blast you all', 'Well, that's that'—these were hardly the expressions of a holy man dwelling in obscurity in India.

In the same book, he scrawled several offensive words for Prime Minister Nehru for whom he had a distinct dislike. Otherwise dignified, Bhagwanji lost his cool while pondering over India's humiliating defeat—a subject which dominated his talks with Pabitra during their meeting at Naimisharanya in December 1962 and subsequently. On page 316 of Dalvi's book, against the PM's quote, 'We were stabbed in the back', Bhagwanji scribbled: 'A lie—black as hell. He was a clown and a knave at that.' The Indian soldiers to him were 'simple honest sons of India' who were 'offered as a "free sample" at the altar of total stupidity, ego and greed!' Bhagwanji did not approve of Dalvi lauding a certain Army commander. 'Aren't your high praises sentimental?' he asked, adding that 'I know' the General 'only as a "yesman-lapdog" to the High Command and the political bosses'.

Quite a few books Bhagwanji possessed had interesting subject matter: *International Military Tribunal for the Far East: Dissentient judgment of Justice Radha Binod Pal*—which he underlined at several places; RC Majumdar's epic *The history of the freedom movement in India*; Leonard Mosley's *The last days of the British Raj*; Peter Sengar's *Moscow's hand in India*, Rajni Mukherjee's *Moscow's shadow over West Bengal*, Sita Ram Goyal's *Nehru's fatal friendship* and Aleksandr Solzhenitsyn's *The Gulag Archipelago*.

The collection even included *Gulliver's travel* by Jonathan Swift, *The Odyssey* and *Iliad* by Homer, *The Bermuda Triangle* by Charles Berlitz, *Flying saucers farewell* by George Adamski, *Life beyond death* by Swami Abhedanand, *Celebrated Crimes* by IG Burnham, *The Hunchback of Notre Dame* by Victor Hugo, *Tropic of Cancer* by Henry Miller, *Alice in Wonderland* by Lewis Carroll and *Rubaiyat* of Omar Khayyam.

The holy man's daily dose of news came from a number of English, Hindi and Bangla newspapers. *The Pioneer* was said to be his favourite, but from the *TIME* magazine to the RSS mouthpiece *Organiser*, he lapped up a variety of magazines. He took note of events by underlining the newspapers. For example the death of British botanist and birth control advocate Marie Stopes in 1958, and the assassination of Bangladesh President Ziaur Rahman in 1981.

When he was not reading, Bhagwanji played records of Pannalal Bhattacharya, KL Sahgal, Juthika Ray, Ustad Faiyaz Khan, Sumitra Sen, Govinda Gopal Mukherjee, Atul Prasad Sen, Bismillah Khan, Ustad Vilayat Khan, Pandit Ravi Shankar, Pannalal Ghosh, Dilip Kumar Roy, Kazi Nazrul Islam, Firoza Begum of Bangladesh and more.

Among the popular musicians, he admired Bollywood great Naushad Ali not only for the music he created but also for his politeness and willingness to help friends from his rainy days. *The jewel amongst your radio announcers is Melvin de Mello.*

Don't worry, he will not die, Bhagwanji told his youngest follower, Nirupam Mishra, when Amitabh Bachchan was battling for life in 1983 and the entire country was praying for him.

The watches Bhagwanji probably wore on his extended tours outside—but never displayed to any local person in UP—were Rolex and Omega Gold. When these watches were discovered at Ram Bhawan, quite a commotion followed because Bose always wore round watches, ever since his parents presented him a round Omega Gold watch in his younger years.

Followers recalled that he spoke like a bureaucrat while talking of the Motor Vehicles Act and like a counter-intelligence expert when alluding to the rings of spies in the nation. He claimed that in UP alone there were nearly forty meeting points for international spies, and the Indian agencies had penetrated only three of them.

When Bhagwanji's belongings were being inventoried in Lalita Bose's presence, several pictures of the Bose family members, especially of Subhas's parents, were recovered. Those who had sent these thought they were Bhagwanji's parents as well. One of the holy man's most treasured possessions was an old-fashioned umbrella sent to him from Calcutta with a note that it was of 'father Janaki Nath Bose'.

Lalita Bose also came across a typed copy of her father's lengthy testimony before the Khosla Commission on 17 August 1972. It turned out that Suresh Bose had insisted that his brother was still alive at that time. This assertion of his had been duly recorded in the testimony. She noted that the typed copy bore corrections in her father's handwriting. She was dumbfounded when the summons sent by the Khosla Commission to her father in West Bengal was located in Bhagwanji's room at Ram Bhawan.

Lalita was not around when a copy
of her freedom fighter cousin Dwijendra
Nath Bose's testimony before the same
commission was located among the heaps
of papers at Ram Bhawan. Suresh Bose
was not the only family member who
had 'fantasized' about a living Subhas
Bose, more than two decades after his
reported death. During his examination,
Dwijendra Nath, son of Subhas's eldest

Suresh Bose is seen paying homage to
Leela Roy in a picture which was sent
to Bhagwanji

brother Satish, was pointedly asked if he had tried to find out the identity
of Pardawala baba, or the holy man behind the curtain, a name by which
Bhagwanji was sometimes referred to in Naimisharanya and Basti. He denied
that he was his uncle. But then, many confirmed followers of Bhagwanji like
Pabitra Mohan Roy and Samar Guha also deposed before this commission
and said absolutely nothing of their holy man connection. They followed as
an article of faith his directive to make endeavours to get the air crash theory
dismissed, and not go beyond.

Dwijendra Nath strayed into the areas deemed forbidden for
Bhagwanji's followers. He was asked by a counsel, if he had indeed made
a statement on 6 March 1966 in Thiruvanathapuram that 'Netaji was still
alive and was working in a place very near the borders of India'. 'Yes I
did say', Dwijendra Nath affirmed during his 1972 deposition before the
Khosla Commission. An *Amrita Bazar Patrika* report on his statement was
quoted and brought on record: '"I can tell you that last September, Netaji
had an attack of pneumonia and was examined and treated by some very
eminent doctors whom I know, but I won't name", Mr Bose told reporters.'

'Yes, I did say that', Dwijen accepted without any hitch.

A letter available with a Bhagwanji follower proves that in 1966 the
counsel of Dr SK Das, former personal physician to President Rajendra
Prasad, had been sought for then ailing Bhagwanji. Was Dwijen making an
allusion to this?

Asked why Subhas Bose was still in hiding, Dwijendra retorted that 'it
is not correct to say that'.

'He is still working for India. He will come out...at the appropriate
time....'

'Therefore, may I understand that your case is that though all these
sadhus are not Netaji, but Netaji is still alive?' the counsel put to him.

'Yes', said Dwijendra Nath.

Seven

In January 1963, Pabitra Mohan Roy was a troubled man. Back to his Dum Dum residence from his surreptitious sojourn in Naimisharanya, he wondered how with his limited means was he going to arrange for the articles Bhagwanji wanted him to bring by the month end.

A chronometer wristwatch which must give absolutely correct time, without fluctuating a second; a pair of binoculars which must be the most powerful, highest powered, longest range, utmost clarity, to be used by hands only; a transistor, extremely powerful in shortwave and midwave; cigars and a Fowler's Dictionary.

The reasons given by the holy man why he needed all these foxed Roy.

One very learned scholar, a Siberian Deputy of Supreme Soviet, several times requested me to get it [Fowler's] *for him. He can never dream of getting it licitly there (you know the reasons). He shall then become a 'suspect'. He has become very attached. And he is a very great help to your Dead Man's....*

For a while he couldn't think of anyone he could go to for help. '*Didi!*' Pabitra then thought of Leela Roy, the big sister of all revolutionaries, founder of

Leela Roy in 1946

Sri Sangha, someone who had known Subhas since the 1920s and treated him as an equal.

On 7 January 1963, Pabitra let Leela Roy into the secret—that he had met 'Netaji' at Naimisharanya. Stunned, Leela Roy recorded in her personal diary that evening: 'A bewildering truth was revealed today afternoon. Unthinkable are its possibilities; everything associated with it is unimaginable.' [Translated from Bangla]

Hurriedly, she called a meeting of her Sri Sangha confidants and close relatives. Sunil Das, Shaila Sen, Santosh Bhattacharya, Bijoy Nag; Basana Guha and her husband Professor Samar Guha were among those who attended. On March 23, accompanied by Shaila Sen, Samar Guha and Anil Das, formerly of INA secret service, Leela Roy arrived at the Shiva temple in Naimisharanya.

She noted in her diary how 'greatly depressed' she was after the first attempt to meet 'Leader' was unsuccessful. Initially she 'decided to leave the place next morning', but in the morning thought she 'would stay on' till she met him. Leela Roy, Samar Guha and Anil Das 'tried to ingratiate themselves' with Saraswati Devi, the attendant. 'But impersonations were not much effective; my inner pride could not be concealed, felt deep humiliation….'

The next morning, she noted that she was, 'almost sure that he has got the news of our presence'.

Eventually, a meeting did take place. It was made possible in part by Srikant Sharma, who acted as a go-between as the visitors begged for an access to the holy man. Bhagwanji told him to communicate only with Roy. 'Samar Guha was just a child when I left India.' In the process, Srikant got summoned inside and had the thrill of beholding an 'aged Netaji'. His observant eyes noted that 'he' had put on weight, his hairline had receded further but the characteristic gap in his teeth was there still.

Bhagwanji gave an inconsolable Leela Roy an instruction in writing. *My hands trembling—had to write every* (Bangla) *letter, remembering after two decades of lapse. Please transfer it to your own writing and return the paper.* He was not going to let her have a specimen of his handwriting. But this was not the moment.

'Do not tell anyone that I am here, or India will suffer!'

Convinced that Bhagwanji was Netaji, Leela Roy told her adopted son and nephew Bijoy Nag, on her return to Calcutta, about the incredible turn of events. 'He has done so much for the country. He is suffering even now.' And then she got on to the tasks Bhagwanji had assigned her.

First of all, Leela Roy dispatched alternative medicine practitioner and former freedom fighter Kamalakant Ghosh to Naimisharanya to take care of Bhagwanji's immediate medical needs. Then, one by one, she started informing a few selected people about the 'return' of Subhas Chandra Bose: Subhas's eldest surviving brother Suresh Bose, childhood friend Dilip Kumar Roy, political compatriots Trailokya Nath Chakravarty, Maulvi Ashrafuddin Ahmed Chaudhury and Swami Asimanand Saraswati, and industrialist Ashutosh Ganguly (founder of Metal Corporation of India which has evolved into the present-day Hindustan Zinc). Not everyone was going to believe her, because they thought if he was indeed back, he would have contacted them before anyone else. Leela Roy was rebuffed when she tried to reach out to some other Bose family members.

Her message to Dilip Kumar Roy, who had studied with Subhas in London but became a holy man afterwards, was conveyed through a hand delivered letter in 1963.

The picture on left was taken at Cambridge University in the early 1920s.
Dilip is sitting on the left and Subhas is standing on the right.
The other picture shows Dilip around mid-1970s in Haridwar.
Courtesy: Hari Krishna Mandir Trust, Pune

Wrecked physically by a recent stroke, Leela Roy wrote with a shaking hand…

I wanted to tell you about your friend. I am not entitled to speak much, but I can only inform you that **'He's alive—in India.'** He has mentioned about your friendship with him many times. For example, **'It was Dilip who always wanted to make me a mystic.'** For this reason, this letter is important.... If you trust me, then it is 100 pc correct. No one else should know about it—this is the **stern injunction** on me.

[Translated from Bangla, except the words empasised]

Reaching Trailokya Nath Chakravarty was not easy for he was in east Pakistan, the present-day Bangladesh. 'Maharaj' had troubled the British during the freedom struggle—so much that they had kept him locked up for thirty unimaginable years in all; more than ten of which were in the notorious prison hell in Port Blair.

Leela Roy asked former revolutionary Sailendra Roy, who died just a few years ago, to sneak into east Pakistan and deliver her message. The formidable Chakravarty was completely shaken upon receiving it. In 1963, he wrote Bhagwanji a letter that was recovered from Ram Bhawan:

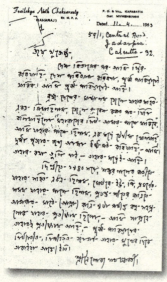

The person with whom I was lodged in Mandalay Jail, played tennis and participated in Durga Puja—I have not forgotten him. I'm still with him. In Delhi, in the year 1940, at Shankar Lal's residence I was accompanying him. I was by his side while we toured United Province. On a chilling winter night in the Agra ground, hundreds of people were waiting for him till nine at night. I'm eagerly waiting for the same person. The oppressed and tortured people of east Pakistan are waiting for him. [Translated from Bangla]

The word 'Subhas' was nowhere used but the context made it very clear that it was he that Chakravarty had in mind. Shankar Lal was Forward Bloc's general secretary. It was at his Delhi residence in

1940 that Trailokya had last met Subhas. He was also with Subhas when he was bundled to the dreaded Mandalay Jail in the 1920s.

After he was ousted from the Congress in 1939, Subhas Bose tried to create a broad platform by bringing diverse groups (Leftists, Hindu leaders, Muslim League) together. At Subhas's behest, Chakravarty had then met old friends: Keshav Baliram Hedgewar, the founder of the RSS; Bhai Paramanand, the Arya Samaj nationalist; Veer Savarkar and his younger brother Ganesh in an attempt to organise a revolutionary upsurge across the country. The response was not encouraging but Maharaj persisted. However, before long, Bose and his key associates were back in jail.

Indefatigable Chakravarty would go on to play a part in the Bangladesh liberation movement as well. In 1970, he visited New Delhi and was on 8 August felicitated at a reception party attended by Prime Minister Indira Gandhi, Lok Sabha Speaker GS Dhillon and several MPs. In the wee hours of 9 August, Chakravarty would pass away. Prime Minister Gandhi, who out of her deference for the 83-year old Anushilan stalwart had personally served him sweets, was shell-shocked at his sudden demise. 'Meeting him was a moving experience', she said, according to the book *Biplab Tapas Maharaj Trailokya Nath*, by Lalit Kumar Sanyal. He was so 'relaxed and full of future', she had added, according to another account in *Indian revolutionary movement* by Bejoy Kumar Sinha.

Former revolutionary Sunil Das was to become another informer of Bhagwanji. He passed on to him the inside stories concerning Subhas Bose. On 24 January 1964, for example, he reported his running into former revolutionary- turned-Nehru-loyalist Surendra Mohan Ghose at the office of Bengal Chief Minister Prafulla Chandra Sen. Describing Ghose as 'an agent of Sri Jawaharlal Nehru', Das narrated:

> [Ghose] went on to say the Allied Powers (this is Govt's opinion) have by common consent struck off the name of Netaji from the list of war criminals because they have officially concluded that Netaji was dead.

An average-looking person, Das wasn't an average revolutionary. Bright enough in his student days to have his paper published in *The American Journal of Physical Chemistry*, he chose to be a freedom fighter like his siblings, all three of whom died for the nation, unsung. So long as he lived, Das kept his mouth shut about his Bhagwanji connection, even though he was part of Calcutta's intellectual circle. Professor Leonard Gordon listed him as one of the sources for his definitive biography of Subhas and Sarat, *Brothers against Raj*. GD Khosla described him in his report as 'a political worker and a close associate of Bose for some years'. But there was more to all that.

When Sunil Das was being examined before the Khosla Commission in 1972, the counsel for Forward Bloc and Sunil Gupta's senior Amar Prasad Chakrovarty, a Member of Parliament later on, tried to get his secrets out.

'The point that I want to ask from you is that you knew Netaji intimately so as not to mistake his identity?'

'His identity? So far as I am concerned, good heavens, never. How can I mistake his identity?'

'Do you think that if Netaji is really alive, there is something really insurmountable which would prevent him or would actually prevent him from coming into the arena when the country is in utter confusion and chaos?'

'Your question has two parts. Regarding the first part of the question my reply is, I believe that Netaji is alive. Regarding the second part I have no competence to go into it.'

'How many times do you think Mrs Leela Roy met Saratbabu?'

'I think almost every day.'

'Were there any discussions regarding Netaji's alleged plane crash?'

'As far as I remember, Saratbabu never believed it.'

Right to left: Sunil Das, Sunil Gupta, Amar Prasad Chakrovarty in suit, and ND Mazumdar.
Courtesy: Jayasree Publications

'Did Didi ever write regarding the disappearance of Netaji?'

'There were occasions when this subject cropped up in editorials [in her magazine *Jayasree*] after 1963. I should say, we noticed a change in her—within herself. Although I happened to be her closest colleague and in many matters she shared counsel with me—as you know, we had been trained in the crucibles of secret revolutionary politics, and we have developed a code and we maintain the code in this way. Unless I am specifically told, if somebody in the hierarchy wants to keep something within himself or herself, we do not try to get it. That has been our training. Up till now I carry that thing with me.'

The list of such amazing persons of unquestionable integrity who took Bhagwanji to be Netaji is quite impressive. Ashutosh Kali was another senior revolutionary, who came to know Bhagwanji's secret through Pabitra. An Anushilan Samity veteran, Kali too had been prevented by long years in prison (1916 to 1938 and 1940 to 1946) from playing a bigger role in the freedom struggle. In May 1963, he offered his services to Bhagwanji.

> The moment we received your instructions, we started maintaining secrecy. ...I am determined not to allow any laxity on our part...any danger to your existence is not just so for you, but also for us all. It can result in a great disaster as well as an immense damage to the nation. [Translated from Bangla]

Before he died in an accident in 1965, Kali visited Bhagawaji in May 1963. Another undated letter of his was found among Bhagwanji's belongings in Ram Bhawan:

> Ever since we got news of you, all of us, the entire Anushilan group, have been yearning to gain from your guidance and work under your instructions. ...I have crossed the age of seventy (but) the idealism that I imbibed from the valiant revolutionaries, the courage with which I fought everything is still burning bright within me. ...If you give the clarion call, even at this point of life, I will not hesitate to join the movement. I wanted to inform you that Basanti Devi is desperate to receive news of you. She has requested us to let her know about your whereabouts. [Loosely translated from Bangla]

The reference to Basanti Devi in Kali's letter was probably to Subhas's mentor Chittaranjan Das's wife, a motherly figure to him. There seems no doubt that Subhas's brother Suresh took Bhagwanji to be his brother. After being sounded out by Leela Roy, Suresh Bose told his confidant Sunil Krishna Gupta to go to Basti and contact 'Subhas' there.

Without offering any details, Suresh Bose asserted before the Khosla Commission that his brother was alive at that time. Asked to 'take this commission into confidence and to say what are the reasons for believing this', he curtly said, 'There is no reason why I should take this commission into confidence'.

Evidently, Suresh Bose did not even tell his own children about his secret contact with his brother. When Bhagwanji's belongings were being inventoried, Lalita Bose, his daughter, was there for a while. She told *The Pioneer* on 1 April 1986 that the personal effects of Bhagwanji 'were in one way or the other related to the kith and kin of Netaji'.

The most remarkable point is that when I went through the effects, I found an unusual Bengali silk in which a well-wrapped photograph of my father, late Mr Suresh Chandra Bose, was found.

...I kept asking my father who is that rustic-looking man who comes to you often from Basti. My father parried my frantic enquiries. He used to chat for hours together with this man in his private room.

Suresh Bose passed away in 1972, Lalita in 1998 but Sunil Gupta lived up to 2010 to tell his incredible tale. There is no way one can ignore this remarkable man's words—and those of Bhagwanji's living followers Dulal Nandy, Bijoy Nag, Surajit Dasgupta, Dr Madhusudan Pal and Professor Nandalal Chakravarty—after getting some idea about their antecedents. To see them move around normally like everyone else, one cannot imagine the experiences they have been through. Nandy and Nag reminisced that even their wives had no clue for a long time whom they were visiting every 23rd January. They would carry hilsa fish in an ice box and custom-made cake from Nahoum, the legendary Jewish bakery at New Market in Kolkata.

From left: Bijoy Nag, Madhusudan Pal, Dulal Nandy, Anuj Dhar, Nandalal Chakravarty and Surajit Dasgupta in 2013

Because Sunil Gupta died in penury, an unsung man, people have trouble recalling his name. Secret records however 'certify' what Gupta really was, apart from being the uncle of martyr Dinesh Gupta of the BBD Bagh fame. On 17 August 1956, Intelligence Bureau Deputy Director S Balakrishna Shetty, who's assigned duty it was to keep an eye on matters relating to Netaji, wrote to the Home Ministry:

We reliably understand that some of the Top Secret papers of the Government of India made available to the Chairman of the Netaji Enquiry Committee are now in the possession of one Sunil Krishna Gupta.... He appears to have obtained them through his friend Mr [Suresh] Bose....

Then Bengal Chief Secretary SN Ray's Top Secret DO, dated 10 June 1957 had this to add:

Sunil Krishna Gupta...is well educated, possesses considerable cultural attainments and is intimately known to the Bose family. All the members of Sunil's family, including his two grown up sisters, were associated with the political movement in the Far East sponsored by the late Subhas Chandra Bose.

Another person who became a die-hard Bhagwanji follower was Anil Das of INA secret service, the one who had accompanied Leela Roy to Naimisharanya in 1963.

Declassified in 1997, and now available at the National Archives in New Delhi, is an intelligence report which reads that on his last night in Bangkok Subhas Bose talked to Anil Das about the underground work after the Japanese surrender. Another report speaks of the CSDIC's anxiousness to nab him, as Das had gone missing after Bose's reported death.

Yet another record shows Bose writing to Hikari Kikan to hand over to AC Das fifty revolvers, some wireless sets and some British currency for post-war work.

None of these documents were in the public domain so long as Das lived. But his letters found at Ram Bhawan added to the account given in the official records. His first, 1964 letter was something of an aide-memoire for Bhagwanji, vetted and approved by Leela Roy. In it Das recapitulated his role in the freedom struggle, beginning in the 1930s and lasting beyond 1945.

> On the night before he left Bangkok, Netaji took individual interviews of a number of people. I was one of them. When Netaji called me, it was half past 2 am. He told me about the post-war work and cautioned me against getting arrested. He gave me a letter addressed to Hikari Kikan. ...Netaji said that wherever he may go, he would remain in contact with us via wireless....

> When I heard the news of the crash of Netaji's plane, I knew such news would come and it would not be true. I waited for over a decade and in 1956, I visited India and told everything to auntie [Leela Roy]. In 1961, I left Bangkok for good and last year, auntie sent me to Naimisharanya and thereafter, whatever small or big news I wanted to know, I came to know from her. Now I am waiting for your orders. [Loosely translated from Bangla]

After perusing this letter, Bhagwanji specifically asked Das about what had really happened after 16 August 1945 and what statements were given by the captured INA personnel. Das elaborated in another letter that he

> received 2 wireless sets and a few revolvers, pistols and stenguns from Hikari Kikan. They could not give me British currency. Then I went underground. Within 6-7 days the British Military reached Bangkok. ...First

Debnath Das surrendered before British military authority, and he was let off after his statement was taken. [Loosely translated from Bangla]

And when Das came to meet him, Bhagwanji actually corrected a few details about 'their' meeting in Bangkok.

There is no way of knowing now who all kept in touch with Bhagwanji believing he was Subhas Bose. Letters of a certain Bhoop Babhdur of Cooch Behar and one VR Mohan were found in Ram Bhawan. The names sound like those of the former king of the region where Shaulmari ashram was located and a well-known distillery industrialist. The holy man would destroy much of his correspondence. Some that have survived the destruction tell their own story. The following note, for instance, was presumably written by former West Bengal Chief Minister Prafulla Ghosh.

The writer, 'Malikananda Ghosh', which was Prafulla's alias, laments that his life would have taken a different turn if the events of 'the Haripura session leading to the Wellington Square happenings' not taken place. Haripura Congress session witnessed the rise of Subhas Bose as the Congress president, and at the Wellington Square session he was forced to step down. Bhagwanji

discouraged his followers to speak or write about his identity, but most could not stop themselves from dropping hints that they were aware of it.

Now, this should give goose bumps to the RSS-BJP rank and file. The *Guruji* of the entire current top brass of the Sangh Parivar—former Prime Minister Vajpayee, former Deputy PM Advani, former HRD Minister MM Joshi, RSS chief Mohan Bhagwat, his predecessor the late KS Sudarshan and, above all, Prime Minister Narendra Modi—held Bhagwanji in the highest esteem. This is evident from a letter written by Madhav Golwalkar to him. This too was found at Ram Bhawan.

॥ श्री ॥

राष्ट्रीय स्वयंसेवक संघ, केंद्र-नागपुर

सरसंघचालक : मा. स. गोळवलकर   सरकार्यवाह : म. द. देवरस

Golwalkar starts his letter with the salutation: 'I bow before you a hundred times'. The content of this letter gives the impression that Golwalkar, who ran India's biggest social organisation, was taking orders from a seemingly non-descript holy man who hardly left his room.

While it is not known whether Golwalkar ever met Narendra Modi, it is clear from Modi's 2008 biography of the second RSS chief [picture] that apart from Swami Vivekananda, Guru Golwalkar is the second most important influence on the present Prime Minister's extraordinary life.

A close follower remembered Bhagwanji meeting certain RSS functionaries. A Sangh Prachark in a foreign country, who wishes to remain anonymous, claimed to a friend of this writer that Madhukar Dattatraya Deoras, the RSS chief after Golwalkar, maintained a contact with Bhagwanji through his brother. Bhagwanji did laud the Sangh for its idealism and devotion to the nation. He praised the Sangh for its resistance to the Emergency (1975-77). Once he noted how a big RSS camp was meticulously organised in one place without troubling the locals in any way, contrasting that to an earlier NCC camp that had left the surrounding vegetation devastated, angering the local Muslim populace. He recalled RSS volunteers lining up to donate blood at front line field hospitals, sometime during the India-Pakistan war after the locals showed little enthusiasm. *Local Army commander had requested for blood to the zonal organiser of the RSS. No news of this came out in the dailies though Government, police and Army all knew,* he said in Bangla.

All the same, there was a certain Aulia Saheb, who knew who Bhagwanji really was and helped him. The holy man even wrote letters, probably anonymously, to Balasaheb Thackeray and ABA Ghani Khan Choudhury, the late Congress leader from Malda. He would say that 'his men' were 'in every key place (here and overseas)': in Army, Government and in foreign nations. *Their garb is legal. They simply cannot be touched or detected.*

Whoever Bhagwanji was, he attracted people across all divides. A certain Abdul Hafiz wrote to 'respected secret sadhu' in Hindi that he prayed to the Almighty for fulfillment of Bhagwanji's desires. 'Please take your original form at the earliest!'

It is not very common for Hindu holy men to have Muslim followers. Bhagwanji actually had a Muslim attendant at Basti. And he often quoted from the Bible. *To everything there is a season. And a time to every purpose under the heaven.* Gurucharan Singh Bedi of Dera Baba Nanak, Gurdaspur, who had sent a copy of the Guru Granth Sahib to Bhagwanji, wrote, 'Crores of Indians have put their eyes upon you'. There was a letter from Calcutta likening Bhagwanji to the invincible grand old Mahabharat or Bhishma. Bhagwanji drew the same analogy for himself, saying he was *the legal inheritor of this earth* but was *stepping aside from the path of ruling.*

Yet another letter in broken English by Gurucharan Singh Bedi reads: 'People say you are Mother India's best son Netajee himself.' Bhagwanji himself used the metaphor for himself. 'I am a son of the motherland', he wrote in Hindi in an undelivered letter to Vibhuti Narayan Singh, former Chancellor of Banaras Hindu University and former king of Kashi. Hindi was clearly not Bhagwanji's first language.

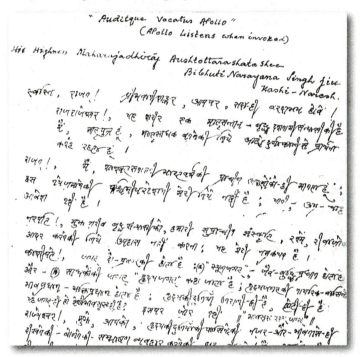

Of course, not everyone who wanted to meet Bhagwanji got to meet him. He was highly selective. At one point, political activist Manu Bhai Bhimani—who had been associated with Gandhi, Subhas and other leaders before 1947—came in contact with a Bhagwanji follower. The follower assessed Bhimani and made a short note for Bhagwanji.

He [Bhimani] came in contact through a common friend. He talks too much. He says that:

1. If Netaji is in India why does he not appear or broadcast? All the people will accept his leadership at once.
2. ....
3. He helped Shri Sarat Chandra Bose all the time till he was alive.
4. He helped Netaji when he escaped from Calcutta to Kabul. Sisir and Manu Bhai went with him. He has a special white bag which he used when he accompanied Netaji.

I verified the points 3 and 4 from Sisir Bose—Point 3 is correct, and point 4 is not correct. Bhimani also sent me a letter which has been sent for your kind perusal.

'He has lied', Bhagwanji commented. He dismissed as 'false' Bhimani's claim that he had helped Sarat Bose until his death in 1950. He crossed out both points 3 and 4 and wrote: 'You don't know facts. *Mejda* helped him. Everyone knows this except you fool.'

In intense investigations minute details add up to create big discoveries. There is something particularly catchy about this letter. The Bangla word for 'elder middle brother'.

In his private moments, not only did Bhagwanji behold pictures of Prabhavati and Jankinath Bose as if they were of his parents, he also addressed Sarat Bose just as Subhas used to.

Mejda.

Eight

A boost for the Bose mystery came from a most unlikely place in the late 1980s. So far only the Indians had been talking about Subhas's presence in USSR after his reported death, but now the citizens of the moribund Soviet state too joined in.

In 1989, an article in the *Soviet Land* discussed the fate of Indian revolutionaries Birendra Nath Chatterjee and Abani Mukherjee who 'had disappeared from the Soviet society without leaving any traces'. The unease about Subhas was palpable as the article continued: 'Mahatma Gandhi, Bal Gangadhar Tilak, Bhagat Singh, Jawaharlal Nehru, Indira Gandhi and other leaders, heroes and martyrs of the India national liberation movement are well known to the Soviet people. Strange as it may seem, few of them have till date known Subhas Chandra Bose. For a long time, Soviet researchers were not allowed even to mention this passionate patriot.'

But why? In 1992, the journal *Echo Plantei* explained the subtext. The editorial note to the article 'The life and death of Netaji Bose', by A Vinogradov, a former *Tass* correspondent to India, said the officials in New Delhi and Moscow were 'keeping silence as regards the true fate of Bose' and that Moscow had 'confirmable documents' as to what the 'true state of affairs' actually were.

In 1994 Victor Touradjev, deputy editor-in-chief of the Russian journal *Asia* and *Africa Today*, published an essay on the basis of secret KGB records. While his basic premise was misplaced, Touradjev reproduced the text of a most vital and hitherto non-existent document: A letter Bose had written in November 1944 to Yakov Malik, the Soviet Ambassador in Tokyo. Bose was desirous of paying 'a visit to Your Excellency and find the way through which your Government can help us for success of our struggle for freedom'.

While everything appeared to be calm on the surface in India, rumblings were going on underneath. The Ministry of External Affairs noted in 1996 that 'from time to time, various articles have appeared in the Soviet/Russian press insinuating, though without any actual proof, that Netaji, in fact, stayed/was incarcerated in the Soviet Union after 1945'.

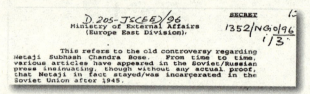

The sort of proof the Indian government was seeking couldn't be had without the government wanting to have it in the first place.

In October 1996, Purabi Roy, professor of International Relations Department with Calcutta's Jadavpur University, and a Russian journalist arranged a meeting at Moscow's President Hotel between Forward Bloc leaders Chitta Basu and Jayanta Roy, and Alexander Kolesnikov, an army veteran turned professor of the Russian Academy of Natural Sciences.

Kolesnikov gave Basu an eye-popping account about his coming across secret 'minutes of a 1946 discussion among Soviet Politburo members Voroshilov, Vyshinski, Mikoyan and Molotov', discussing 'whether Bose should be allowed to stay in the Soviet Union' or not. He advised the Indians to persuade their government to seek access to secret records held at the Russian archives. This idea was to become the leitmotif of Purabi Roy's big push to uncover he truth about Netaji's whereabouts.

Mysteriously, Chitta Basu on his return to India did not make public Kolesnikov's revelation and a written note given by him. He died during a train journey in 1997. Later, a search of his belongings for Kolesnikov's note proved futile. The Russian army veteran had by this time written an article in a local newspaper. While he did not discuss his sensational finding in it, but he did comment that Bose's disappearance was 'a mysterious point in Soviet- Indian relations'. The old conspiracy theory was back in circulation.

Plucky Purabi Roy battled on, making her case through the media: 'I need only a letter from the Government requesting the Russian authorities to allow me to go through classified documents kept in different archives.'

If they are confident that Netaji was actually killed in a plane crash in 1945, why have they always tried to scuttle any fresh investigation? If they are clean, let them provide us access to the two archives and see what's there?

With the issue heating up, the Joint Secretary in charge of Europe East Division (JS [EE]) in the MEA made a realistic assessment of the situation. RL Narayan—who had had two stints in Moscow and would be an Ambassador shortly afterwards—admitted that the official Russian response so far to the Indian approaches seeking information about Bose was not satisfactory.

He clarified that a recent official Russian denial about not knowing anything about him was not based on the 'Stalinist period (KGB archives)'. He explained: 'Papers relating to the Stalinist period (KGB archives) are kept separately and have so far not been accessed by foreign and even Russian scholars.'

Narayan's fair recommendation to the higher-ups was:

It would be unrealistic for us to expect the Russian authorities to allow our scholars access to KGB archives. What we can do is to request the Russian authorities to conduct a search into these archives, and let us know if there is any evidence of Netaji's stay in the Soviet Union. It is recommended that we may request our Ambassador in Moscow to make a suitable démarche to the Russian authorities on the above lines.

Document obtained in public interest

But Narayan's counsel was evidently overruled after then Minister of External Affairs saw his note. Pranab Mukherjee directed Foreign Secretary Salman Haidar to discuss the issue with Narayan 'urgently'.

The outcome of the meeting became apparent with the events that followed. No démarche was ever issued. Making an about-turn, Narayan dropped his sympathetic line and turned hostile. It was as if someone had cast a spell of the black magic of Bengal. In a subsequent note of 7 March, he dismissively wrote that the 'Asiatic Society scholars have unearthed no hard evidence of Netaji's stay in the Soviet Union after 1945' and, therefore, 'it would not be appropriate for Government of India to make a formal request to the Russian government to open the KGB/Presidential archives' as the same 'would amount to our disbelieving the Russian government's categorical and official statement on the subject'.

It would appear that at least for a while, then Prime Minister Narasimha Rao was not in synch with the line taken by the Ministry of External Affairs. Narayan's second note carries the following instruction to the MEA, issued through Joint Secretary (PMO):

> PM would like our Ambassador in Moscow to make discreet enquiries at a high level to ascertain, if possible, the existence of such information in Russia; and the possible reaction of the Russian side if we were to request access. Foreign Secretary may kindly see.

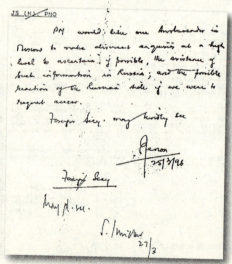

Document obtained in public interest

However, there is nothing on record to suggest that the then PM's direction was acted upon by the Ministry of External Affairs under the able leadership of the Nehru-Gandhi family loyalist Pranab Mukherjee. Whatever the Ambassador did or did not do in Moscow did not change a thing. Writing in a November 1996 note, Narayan charged the Asiatic Society scholars with wanting to access Russian archives 'essentially in order to go on a fishing expedition in search of material on Netaji' which they 'have convinced themselves exists in these archives'. Therefore, India's seeking access to KGB archives 'would serve no positive purpose, but could well have a negative impact'.

2   **SECRET**

6. Obviously, no Government in the world can be expected to throw open its secret archives for general research, on the basis suggested by the Asiatic Society. Equally, it would not be appropriate for the Government of India to seek access to these archives, which have not been declassified so far. We would, if nothing else, be embarrassed were a similar request, on the basis of reciprocity, to be made to us by the Russian Government at a later stage.

Document obtained in public interest

As for the External Affairs Minister, he went on to possibly leak the contents of a secret Russian response to a senior Bengali journalist, linked to Congress sympathisers in the Bose family bent on proving the air crash theory.

By 1997, the United Front government was in the saddle and the political environment had changed dramatically, thanks to a Bhagwanji follower once again. If in 1967, Samar Guha had created the wave for a fresh inquiry, thirty years later, Sunil Krishna Gupta pulled off another one.

In August, then Defence Minister Mulayam Singh Yadav triggered a controversy by innocuously proposing to bring the Renkoji ashes to India. Gupta and his nephews, Surajit and Jagatjit Dasgupta, and their friends, advocate Rudrajyoti Bhattacharjee, Madhusduan Pal and Nandalal Chakravarty—all of whom were either in touch with Bhagwanji or knew about him—approached the Calcutta High Court with a writ petition seeking to settle the controversy first.

In a history-bending order in April 1998, Chief Justice Prabha Shankar Mishra and Justice B Bhattacharya directed the government to 'launch a vigorous enquiry... for the purpose of giving an end to the controversy'. What went in favour of the new inquiry was the government's admission during the United Front days that notwithstanding the reports of the Shah Nawaz and GD Khosla panels, 'there are doubts as to the death of Netaji in the manner reports indicated, and that there was/is a need to have further probe'.

In April 1998, Atal Bihari Vajpayee had just begun his second innings as the Prime Minister of India. As his government dithered in taking a decision, Subhas's kin, researchers and Forward Bloc leaders—Subrata Bose, Purabi Roy, Debabrata Biswas, VP Saini in particular—began lobbying vigorously for a fresh probe.

Mounting pressure on the government was a Forward Bloc-sponsored resolution in the West Bengal Assembly. Adopted unanimously on 24 December 1998, it said the people and scholars of India were still in the dark and urged the Central government to 'make necessary arrangements for availability of records in and outside India' to scholars.

Finally in March 1999 Home Minister LK Advani, Principal Secretary to the Prime Minister Brajesh Mishra, Attorney General Soli Sorabjee and Home Secretary Kamal Pande decided that the only viable option was to comply with the court's order.

The government consequently notified on 14 April 1999 that 'the Central Government is of the opinion that it is necessary to appoint a Commission of Inquiry for the purpose of making an in-depth inquiry into a definitive matter of public importance'. On Chief Justice of India's recommendation, former Supreme Court judge Manoj Kumar Mukherjee was appointed the new commission's chairman.

To an extent the Vajpayee government cooperated with the Mukherjee Commission, but a point came when it became apparent that 'the party with a difference' was not all that different. When Lok Sabha MP Moinul Hassan Ahamed asked a question about Subhas in Russia, then Foreign Minister Jaswant Singh did not tax himself much. On 1 March 2000 he parroted an answer which had been previously drafted for a Congress minister. Not a word different here or there. A fine example of the continuity of official policy, no matter who was holding the reins of power.

Justice Mukherjee learnt at the very outset that the government was not going to be proactive about his inquiry. He had expected that at least, the Ministry of Information and Broadcasting would play a constructive role in relaying the news about the Commission's work. Nothing of this sort happened, and having failed to make the officials see reason, Mukherjee shot off a long letter to then I&B Minister Arun Jaitley on 14 April 2000.

Meanwhile the extended last date for submitting statemen affidavit expired and the first hearing of the Commission was held on 23.3.2000. It is really a matter of regret that Sri Shah did not even show minimum courtesy of giving a reply to my d/o letter although the letter was sent by fax and post (a copy of my letter dated 25.2.2000 is enclosed).

May I request you to kindly look into the matter personal and issue appropriate direction to the Prasar Bharati Corporatio of India to give wide publicity to the setting up of the Commission and the matters of inquiry before it, both in India and abroad, through the electronics media for at least 5 consecutive days ?

A copy of each of the Notifications, referred to above, and a copy of the Order passed by the Commission in its first hearing on 23.3.2000 are enclosed for ready reference.

Expecting an early action, and with personal regards,

Yours sincerely.

(M.K.Mukherjee)

Sri A.K.Jaitley
Hon'ble Minister of Information and Broadcasting
Government of India
Shastri Bhawan
New Delhi-110001.

The Minister was told that Doordarshan and Akashvani were not giving any publicity to the commission's work, possibly deliberately. 'I wrote a d/o letter… to Sri Rajiv Shah of Prasar Bharti…requesting him to take necessary steps…Sri Shah did not even show the minimum courtesy of giving a reply to my d/o letter, although the letter was sent by fax and post', the judge wrote.

Nevertheless, Justice Mukherjee pursued all the leads that he could. In all fairness, he did not allow people to make adverse comments against Pandit Nehru or others; he just religiously followed the terms of references assigned to his commission. His inquiries succeeded in some instances and in others, the government came in the way.

For the first time, the urn kept at Renkoji temple was opened. It was seen that it contained skull and jaw pieces.

The commission inquired from a number of DNA experts in India, Japan, Europe and America about the feasibility of a DNA test on these remains. Sir Alec Jeffreys of the Department of Genetics at the University of Leicester (UK) expressed doubts about the success of a DNA test on bones subjected to high temperatures. Regretting his inability to do the job in his laboratory, Sir Jeffreys—a pioneer of forensic use of DNA—told the commission to contact one of the national forensic service laboratories in the UK, for they were fully-equipped to perform the complex analysis required in the case.

The commission sounded off the MEA on 27 January 2003 about Sir Jeffreys' opinion and asked for the particulars of the national forensic service laboratories in the UK. The Ministry remained silent.

Terry Melton of Mitotyping Technologies in the US came up with an offer. Stating that the Renkoji remains were unlikely to yield a DNA profile, he nevertheless agreed to hold a standard forensic mitochondrial DNA test. Melton 'recommended a thorough anthropological evaluation of the remains' and 'apprised the commission of his requirements for performing the DNA analysis, and stipulated certain preconditions which included the anthropologist's report being made available to him prior to his proceeding to do the job'.

Such a test might have helped determine whether or not the pieces of skull and jaw did actually belong to an east Indian man who was around 48, when he was cremated in 1945. In March 2003, when the BJP was still in power, the commission appraised the MEA of Milton's views and directed them to do the needful. From that point on, the government began dragging its feet. And the result was that no scientific test could ever be carried out on the Renkoji remains.

When he went to Japan, Justice Mukherjee learnt that Dr Tenyoshi Yoshimi, the only surviving witness to Netaji's alleged death in 1945, was making up stories. Not only did the doctor make a false claim about issuing a death certificate for Bose, he admitted to having issued a fake one in 1988. This manufactured certificate had, in those days, landed with a researcher assisting the Government of India in proving the Taipei death story.

In London, Justice Mukherjee was helped by the House of Lords member Peter Archer. Lord Archer took up the issue of still secret documents concerning Bose with Alexander Irvine, the then Lord Chancellor, the Keeper of Public Records in the UK. Irvine wrote to Archer on 1 December 2001 that he 'looked into this thoroughly' and understood that while a few records were still being held by intelligence and security agencies, they did not 'contain any additional information relating to Subhas Chandra Bose's death that is not available at the Public Record Office or the British Library'.

Of the documents that were declassified and available at the National Archives in Kew, Irvine specifically mentioned two files—one of which talked about certain investigations in Taiwan in 1956. Justice Mukherjee was going to find this file immensely useful.

Records made available to Mukherjee by the Ministry of External Affairs showed that following a request from the Shah Nawaz Committee, the Ministry had approached the British High Commission to make an inquiry in Taiwan (Republic of China). Some progress appeared to have been made. For instance, a 24 May 1956 telegram from TN Kaul in New Delhi to the Indian Embassy in Japan said that the Taiwanese authorities were 'willing to allow five Chinese, whose names were given by the committee, to be examined by the British Consul in the presence of Formosan officials. They are however not prepared to let them to go to Hong Kong, to appear before our committee'.

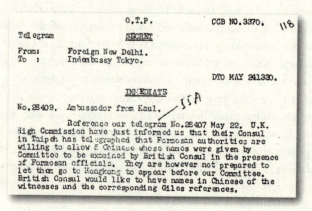

At the time, New Delhi failed to view this as a positive development. The Taiwanese government's decision not to let their citizens appear before a panel appointed by a government which did not recognise it, made the then MEA smell a conspiracy when there was none. The telegram went on to speculate that the Taiwanese 'may possess their witnesses and make them give wrong statements which may only complicate the work of the committee'.

3.   Formosan authorities' refusal to allow witnesses to go to Hongkong is significant. It is possible that they may tutor their witnesses and make them give wrong statements which may only complicate the work of the Committee. Our opinion therefore that Committee should not visit Formosa is confirmed. Please consult and ask them whether they would still like British Consul in Formosa to examine Chinese witnesses. Our advice would be that you should wait till you hear from the Japanese authorities in response to your approach.

PPS TO PM: PS TO PM(4): MINISTER WITHOUT PORTFOLIO: MINISTER: DY MINISTER: SG(2): FS(2): CS(2): JSE: DSXP: SOFA: USFEA(2): SONGO AND CAB SECY.

BHATIA(24).
24-5-1956.   Superintendent UCB.

There was nothing in the files to suggest what the British found out eventually, and whether or not New Delhi was informed about the outcome of the inquiry in Taiwan. Opening the 1956 British file, Justice Mukherjee found out why.

The specific queries of the Shah Nawaz Committee—which were mostly based on inputs provided by government-friendly journalist Harin Shah— were forwarded by the British to the Chairman of the Taiwan Provincial Government who, in turn, ordered the Department of Health to carry out an investigation. The findings were conveyed to the British.

A Franklin, the British Consul in Tamsui, Taiwan, reported to the Foreign Office in London on 10 July that 'it will be seen that most of the witnesses the Indian authorities requested us to obtain evidence from, have either died, disappeared or know nothing'. The old Japanese records, said to be that of Subhas Bose, actually turned out to be of a soldier.

The Taiwanese had in 1956 even traced the municipal bureau clerks who had supposedly seen 'Bose's body' prior to issuing the cremation permit in 1945. One of them clarified that all he saw was a body, 'packed in powdered lime, swathed in white cloth' whose 'only the eyes, the nose and the lips were visible'. The clerk had added: 'We were not acquainted with Bose in his lifetime; it therefore follows that we could not identify him after his death.'

In other words, there was no real proof of Bose's death.

The most damming of all the papers appeared at the end of the British file. It stated that not one, but five copies, of the British/ Taiwanese report were handed over to the Ministry of External Affairs in Delhi on 10 August 1956. Nehru himself was the Minister of External Affairs in those days.

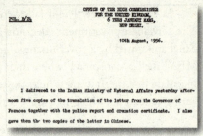

The National Archives, Kew

That the MEA under both the Vajpayee and Manmohan eras chose not to share with Justice Mukherjee a most credible report not supportive of the government view about Netaji's death was an undeniable proof of cover-up at the highest-level.

More shocks were in store for the former Supreme Court judge. The same Atal Bihari Vajpayee who had in 1972 opposed Indira government's initial decision to bar the Khosla Commission from visiting Taiwan remained passive when his own government did virtually the same to the Mukherjee Commission.

It was way back on 5 October 2001 that the Mukherjee Commission first approached the MEA to seek relevant information from Taiwan. In November 2002, the Ministry was requested to 'persuade the Government of Japan to get from the Government of Taiwan, the original register of cremation permits for the period from 18.08.1945 to 21.08.1945'.

In June 2003, the MEA told the commission that no 'relevant' documents were available in Taiwan. In the same month, a breakthrough was made by this writer under the aegis of *Hindustan Times*.

The paper's online division had already carried out an enquiry of its own into the entire controversy. The *HT* probe—with which I was closely associated as a staff journalist—concluded as early as 2001 that 'on present evidence, it would seem improbable that Bose died on August 18, 1945'.

In June 2003 this determination was bolstered as I beseeched the Republic of China (Taiwan) Government on behalf of all Indians, to state facts about Netaji's reported death in their country. Within days, Taipei Mayor Ying Jo Ma's office responded that 'according to the historical documents in Taipei city archives, there is no such record of a plane crash in Taipei on that day'.

This was followed up with a similar appeal to President Chen Shui-bian. His office forwarded my mail to ROC Minister of Transportation and Communications, Lin Ling-San, whose reply stated that a thorough analysis of the records left by the Japanese showed that there had been only one major air crash during that period. In September 1945, an American

C-47 transporter carrying about twenty-six released POWs had crashed near Mount Trident in Taitung area, around 200 nautical miles away from Taipei. There was 'no evidence' to show that any plane carrying Netaji had ever crashed in or around Taipei between 14 August and 25 October 1945.

Informing the commission about the Taiwan government's response, I advised its officials to contact the Taipei Economic and Cultural Center in New Delhi. After hearing me out, one commission official bitterly complained that the Government of India had not even told them that such an office existed in the national capital.

In September 2003, two things happened. One, the MEA forwarded to the commission the Japanese government's response about the cremation records for 1945 that was obtained, it said, 'after repeated reminders and follow-up' by the Indian embassy. The Japanese government had said:

> We have tried our best to find out in our old files, a copy of the documents (relating [to] "cremation permits") required by Justice Mukherjee. However, we are not able to find it so far. You may understand how difficult it is to find out nearly half-a-century old documents.

Two, in view of my informing the commission about Taiwan government's rejection of the air crash theory, the MEA called for 'full details of the communication received from the Taiwanese side', with the request 'that any information required to be obtained from Taiwan may be referred to the Ministry'. The then government was obviously not pleased. It ticked off the commission, telling it that 'we do not recognise the "Republic of China" or "Taiwan" and hence, we do not have any official dealing with them'.

It was Indira Gandhi's days redux. In 2003, a foreign newspaper had reported about India's secret military ties with Taiwan. Thinking about Samar Guha's claim about similar ties in the 1970s, I wondered how did that square with 'no official dealing with them' policy.

Soon it transpired that the MEA was miffed with the Mukherjee Commission over its contacting the Taiwanese authorities and asked for an explanation. In November that year, the commission sent a letter to the MEA, detailing the circumstances that had 'compelled the commission to directly approach the authorities concerned in Taiwan', notwithstanding the MEA's previous objections.

In November only, the MEA again parroted that the commission 'should not send such communications directly to Taiwanese "Government" authorities', for it was 'considering alternative options for seeking the assistance of other agencies/organisations for obtaining the requisite documents'. The Ministry promised to keep the commission 'informed of the progress in this regard'.

Thereafter, the commission 'stopped communicating directly with the Government of Taiwan and the Mayor of Taipei with the hope that the Ministry of External Affairs would do the needful to enable the commission to obtain the relevant documents and information from Taiwan'. Sensing the sensitivities of the matter, the director of Taipei Economic and Cultural Center in New Delhi had refused to be of any assistance to the commission.

When nothing further was heard, the commission sought a 'progress report' from the MEA on 8 January 2004. On 15 March, the ministry reverted with 'the outcome of efforts made by India-Taipei Association (ITA), a non-government office in Taipei'. There was no outcome. ITA was beating about the bush, making enquiries in the archives rather than getting facts straight from the Taiwan government.

The Government of India made a last-ditch effort to stop the commission from visiting Taiwan. It told the commission that it was 'not inclined to fund its visit to Taiwan'. Justice Mukherjee now had reasons to get annoyed. He tried to raise the matter personally with the then Foreign Minister. But Yashwant Sinha dodged the meeting, saying he 'would not be able to meet him [Justice Mukherjee] before the elections'. Those were the days of 'India shining'. The BJP was flying high, disconnected from ground realities, insensitive to public perception and expectations.

Justice Mukherjee commented that 'the government stand regarding the commission's Taiwan visit...seemed to be something different than what it was when this commission was set up'. Elections took place and the BJP bowed out of power. Now was the time for a tug of war. Justice Mukherjee had great success with the new Foreign Minister. Kunwar Natwar Singh may have been a committed Nehruite, but his gracious appearance before the commission as a witness previously had left no one in doubt that he respected Bose as well. Singh cleared the commission's visit to Taiwan and earned the gratitude of the commission officials, who contrasted his action with the 'inaction' of the BJP ministers, Jaswant Singh and Yashwant Sinha.

But the Ministry of Home Affairs, the nodal ministry over the Bose mystery matter, was not very pleased with the commission's inquiry. In October 2004, the MHA, under Shivraj Patil, sent the commission a letter that 'made certain highly objectionable queries'. Justice Mukherjee felt it would be 'humiliating for the commission to reply to the queries'. On 15 October, he told disinterested media persons in Kolkata that the commission 'was ready to place its report on the basis of documents available to it, if the Centre did not cooperate with the probe panel'.

Justice Mukherjee also had to endure an insult at the hands of the then Home Minister. Meeting Patil's predecessor LK Advani was not as fruitful as the judge had expected, but the senior BJP leader was always courteous, always respectful. Patil's undignified manner, on the other hand, was unbecoming of a man holding the Home portfolio. He did not ask Justice Mukherjee to sit down, but gave him a dressing down. He lectured that 'the inquiry had gone on for too long, and that too much money has been spent on it'.

The Home Ministry's posturing foretold the government's intention to somehow put an end to the commission's inquiry. In November 2004, Finance Minister P Chidambaram told the media in New Delhi of the Cabinet decision that 'no further extension' would be given to the commission beyond May 2005. From this time on, it was a race against time for the commission. Until the last moment, one did not know if the visit to Taiwan would be possible. Russia seemed a remote possibility.

In the end, the Manmohan Singh government could not stop Justice Mukherjee from visiting Taiwan. It watched helplessly as he held direct consultations with government officials in Taipei. They testified that the e-mails sent to this writer were genuine. But they were not too keen to share all the sources of their information.

Justice Mukherjee requested Taiwanese Foreign Ministry official Sean Hsu to locate the cremation register for the period during which Bose had allegedly died. 'Mr Hsu was kind enough to assure that he would do the needful within a fortnight'. It was the same job the Japanese had said could not be done because it was very difficult to trace half-a-century old documents.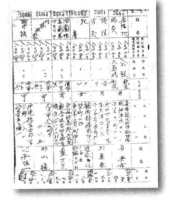

Fulfilling its promise, the Taiwan government did provide the commission the 1945 cremation register from the old crematorium of Taipei city. The record was quite comprehensive and meticulous. Running into 25 big-sized pages, it listed details of about 273 persons—Japanese, Chinese, British—cremated or buried in Taihoku in between 17 and 27 August 1945.

A minute study of the register carried out by an expert recommended by the Japanese consulate in Kolkata showed that neither Subhas Bose, nor General Shidei, nor the pilots had been cremated in Taipei in between 17 to 27 August 1945. No plane had ever crashed and there was no cremation of the people supposedly killed. The official theory now stood turned on its head.

Nine

What happened to Subhas Bose if he did not die in Taiwan? The Russian angle now loomed large before the Mukherjee Commission.

Two instances deserve to be spotlighted. Ardhendu Sarkar, an affable retired chief engineer of the Heavy Engineering Corporation, was circumspect with every word he uttered to me in his spacious flat in a high-rise in Kolkata. He had nothing whatsoever to gain by testifying before the commission, and repeating to me, that Netaji was in Russia after his 'death'.

In the early 1960s, Sarkar was on a deputation to the Gorlovka Machine Building Plant near Donetesk in Ukraine, then part of the Soviet empire. His senior colleague there happened to be a German Jew, who had been brought to the USSR, sent to a Siberian camp for indoctrination, given a new identity and married to a Russian.

In one of their moments of camaraderie, BA Zerovin, as he was now called, let it slip to his colleague from Bengal that he had met Subhas Bose in Berlin, and 'again in 1948', in a gulag somewhere beyond the end of the trans-Siberian Railways. According to Zerovin, 'Bose' was apparently being treated fine, given a car and was moving around with two guards. In their short exchange, 'Bose' told Zerovin that he expected to go back to India soon.

Zerovin realised after his moment of indiscretion that he had spoken too much. He cautioned Sarkar to keep his mouth shut as long as he was in the USSR. But Sarkar 'naively' walked into the Indian Embassy in Moscow—and shared the information with a Second Secretary.

The Secretary was not amused. 'Why have you come to this country?' he lashed out.

'Does your job involve poking your nose in politics?'

Sarkar's blood ran cold. The Secretary saw fear in his eyes and advised him not to 'discuss this with anyone'.

'Just do your work and forget what you've just said.'

Soon Sarkar was sent back to India. He returned home in a state of shock, and kept his mouth shut in the interests of his family. He could summon courage to recall his experience only after his children had settled. It was good that he deposed before the Mukherjee Commission, because there were many who did not for fear of some sort of retribution.

Luckily, Rai Singh Yadav was out of harm's way by the time he decided to testify. This former director of pre-R&AW era Information Service of India of the MEA had loads of nuggets to share when I met him subsequently. Angst and helplessness writ on his face battered by age, Rai Singh [picture] thought back to his time in Europe when a Russian diplomat, who he thought was a KGB man, teased him. 'Your Quisling was with us!'

'Our people did not want to disturb relations. They knew Netaji was in Siberia. He was left out in the cold!' Rai Singh charged.

And what he said in support of this was rather harrowing. Rai Singh Yadav had been friends with Tibetologist Ram Rahul, whose distinguished friends in turn included a judge of the US Supreme Court and a low-profile former Soviet official. Time was when Babajan Gouffrav was a man of influence in Soviet Russia, because he knew Stalin and was director of the prestigious Institute of Oriental Studies in Moscow.

'Ram sent for me when he was on his death bed. He said, "I don't want to go to my funeral pyre with this. Listen to this carefully."'

Rai Singh reminisced further. I listened with increased interest.

'Release this information when India is ready to ask questions about Netaji', were Ram Rahul's words to Rai Singh.

Singh's heart thumped as the professor unburdened himself in his last moments, disclosing an admission by the venerated Gouffrav, by then dead. Gouffrav had told Ram Rahul that:

'Netaji had crossed over to the Soviet Union in 1945 via Manchuria.'

According to Gouffrav, India's Ambassador in Moscow—whom Rai Singh identified as Sarvepalli Radhakrishnan—was allowed to see Bose on the condition that he would not try to speak with him. After this strange meeting, Ambassador Radhakrishnan(1949-52) informed New Delhi about Bose's presence in the Soviet Union.

When Radhakrishnan returned to India, Nehru proposed his name as India's first Vice President in a Cabinet meeting. Rai Singh said that Abul Kalam Azad and others protested because though Radhakrishnan was an internationally-renowned philosopher and had been knighted by the British for his excellence in this field, he had played no role in India's freedom struggle. Rai Singh repeated a jibe attributed to the Maulana by another Congressman:

Kya hum sab mar gaye hain? Ye Sir Sarvepalli kahan se aa gaye hamare Vice President banane ke liye? 'Are we all dead? From where did this Sir Sarvepalli come to be our Vice President?!'

February 2001 onwards, the Mukherjee Commission repeatedly asked the government to make arrangements for its visit to the Russian Federation. In 2003, the MEA was requested to 'approach the Government of Russia for access of the Commission to the archives of the KGB, Federal Security Bureau'.

There was no sign of the Russia visit happening even in February 2005. As the commission's tenure was coming to an end with the government's refusal to give it another extension, Justice Mukherjee decided to write his report on the basis of what had happened thus far. His staffers spoke to the Home Ministry officials for arrangements about their handing over the report. Justice Mukherjee had made up his mind never to see Shivraj Patil after he had been humiliated by Patil during their last meeting.

It was under these circumstances that this writer approached former Union Ministers Murli Manohar Joshi and George Fernandes for assistance. 'Why didn't you come to me earlier?' Joshi asked me. He clarified that as the HRD Minister in the previous NDA government, he had not been in the loop over this matter.

Battling the initial stages of Alzheimer's disease, Fernandes was unable to do as much as he could have. It was the erudite Joshi who made the then government extend the commission's tenure to enable it to visit Russia. He pressed for this visit in meetings with Prime Minister Manmohan Singh and Home Minister Patil.

Purabi Roy and I apprised MM Joshi of the facts as we saw them. Joshi then wrote to the Prime Minister that 'it would be necessary to approach the present Government of the Russian Federation at the highest level', so that the commission got access to the relevant documents.

In other words, Joshi requested Singh to take up the issue with the Russians personally. One cannot get classified information and records from a foreign government just like that. A foreign state will not easily give out a secret which might affect its interests unless it sees signs that the other government means business. And there's no better way to show seriousness than to raise the matter at the highest, preferably the head of the government level.

Take for example the tragedy of Raoul Wallenberg—a young Swedish diplomat who saved thousands of Hungarian Jews from the Nazis in 1944 before his disappearance from Budapest in January 1945. Wallenberg was initially reported dead and then it emerged that he had been abducted by the Red Army. Just as it happened with  Bose, the rumours of Wallenberg's presence in the USSR began swirling. And just as Bose's kin and admirers strove to get at the truth, Wallenberg's influential family, admirers and the people he had rescued began making efforts to find out what had become of him.

From this point on, the two cases begin looking different. That is because the intentions of the Swedish authorities were not mala fide. The moment it got the lead that Raoul Wallenberg could be alive in the USSR, the Swedish government wasted no time in contacting the Soviet authorities. The Swedes did not enjoy close relations with USSR, but that did not come in the way of their quest for truth. Eight written and five oral official approaches concerning Wallenberg were made in between 1945 and 1947.

Persistent Swedish approaches made the Soviets come out in August 1947 with their first ever high-level formal reply. Deputy Foreign Minister Andrey Vyshinsky wrote that an extensive search of the records had shown that 'Wallenberg is not in the Soviet Union and is unknown to us'. He also suggested that he 'had either been killed in the battle for Budapest or kidnapped and murdered by Nazis or Hungarian Fascists'.

Such an answer would have ended all further questions from Sweden, but there were outcries from the Swedish public and media. Their government stood by them and kept on raising the issue. The Soviets retaliated in 1948 through their semi-official Foreign Ministry weekly *New Times* which decried the 'fables' and 'filthy campaign' about Wallenberg's presence in the USSR.

A 1946 article in Soviet mouthpiece *Pravada* had in similarly vituperative fashion 'denounced as "a stupid fairy tale" a report that Subhas Chandra Bose...is in Soviet Russia'. It said the theory was 'a fabrication of dishonest newspaper buffoons endowed with an imagination which is as quick as it is dirty'.

For the Wallenberg case, things began to change in 1955, when many of the Germans and Austrians captured by the Soviets during the Second World War were released. Proactive Swedish authorities traced out some of them and obtained their testimonies concerning Wallenberg. They said they had contacted Wallenberg in prison, through wall tapping.

Even this thin evidence infused confidence in the Swedes. The yearning for the truth made them go back to the Russians. Moscow's harsh response this time was that 'it was impossible to accept the testimony of war criminals whose information was in disagreement with the results of our own, thorough investigation'.

Sweden ignored this aggressive political posturing. When Prime Minister Tage Erlander visited Moscow in 1956, he put the Wallenberg issue high on bilateral agenda despite strong Soviet objections. Their Foreign Minister, Vyacheslav Molotov, noted that 'Erlander persistently asked us to find a solution to the situation, in order to settle the matter' and that 'the Wallenberg issue was such an irritating element in Soviet-Swedish relations that it might have a negative effect on them'.

Cornered by the Swedes, the Soviets finally owned up the basic truth: Wallenberg was indeed in the USSR after 1945. In 1957, USSR Foreign Minister Andrei Gromyko's bombshell of a letter referred to Wallenberg's death following a heart attack a decade earlier in the Lubyanka prison at the KGB's HQ. The same Gromyko was Foreign Minister from 1958-85.

All that the Russians had said up to that time about not knowing anything about Wallenberg, thorough investigation, extensive search of records et al, was part of an elaborate, state-sanctioned hoax.

In contrast, the case of Subhas Bose as it was pursued by India would make your heart sink. India was effectively in the Soviet bloc in the post-Stalin period (that is since 1953). Everything else but the Bose issue was discussed.

In spite of the knowledge that Bose could have made it to the USSR, New Delhi never officially utilised even an iota of its diplomatic and political clout with Moscow to find out facts and get Bose back to India, so long as statesmanly Jawaharlal Nehru and his family of 'world leaders' were at the helm.

The 1950s and 1960s were the decades of denial. Humiliation and intimidation was in store for those who tried to sensitise the authorities. An unverifiable account involved globetrotting Satyanarayan Sinha, a former foreign ministry official and Member of Parliament. Sinha claimed that he had implored the Prime Minister at a diplomatic gathering to informally raise the Bose issue with the Soviet ambassador, but Nehru rebuffed the suggestion out of hand, dismissing it as 'talk of the chandukhana (gossip in a den of opium addicts)'.

Sinha was somewhat of a braggart, but his allegations before the Khosla Commission outraged the Soviets so much that he was accosted by USSR embassy officials in Delhi. 'Do you want Kozlov to be shot in Russia?' they asked him about his Russian contact.

There is a view that India did try to find out about Netaji's presence in Soviet Russia soon after 1947. Since no available official

Soviet Questions to Netaji Probe Witness

NEW DELHI, Oct. 19.

Dr. Satyanarain Sinha, a former official of the External Affairs Ministry, to-day told the Khosla Commission that some Soviet Embassy officials in New Delhi had visited him yesterday and questioned him about his evidence before the Commission relating to the 'disappearance of Netaji Subhas Chandra Bose.

Recalling his evidence that a K.G.B. (Komintern) member Mr. Kozlov, had told him of Netaji Bose being in custody in Siberia, Dr. Sinha said the Embassy officials had asked him: "Do you want Kozlov to be shot in Russia?"

He wanted the Prime Minister, Mrs. Indira Gandhi, who was expected to stop over in Moscow on her way to the U.N. to request the Soviet Prime Minister Mr. Kosygin, to give protection to Mr. Kozlov.

The Commission, however, said it was not responsible if anybody was put in prison if his name figured before the Commission.—UNI.

records allude to this, a conspiracy theory has filled in the knowledge vacuum. It holds that not only Sarvepalli Radhakrishnan but also his predecessor and free India's first representative to the USSR Vijaya Lakshmi Pandit, Nehru's talented younger sister, knew of Bose's existence in that country. This theory has such an appeal that from well-read people of refinement to village yokels think of it as untarnished truth.

It is claimed that when Vijaya Lakshmi Pandit came back from Moscow, she made a statement in private that she knew something whose disclosure 'would electrify India and the resultant happiness would be greater than what the people had experienced on 15 August 1947' The same story holds that Nehru asked Vijaya Lakshmi to keep her mouth shut. And a good sister that she was, she deferred to his judgment.

Rai Singh told me that he once had the privilege of being in attendance to 'Ambassador Pandit' at an airport lounge. He then mustered courage to ask Vijaya Lakshmi about her 'important statement' on return to India from the USSR. When she kept on sipping her drink, he repeated, 'Madam, unfortunately that important statement of yours was not understood by people!' According to Rai Singh, she then sidestepped the issue.

The only time Vijaya Lakshmi Pandit and Sarvepalli Radhakrishnan were properly asked to verify their stand was before the Khosla Commission when a few witnesses revived the charges. 'The last time I met Netaji Subhas Chandra Bose was in Darjeeling in the summer of 1940', Radhakrishnan affirmed in his affidavit. Vijaya Lakshmi stated in hers that she never met Bose after he left India in 1941. These qualified statements did not rule out the possibility of their coming to know of Netaji's presence in Soviet Russia, a revelation of catastrophic political proportions and ramifications. Strangely, these affidavits are not traceable in the declassified records of the Khosla Commission at the National Archives.

There was some argument before the commission whether or not the circumstances warranted their cross-examination by lawyers. The commission's counsel TR Bhasin on 6 July 1972 'reiterated his demand to summon former President S Radhakrishnan, Mrs Vijaya Lakshmi Pandit and others as witnesses before the commission'. 'Radhakrishnan to be examined', the *Times of India* reported on 24 December 1972.

In his final report, Khosla justified not summoning and examining the two personally because 'Dr Radhakrishnan was too ill to be examined orally'. He wrote that there was 'no reason whatsoever for disbelieving' Vijaya Lakshmi Pandit's affidavit. 'It is far more reliable and acceptable than the evidence of a host of witnesses who have made incredible statements about encounters with Bose at different times and at different places.'

The explanation sounds fine to me on the face of it. But somehow it doesn't square with 'chairman' Khosla's own announcement as it appears in the recently declassified record of the commission's proceeding dated 24 July 1973.

> SECRETARY: The Other Witnesses fixed for 25th, summons have been issued, but we have not heard anything to the contrary, whether they are coming or not. We have made efforts to get them to appear before the Commission.
>
> CHAIRMAN:: Mrs Pandit will come on 26th.
>
> Mr. Mullick will come, he is out of Delhi now. He will come on the 7th.

Document obtained under the Right to Information

Despite Khosla's assertion that 'Mrs Pandit will come on the 26th', she never did.

And he, a personal friend of Nehru, never complained.

Going by official records, hectic lobbying by Samar Guha and Chitta Basu made the VP Singh government raise the Bose issue with the tottering Soviet government in 1991. A 'note verbale' sent by the Indian Embassy in Moscow to the USSR Ministry of Foreign Affairs sought 'any material available in the archives of Soviet organisations, including security organisations, which could shed light on the fate of Netaji'.

Now what in the world is a note verbale? It is an unsigned, Demi-Official (DO) letter, which is used when one government does not want to communicate with another in a fully official manner. It constitutes contact at the elementary level. High level contacts start with the issuance of a démarche. Depending upon how important the matter is, personal approaches by the ambassador, official, minister or head of the government follow.

Obviously, our worldly-wise officials know what does the trick. Actually, it all depends on what the issue at hand is about, who are the affected parties and how much stink is being raised in the media, etc.

Speaking in Parliament in August 2015, External Affairs Minister Sushma Swaraj pulled back no punches as she tore into the Congress party for all that had built up in the months of July-August 2015 over the so-called 'Lalitgate' scam. She taunted Rahul Gandhi to question his mother Sonia on why his father Rajiv Gandhi had a quid pro quo arrangement with the US, and why he allowed Union Carbide chief Warren Anderson to run away from India? Sourcing her information to late Congress leader and the then Madhya Pradesh chief minister Arjun Singh, Swaraj claimed that Rajiv allowed safe passage for Anderson to secure the release of his childhood friend, Shahryar, who was serving a thirty-five-year sentence in a US jail on a fraud charge. Overlooked in this spat was the fact that about six months had elapsed between Anderson's escape in December 1984 and the June 1985 Presidential pardon for Shahryar, efforts to seek whose release were going on for quite some time.

So, even as Sushma spoke in Parliament, I thought back to several years. At the car park of the India International Centre (IIC) in New Delhi, an elderly gentleman had spoken to me in a soft but firm tone bearing a tinge of bitterness. He claimed that the stupendous Indian efforts in securing Shahryar's release had a link to his missing uncle.

After Shahryar was sent behind bars in 1982 for offences which included an attempt to blow up a ship, his devastated father, Mohammed Yunus, scrambled to get his only child released. He was able to pull some strings, for he was, to quote a leading journalist writing in *India Today* a few years ago, 'a former foreign service official and long-time sycophant of the Gandhi family'. The claims of 'friendship' between Shahryar and Rajiv were somewhat exaggerated in my understanding. 'The Nehru-Gandhi family has ruled the country. They are king and we commoners', Amitabh Bachchan famously said in 2004.

Yunus tried in various ways with the assistance of the Government of India to get his son released. 'The case is very sensitive and has high visibility in India. Indian officials have already been (able) to see the assistant US attorney', notes an August 1982 letter written to the then US Attorney General William French Smith by his special assistant John Glover Roberts Jr, who is now the Chief Justice of the United States.

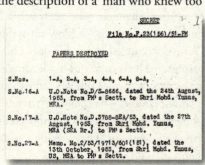

Roberts's letter referred to Hollywood legend Charlton Heston writing to the then US Attorney General, seeking 'fair treatment' for the son of his friend. Yunus was described by Heston as 'a highly respected member of both of Mrs Ghandi's [sic] governments, and a key figure there since before Independence, when he was a close friend of Mahatma Ghandi [sic]'.

The correspondence shows how desperate Indian officials were to get Shahryar released. One official in Delhi even took a swipe at the US, telling Heston that America was 'a strange country, where a man could shoot the President and get off scot-free, while another could launch a failed fraud and get thirty-five years'.

However, Smith expressed his inability to do anything.

Shahryar was not set free until, as the story goes, Rajiv Gandhi had made a personal intervention. And thereby hangs a conspiracy theory, which was precisely what was conveyed to me at the IIC car park.

'Yunus threatened Rajiv that he would unmask his grandfather in the Netaji matter if he did not seek his son's release', were the words of late Pradip Bose, a nephew of Netaji.

Was Yunus someone who fitted the description of a 'man who knew too much' about the controversy related to the fate of Subhas Bose? It has been claimed over the years that Jawaharlal Nehru entrusted Yunus with the safekeeping of the secret files on Bose. Now that Yunus is dead, we may never know the truth. Partly because several classified Nehru-era records concerning Bose and the Indian National Army (INA) properties were illegally destroyed when Indira Gandhi was the Prime Minister. What has survived in a secret prime minister's office (PMO) file today is a note bearing Yunus's name.

The issuance of a mere note verbale in the case of Subhas Bose signaled to the Russians that the Indians did not consider the issue a very serious matter. Otherwise, what does it really take to say a few words politely to a minister or ambassador of an extremely friendly foreign nation? Wallenberg was just a junior official, but his heroism made the Swedish Prime Minister pitch in for him. Subhas Bose, head of the Provisional Government of Free India in exile, deserved far greater efforts than were made by the people who reaped the harvest of his struggle!

Obviously, Manmohan Singh did not approach his Russian counterpart. Apart from MM Joshi's letter, there was nothing to exert pressure on him to do so. Pressure builds up only when something, irrespective of its significance, hits the headlines and people get agitated. This was demonstrated when a major story broke in 2011 about the Norwegian authorities' taking custody of two children whose Indian parents were allegedly not looking after them properly. According to a report in *Hindustan Times*, the couple 'accused the [Norwegian] authorities of unfamiliarity with Indian cultural practices'. As the news broke across channels, a massive commotion ensued across India over the perceived unfair treatment meted by Norway to the Indian couple and their children. So much so that the then Opposition party leaders organised sit-ins in front of Norway's Embassy in New Delhi. Then Leader of Opposition, Sushma Swaraj, said, her party was 'angry and upset' and demanded 'firm and decisive' action from the government against Norway. As a result of all this, then External Affairs Minister, SM Krishna, as reported by NDTV, 'called the Indian ambassador in Norway and urged him to speak to the Norwegian Foreign Minister, demanding the kids be sent back to their parents'. When the children returned to India in April 2012, they were received at the airport by the Minister of State for External Affairs in person. The real story emerged later on, as the husband publicly accused the wife of having 'a schizophrenic streak' and beating him and their children.

India never tried too hard to get facts about Subhas Bose. The 1991 note verbale was unlikely to yield anything and it did not. On 8 January 1992, the Foreign Ministry of the Russian Federation, which had taken the place of the USSR, sent a flat denial to New Delhi:

> According to the data in the Central and Republican Archives, no information whatsoever is available on the stay of the former President of Indian National Congress, Netaji Subhas Chandra Bose, in the Soviet Union in 1945 and thereafter.

Anuj Dhar

The Russian note bore a striking similarity to the Soviet missive over the Wallenberg matter—'he is not in our country and is unknown to us'.

Another note verbale was issued by the Russians in 2003, when the NDA government had to again take up the issue at the prodding of the Mukherjee Commission. The Government of India's favourite judge, GD Khosla, never thought of anything like that even after the Russians came up with their first and last official statement on the Netaji issue. Rattled by Satyanarayan Sinha's charge that he was accosted by USSR Delhi embassy officials, who threatened to execute his Russian contact, the embassy on 3 November 1970 tersely stated 'with full responsibility' that the Soviet authorities 'had absolutely nothing to do with the fate of Subhas Chandra Bose'.

According to the 2003 note sent by the Russians, a 'search was made for documents related to the fate of SC Bose in the following federal archives: Russian State Military Archives (RGVA), Russian State Archives of Socio-Political History (RGASPI), State Archives of the Russian Federation (GARF), and Russian State Historical Archives of the Far East (RGIADV). The information requested for was not found on the GARF, RGVA and RGIADV archives'. The note squarely stated that

> no information has been found about the fate of SC Bose in the Central Archives of the Russian FSB, the Central Archives of Ministry of Defence of the Russian Federation, in the manuscript section of the Russian State Library or in the State Archives of Photographic Documents (RGAKFD).

To break it down in comprehensible language—the Russians said they did not know where and how Bose had died.

This stand of Russia could not be treated as canonical, as Indian governments did, because of a number of reasons. First, we had the precedence of the Wallenberg issue, and another matter which was even more damning than that. For nearly half a century, Soviet Russia had feigned ignorance about the slaughter of virtually the entire top Polish brass, some 22,000 officers, in 1940 (by the NKVD, Stalin's secret police). They had once even set up a commission, which, after what they called 'rigorous inquiry', fixed the blame for the Katyn Forest massacre on the Nazis.

As long as Poland remained in the Communist bloc, the demands for the truth were successfully suppressed. Then Poland became democratic and its people and government did what the Swedes had done for Wallenberg. The outcome couldn't have been more dramatic. Mikhail Gorbachev, General Secretary of the Communist Party of the Soviet Union, went live on TV in 1990 to accept the Soviet guilt. The same Gorbachev who, according to a 2001 story in *Hindustan Times*, would evade 'a direct answer' to a researcher's query about Bose and say that 'it was up to both governments to solve the issue once and for all'.

Second, the list of archives searched for Bose-related records did not include many important archives. Left out of the preview were the all-important archive of the President of the Russian Federation, containing mostly Top Secret records of the President of Russia as well as those of the former Communist Party of the Soviet Union, and the archive of SVR—the Russian foreign intelligence service.

In an email to this writer, Gabor T Rittersporn of *Center National de la Recherche Scientifique*, Paris, wrote: 'Documentation on cases resembling the Bose affairs are kept in inaccessible archives of the security agencies [in Russia]'.

Three, there was no guarantee that even the archives searched for were gone over with a fine tooth comb. A case in point was an acclaimed 1995 BBC documentary *Hitler's Death: The final report* in which the then director of Moscow state archives, Sergei Mironenko, was shown making an interesting observation about the secret 'Operation myth' files about the investigation into the death of Adolf Hitler. 'We only discovered these files about two years ago. Before that they were so sensitive that their very existence wasn't even recorded here.'

The Mukherjee Commission's much-awaited visit to Russia took place from 20 to 30 September 2005 during Vladimir Putin's presidency. Wherever Justice Mukherjee went, he was told that evidence of Subhas's sojourn in Stalinist Russia, if any, would only be found in some intelligence- and security-related archive. But there was no way the commission would get access to such archives.

The only place where the commission was offered some records was the Russian State Archive of Socio-Political History. Its director told Justice Mukherjee that they had one file each on Subhas and Sarat Bose. The one on Subhas contained reports about him and the controversy surrounding his death and possible survival from Indian, British and Chinese newspapers for the period 1942-1956.

Why was Soviet Russia interested in Indian media coverage about Bose's disappearance till 1956?

The commission also examined some Russian witnesses, whose names were suggested by Purabi Roy. The presence of all of them was 'arranged with their consent by the Indian Embassy in Moscow'. But the Embassy and the Russian Foreign Ministry could not trace, even after repeated reminders, the most important of them all. Alexander Kolesnikov—the one who had seen a record showing Subhas's presence in the USSR in 1946—was finally located after Justice Mukherjee had reached Moscow. It turned out that Kolesnikov had joined the Russian diplomatic service and was out of the country. But how was it possible for a diplomat to be untraceable? The Russians were clearly evasive.

The examination of the other Russian witnesses who did appear before the commission was an exercise in futility. Purabi Roy said that they had 'turned hostile' under official pressure. All four of them responded in short, evasive sentences that they had no knowledge about the possibility of Subhas being in the USSR after 1945. World War II history expert Professor Boris Sokolov went so far as to say that

> if really Mr Bose was transported to USSR in 1945, then it should be kind of a big special operation and the preparation of such kind of operation should cover more than one month. I have no proof, really that he was in USSR in 1945 or later. But, there should be documents in the Archives of Special Services only if Mr Bose really was in the Soviet Union in 1945 or later. I never worked in FSB Archives and could not prove or deny that fact.

Despite limitations and official stonewalling, Justice Mukherjee made several path-breaking findings. Unlike GD Khosla's report, his was a transparency-seeker's delight. Of the three volumes of the report, two contained status reports issued by him right from the inception, laying bare his conduct and approach—also that of the then governments.

The main report comprised a concise narrative which did not stray from the subject matter germane to the inquiry, something GD Khosla did quite often in his lengthy report. More than half of the Mukherjee Commission report comprised copies of the exhibits relied upon by the judge to arrive at his findings. The Khosla Commission report had none.

There can be no better way to summarise Justice Mukherjee's findings than to excerpt his legalistic report in points:

- Recording a firm finding on this issue [by merely] treating the oral evidence of the eyewitness about Netaji's death and cremation as axiomatically true would be non sequitur and over-simplification of and a superficial approach to this complex issue.
- If...[the contradictory evidence of the eyewitnesses to Bose's death] is accepted at its face value, still, it must be said, definite findings about Netaji's death and his cremation can be arrived at, if and when the evidence passes the two basic litmus tests of appreciation of evidence, namely, probability and the aphoristic saying, 'Men may lie but circumstances do not'.

- Best corroborative evidence which can unmistakably prove the factum of Netaji's death and cremation, as deposed by the eye witnesses, will be the contemporaneous official records relating thereto.

- Proof of a secret plan, as also the manner of its execution, is largely inferential but the inference to be drawn must be a reasonable one, supported by attending facts and circumstances.

- That Netaji's decision to go out of Japan was pursuant to a plan formulated on the advice and with the active cooperation and support of the Japanese military authorities stands established by overwhelming evidence adduced before the [Shah Nawaz] committee and the two commissions. [Mukherjee accessed records of Khosla and Shah Nawaz panels in view of the fact that most witnesses had died much before his inquiry started.]

- A secret plan was contrived to ensure Netaji's safe passage, to which Japanese military authority and Habibur Rahman were parties. ...The purpose of his (Netaji's) flight was to go to the Soviet Union....

- Netaji could not have thought of taking the decision to escape—not to speak of translating that thought into action—without the active support and cooperation of the Japanese military authorities.

- The death of Ichiro Okura [a Japanese soldier] owing to heart failure on August 19, 1945 and his cremation on August 22 1945 on the basis of a permit issued on the previous day, were passed off as those of Netaji.

- The very fact that the Japanese army authorities wanted to pass off the death and cremation of Ichiro Okura as those of Netaji is an eloquent proof of their ensuring Netaji's safe passage by creating a smokescreen.

- Obviously, in cooking up the story of Netaji's death in the plane crash and giving it a modicum of truth, they (the Japanese military authorities and Habibur Rahman) had no other alternative than resorting to suppression of facts and in doing so, they not only invited material contradictions in their evidence...but also left latent loopholes which have now been discovered.

- Lest the identity of the dead body of Ichiro Okura should have been discovered by the Taipei Municipal Bureau of Health and Hygiene, people who were not likely to be party to the escape plan, the Japanese army officers restored to various precautionary measures at the time when the dead body of Ichiro Okura was brought to the Bureau for regulatory inspection....

- That Habibur Rahman was also a party to the escape plan is evidenced by the prominent role he played in ensuring that the Bureau people could be misled into believing that the body which was going to be cremated was that of Netaji.

- The very fact that the Japanese Buddhist custom, viz. preservation of the dead body for three days before cremation—which fits in with the Ichiro Okura's death on the 19th and his cremation three days thereafter, ie. on the 22nd, and picking up of bones from every portion of the body after the cremation and keeping the same with the ashes was adhered to—is another circumstance which indicates that the body was cremated and the mortal remains were of Ichiro Okura and not Netaji.

- The eloquent proof of Habibur Rahman's role in the escape plan and also the manner in which he wanted to execute the same is furnished by the fact that he ensured the photographing of the dead body, minus the face.

- If this evidence of Habibur Rahman [that the plane nosedived from a fairly high altitude] is to be believed, then none of the 12/13 passengers…could have survived.

- If Netaji had really died in the manner as alleged, it was expected that he (Habibur Rahman) would, as the only surviving member of INA, immediately report about it, more so when it related to the death of his Supreme Commander, to his superiors in the army and his colleagues in Bangkok, Singapore, Saigon and Tokyo. His conspicuous silence cannot be explained in any way except that he was playing a very vital role along with the Japanese army authorities in formulation and execution of Netaji's escape plan.

All of this made Justice Mukherjee arrive at his momentous finding on 'the basis of robust circumstantial evidence on record':

> It stands established that emplaning at Saigon on August 17, 1945 Netaji succeeded in evading the Allied Forces and escaping out of their reach, and as a camouflage thereof, the entire make-belief story of the air crash, Netaji's death therein and his cremation was engineered by the Japanese army authorities including the two doctors and Habibur Rahman and then aired on August 23, 1945 through a statement prepared by Shri SA Ayer at the direction of the aforesaid authorities to give imprimatur of the INA to the death news of Netaji.
>
> …The question whether Netaji thereafter landed in Russia or elsewhere cannot be answered for dearth of evidence.

Ten

On 18 May 2006, the Mukherjee Commission report was placed before Parliament with a single-page Memorandum of Action Taken that was less detailed than a school report card. The government rejected the findings that Subhas had not died in Taiwan and the ashes presumed to be his were of someone else.

When they rose against this arbitrary move, the Opposition MPs were taken head-on by Pranab Mukherjee, who made light of the dismissal saying: 'There are umpteen number of cases where the reports of the commissions have been rejected by the government. Here is nothing new.' Nothing new? Right from 1997 (when the Calcutta High Court began deliberating the matter) to 2005 (when Manmohan Singh's government was in place for several months), the government's stand had more or less been against the air crash theory. But after the commission's report was submitted with the conclusion that rather than dying in Taipei, Netaji had escaped towards USSR, the government did a 180-degree turn.

In a somersault that can only be inspired by political considerations, the government reverted to the findings of previous inquiries set up during the Congress rule. GD Khosla was hailed as someone having the 'acumen to evaluate the evidence produced before him' and upright Justice Mukherjee painted as someone confused.

The Russian angle was completely wished away. 'Now, you know Japan had fought against Russia or the Soviet Union. ...And even after this do you think he would have gone to Russia?' Home Minister Shivraj Patil asked rhetorically in Parliament.

If only someone could tell him that the government was hiding away records which provided the answers. For instance, in 1952, Anand Mohan Sahay sent a Top Secret report to the Foreign Secretary saying:

> Netaji said that he could see the end of the war in course of months, and he wanted me to try to persuade the Japanese to allow us to establish direct contact with the Soviet Embassy in Tokyo. I was in Tokyo in the beginning of February 1945. I met General Tojo and the Chief of the General Staff and discussed the matter at length. I told them that if we could deal with the Soviets directly, we might be able to help in improving the Russo-Japanese relation that was necessary to strengthen Japan's position.

> The plan was to proceed to Manchuria and be there when the end of war comes, so that we may be within Soviet sphere after the surrender of the Japanese. War came to an end on 15th August. A special messenger from Netaji came to see me on 16th from Bangkok with a letter from him asking me to get ready to secure transport from the Japanese and to leave for Manchuria, and to meet him there. He suggested that although the Soviets had declared war against the Japanese, it would be desirable to be arrested by the Soviet authorities in Manchuria, because we could later negotiate with them and might persuade them to accept us as their friends and not enemies.

Moraraji Desai's dismissal of Khosla's and Shah Nawaz's reports was junked because, Patil said, the former PM's 1978 'statement could have been motivated, not by reasons of law, but by reasons political'. What reasons political could have motivated Desai to tell lies to the nation over a man he was not very particularly fond of? Didn't Patil know that Desai was engaged in trying to queer Subhas Bose's pitch in pre-Independence years?

As a minister in Nehru's cabinet, Desai was never heard, even on the grapevine, saying anything which might be construed as favourable by those seeking the resolution of the controversy. As Prime Minister, he made remarks far more cynical than Shivraj Patil's and was all for continuing with the official policy on Bose's fate. He could not sustain it in the brazen fashion of his predecessors because of the offensive mounted by Samar Guha and other lawmakers. He gave in and admitted what was true—the evidence for Bose's death was sketchy, riddled with contradictions and there were contemporary records to disapprove it.

The UPA government used a shady logic to discredit Desai. It goes something like this: It is eternal truth when the 'eyewitnesses' back the Taipei crash theory with contradictory statements and no supporting documentary evidence. But it is telling lies when a Prime Minister of India, a top notch follower of Mahatma Gandhi, makes a statement in Parliament repudiating the crash theory. Why? Because the government can't find the 'contemporary records' Desai referred to.

But which government is it that can't find the records? The one which by its own admissions to the Mukherjee Commission illegally destroyed and misplaced several Netaji-related records in the past?

If there were any lingering doubts about the government's lacking bona fides over the Netaji disappearance issue, they were put to rest when Rudrajyoti Bhattacharjee, Sunil Gupta and others—whose writ petition had led to formation of the Mukherjee Commission—went back to the Calcutta High Court, seeking justice.

A plain reading of the affidavit-in-opposition filed by the PMO and the MHA in October 2007 was enough evidence that the government was not treating the matter objectively.

The affidavit asserted, without any elaboration of course, that the British and American intelligence investigations had corroborated the air crash theory. It said there was no evidence/document to prove that Subhas had a plan to escape and that he did not die in the plane crash. It took refuge in the fact that the 'the findings of the Khosla Commission were accepted by the Government of India and placed before the Parliament'.

Surely the government accepted these findings in the Nehru and Indira years. But who told the court in 1997 that a fresh inquest 'is required and the information that Netaji died in the plane crash on August 18, 1945 is full of loopholes, contradictions and therefore inconclusive?' Who else but the learned government counsel. And who was it that asserted before the Mukherjee Commission in 2005 that 'there were glaring discrepancies in the evidence' and wanted the government to be credited for helping find evidence in Taiwan that Subhas had not died there? None but the senior counsel appearing for the Government of India!

The government affidavit said the witnesses appearing before the first two probes were recalling an event that took place eleven and twenty-five years earlier. 'It would be well-nigh impossible for the witnesses to remember every detail of the accident. It is reiterated that discrepancies do not disprove the air crash story.' If that was so, why did the government not tell this to the High Court and the commission? There were many discrepancies even before the intelligence teams which had scoured for evidence immediately after the news of crash came in. Habibur Rahman made contradictory statements within a month of the alleged crash.

How could the so-called eyewitnesses ever forget for the rest of their lives the horrific sequence of Subhas Bose coming out of the plane wrapped in fire and one of them risking his life to try to save him? Who was the one to lunge forward to aid Netaji? Rahman said he tried his best all by himself; Major Takahashi claimed that he helped Bose roll on the ground to put out the fire. Nonogaki said he and Rahman, together, did their best and ground engineer Captain Nakamura insisted that he 'and three of his men took off his coat and stripped him of all his clothing'.

```
14.4.1971.                                                    ·2324

Mr. Trikha:  So when Chandra Bose followed your advice and
             crawled on the ground the fire extinguished?
Mr. Takahashi:  I remember I caught his legs and showed him
             how to roll.
Mr. Trikha:  After when you helped Chandra Bose to roll on
             the ground, his fire was extinguished?
Mr. Takahashi:  Yes.
```

Record of Takahashi's examination before Khosla Commission obtained under the RTI Act

If four people claiming to have witnessed one big event of history give out four different versions, only a kangaroo court will take them seriously.

Justice Mukherjee's attempts to test the veracity of the eyewitness accounts by tracing 1945 vintage records were not acceptable to the government. The government affidavit said that the commission's not finding any such record did not disapprove 'the fact that Netaji died in the plane crash'.

If that were the case, why was the government itself looking for such records in the days of Nehru? And why did it not tell that to the High Court that it had in its possession records, including secret ones, demonstrating just how right Justice Mukherjee's approach really was? Actually, even prior to independence, the investigators were of the view that in absence of any direct evidence of Bose's death, tracing of records concerning treatment, death and cremation was of paramount importance. Colonel Hannessy of Military Intelligence put it succinctly to the US consulate in Bombay in May 1946:

> Bose must have been treated in a hospital by some physician; that if he died there must be people who had first-hand knowledge of his death and that there might conceivably be some record of his death; and that further, in the event of his death, there must be a person alive today who had some knowledge of his cremation.

CSDIC's Colonel Anderson wrote this to the Intelligence Bureau in February 1946:

> For final and positive proof, a British investigation team would need to be sent up to Formosa [Taiwan] from Saigon and Hanoi to examine the hospital records at Taihoku.

In 1951, BV Keskar, Minister of State for External Affairs, read out in Parliament a statement made in 1946 by Nehru that the main proof of Bose's death was a death certificate issued in Taiwan.

The truth is that it was merely *claimed* that such a certificate for Subhas was issued. In reality, when it was searched for, there was no sign of it. Prime Minister Nehru knew it for himself, because one of the requests his government made to the British in 1956 pertained to procuring Subhas's death and cremation records from Taiwan.

> Indian government have asked whether HM Consul in Tamsui could seek certain Formosan witnesses and obtain a copy of cremation certificate.

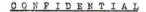

CONFIDENTIAL

Inward Telegram to Commonwealth Relations Office

FROM: U.K. HIGH COMMISSIONER IN INDIA

RPTD: TAMSUI
HONG KONG
BANGKOK)
TOKYO   ) (SAVING)
RANGOON)

C1852/1
C1951/2

D: Delhi 14.30 hours 3rd May 1956
R: 16.03 hours 3rd May 1956

CYPHER

No. 701 CONFIDENTIAL

Addressed Commonwealth Relations Office No. 701, repeated Tamsui No. M144, Hong Kong No. M145 , Bangkok No.7 Saving, Tokyo No.M45 Saving, Rangoon No.3 Saving (Commonwealth Relations Office please pass Tamsui and Hong Kong).

In view of persistent though probably unfounded rumours that Subhas Chandra Bose leader of the Indian National Army, during the war was not killed as reported at the time in an air crash in Formosa but is still alive, Indian Government have appointed a committee to investigate and if possible establish facts. Committee is headed by Shahnawa Khan, Parliamentary Secretary of the Ministry of Transport, and has two other members, Bose's brother and S.N. Mitra, I.C.S., formerly Chief Commissioner of the Andaman Islands.

2.   Commission plans to visit Bangkok, Tokyo and Hong Kong and I believe Rangoon but for political reasons is unable to visit Formosa. Indian Government have asked whether H.M. Consul in Tamsui could seek out certain Formosan witnesses and obtain a copy of cremation certificate.

Not only that the Nehru government even pestered the Japanese government for the same records. And when they were not forthcoming, New Delhi developed cold feet.

Justice Mukherjee did exactly what the British investigators wanted to in 1946 and the Government of India did in 1956. And all he got was Ichiro Okura's death certificate and his name on the cremation permit. Would Anderson have

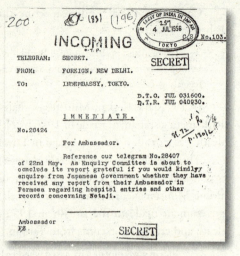

been satisfied that it was 'the final and positive proof' being looked for?

The government should have commended Justice Mukherjee but its 2007 affidavit offered one weak argument after another. The alibi for the non-availability of any record with Subhas's name on it was that 'it was a war time and the Japanese surrendered to the Allied Forces and as such, either no records were there or whatever records were there might have been destroyed'.

The unstated motivation behind the reference to 'war time' was Khosla's spin in his report that in the 'chaotic conditions' of August 1945, the Japanese lost their bearings and did not carry out even the basic routine jobs. This was a preposterous thing to say because chaos is the hallmark of everyday life in the third world nations like India, where people go berserk on the arrival of a train at platform. The Japanese became an advanced people generations ago. Minutes after Japanese cities were pulverized with nuclear strikes, investigators, researchers, scientists rushed to the affected areas and that's why there is loads of documentation about the catastrophic events in Japan even today. The Taipei city of August 1945 was not Hiroshima or Nagasaki, and the Japanese were never so out of their minds that they wouldn't do basic paper work about people dying in their military hospitals. So the contention that 'no records were there' doesn't stand to reason.

It doesn't even stand to facts. How would the government classify the documents relating to Ichiro Okura's death and cremation if not as 'records'? When the records for an ordinary solider like Okura could be created in August 1945, what stopped the Japanese from creating those for General Shidei, and Subhas Bose?

The assertion that 'whatever records were there might have been destroyed' is nothing but an attempt to subvert the truth. The Manmohan Singh government knew too well that Japan never said the records of Subhas's death and cremation were destroyed. They only came up with the fact that they were created in the name of Ichiro Okura.

In a secret file, there is a self-evidencing communication from the Japanese foreign ministry to its Indian counterpart. The Japanese government was unable to trace the records sought by India despite 'thorough investigations made on the files of doctor's reports, and death certificates, which had been transferred from the former Taipei army hospital to...[the Ministry of Welfare in Tokyo] for custody'. That's because, no such records ever existed as Subhas never died in Taiwan.

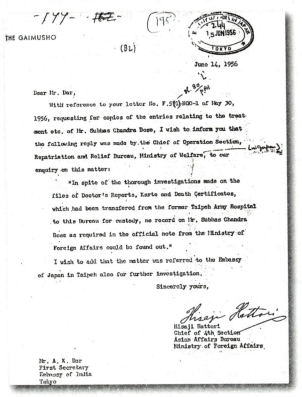

The Indian government insists that Subhas Bose died in Taiwan. So, wasn't he cremated there? Then why isn't his name there in the contemporary Japanese register, detailing each and every person who was cremated in August 1945? Is the cremation record which the Government of India was itself looking for in the 1950s not relevant anymore?

The PMO/HMA joint affidavit states that 'the findings of the Justice Mukherjee Commission were inconclusive and not based on firm grounds and it was, therefore, not possible for the Government of India to accept the same'.

One wonders how Justice Mukherjee could have made himself more convincing? By bending rules? Writing flowery English? Or by hushing up evidence? Maybe badmouthing the Japanese would have been in order. Or, better still, vilifying Netaji as their puppet and pawn would have done some good. Exonerating the government of all wrongdoings would have been a sign of political correctness on the former Supreme Court judge's part.

According to the Standard Operating Procedure adopted by the Congress-led government, anything which did not conform to its worldview was not conclusive. To quote an *India Today* article, 'It took 21 years and nine commissions of inquiry for the victims of the 1984 anti-Sikhs riots to get their first token of justice' in the shape of the Nanavati Commission report. In August 2005, the same Manmohan Singh government, the same Shivraj Patil speaking for it, dismissed the findings of the Nanavati Commission too.

The 'Action Taken Report', in this instance, said that Justice Nanavati was himself not certain of the involvement of Congress leaders and, therefore, 'any further action will not be justified'. Then, the Opposition members and the people of Punjab lunged at the throats of the ruling class and, by jove, a complete about-turn happened. Patil now assured Parliament that 'all the recommendations' of the commission would be implemented by the government 'as it is'.

'It is also reiterated that the report of the Justice Mukherjee Commission was examined in-depth and the Action Taken Report reflects that', trumpeted the then government in its affidavit.

AUTHENTICATED

MEMORANDUM OF ACTION TAKEN ON THE REPORT OF THE JUSTICE MUKHERJEE COMMISSION OF INQUIRY REGARDING THE ALLEGED DISAPPEARANCE OF NETAJI SUBHAS CHANDRA BOSE

By Government of India Notification No. S.O. 339(E) dated 14th May, 1999, Shri M.K. Mukherjee, retired Judge of the Supreme Court of India, was appointed under the Commissions of Inquiry Act, 1952, to inquire into all the facts and circumstances related to the disappearance of Netaji Subhas Chandra Bose in 1945 and subsequent developments connected therewith including –

(a) whether Netaji Subhas Chandra Bose is dead or alive;
(b) if he is dead, whether he died in the plane crash, as alleged;
(c) whether the ashes in the Japanese temple are ashes of Netaji;
(d) whether he has died in any other manner at any other place and, if so, when and how;
(e) if he is alive, in respect of his whereabouts.

2. The Government have examined the Report submitted by the Commission on 8th November, 2005 in detail and have not agreed with the findings that –
(a) Netaji did not die in the plane crash; and
(b) the ashes in the Renkoji Temple were not of Netaji.

3. This Report is placed before the Houses as required under sub-section (4) of Section 3 of the Commissions of Inquiry Act, 1952.

The memorandum of the Action Taken Report for the Mukherjee report tabled in Parliament reflects only one thing: Whitewash.

In 2011, the government's side of the story got a tremendous boost from a book authored by Harvard University don and Subhas' grandnephew

Sugata Bose who is now a Trinamool Congress Lok Sabha MP. *His Majesty's Opponent* was touted as giving out 'an authoritative account of his untimely death in a plane crash [which] will put to rest rumors about the fate of this "deathless hero"'.

The book went on to spawn massive media coverage as most reporters and reviewers could not see beyond the magic combination of Bose being a Harvard historian and Subhas Bose's kin. Sugata hammered the point that the Netaji mystery was 'exploited by a few fringe groups'. But unbeknown to the reviewers and interviewers, not too long ago, Sugata Bose's mother Krishna's famous uncle, writer Nirad C Chaudhury, had told *The Asian Age* that Subhas had become 'a good business proposition' for a section of his family. 'The likes of Sisir Bose cannot shed new light on Netaji's life', he had said, mentioning Sugata's father. 'All that they can do is encash on their *Rangakaka* (uncle Subhas)'. Contrary to what most of us grew up hearing, Sisir Bose was not Subhas' *only* nephew. He was one of many nephews and nieces. What made him stand out was that he and his wife, Krishna Bose, were once loyal members of the very political party that was blamed for downgrading Subhas's legacy and covering up the truth about his fate.

Speaking to *The Times of India* on 23 April 2015, Sisir Bose's sister Chitra Ghosh revealed that 'the entire family, including Sisir, was united in the belief that Netaji had not died in the plane crash. Then something happened in the mid-1970s that led to Sisir changing his stance. It coincided with his moving closer to the Indira Gandhi-led Congress'. The paper quoted her furhter clarifying that 'Sisir, his wife Krishna and their son Sugata toed the Congress line on Netaji because of the crores Netaji Research Bureau had received from successive Congress governments'.

Chitra was merely echoing the views of the majority of the Bose family members. An RTI application filed by Chandrachur Ghose showed that in 2010-11 alone the research centre received a grant of Rs 1.8 crore from the Central government.

Against this backdrop, it was not surprising that Sugata Bose's 'authoritative account' in his book was nothing but amplification of the reports of Congress leader Shah Nawaz Khan and GD Khosla, Indira Gandhi's hagiographer. Sugata has joined the league of some extraordinary men—Jawaharlal Nehru, his minister Shah Nawaz, his friend GD Khosla and his ardent follower Shivraj Patil—in branding his own granduncle Suresh Bose a liar. All on the basis of a note created fraudulently by the Government of India nominee on the committee.

The facts of Khosla's closeness to Jawaharlal, his self-proclaimed disagreement with Subhas during their student days in London, his writing the biography of Indira Gandhi during the period he was heading the Netaji Inquiry Commission and his churning out a book from his inquiry, and the apology he rendered to the Bose family did not come in Sugata's way to laud him as an 'eminent judge'. On the other hand, he described MK Mukherjee as a 'retired Bengali judge', to impute partiality to him and even made libelous statements against him.

According to Bose, Khosla's report 'fell victim to political partisan' whereas the Congress-led government 'quite sensibly, rejected outright' the Mukherjee report. He was disheartened that Indira Gandhi's government lost the elections in 1977 and the Janata government set aside Khosla's findings. He did not care to explain that between September 1974, when Khosla's report was tabled in Parliament and 1977, when Morarji Desai became Prime Minister, India had, for the most part, been under an authoritarian rule.

It was during those dark days that Khosla's report was finally approved in Parliament sans Opposition. The people who fought against the Emergency were also the people who raised voice against Khosla's report. They included politician Samar Guha, lawyer Gobinda Mukhoty and journalist Barun Sengupta.

Since Sugata Bose has such a knack for writing beautifully in English, his arguments in favour of the air crash theory, while appearing to be convincing, actually create a 'wilderness of mirrors' where distinguishing the real is impossible, unless one is aware of the nitty-gritty. Take for instance his claim in his book that an inquiry headed by IB officer Finney 'reached definite conclusion' that Subhas Bose had died. The shocking truth is that Sugata Bose has only perpetuated a fraud which began during Nehru's time and was continued by GD Khosla.

When the charade of the Shah Nawaz's inquiry was on in 1956, the then IB chief BN Mullik, the big daddy of all Indian spooks, provided Shah Nawaz a dossier of the British-era intelligence reports. The selection was made in such a way so as to dip the needle in favour of the air crash theory. The first report in the dossier was from PES Finney. Dated 5 September 1945, it ran into three pages and ended with the 10th and last paragraph that appeared to support the air crash theory.

But this report—used to the hilt by the committee and the Khosla Commission and now Sugata Bose—had been doctored to shore up evidence in favour of the governmental line. That's because the original report had twelve, not ten points. The IB removed the last two points before supplying the report to the inquiry panels. Finney had reached no definite conclusion and that's why he listed out more areas of inquiries in the deleted paragraphs.

Placing the original and the doctored reports side by side brings out classic 'before' and 'after' miracle.

whereas the series is incomplete. Although at this stage one cannot rule out the possibility of Bose being still alive, and of these telegrams being part of a deception plan regarding himself, (particularly in view of his previous intentions of escaping to Russia), the general impression gained from the study of these documents and the talk with Isoda and my informant is that Bose did actually die as stated.

11. The following line of investigation is suggested :
(a) tracing and examining of staff officer TADA in Japan.
(b) examination of Swami in Penang.
(c) Further examination in detail of Lieut.Gen.Isoda.
(d) examination of Hikari personnel in Saigon.
(e) search of Hikari documents in Saigon.
(f) examination of Chief-of-Staff or other staff-officers of Southern Army in Saigon who know about these telegrams.
(g) tracing and examination of Col. Habibur Rahman.
(h) search of photographs, remains or ashes, etc. of Bose in Saigon, where they may have been sent, or in Tokyo.

12. Considerable time is being spent on these enquiries, and it is therefore requested that any conclusive information, one way or the other, should be circulated as soon as possible.

Sd/-
Asst. Director,
Intelligence Bureau,
Govt. of India,
attached I.A.U.
7 Divn.
Bangkok.

BEFORE

-3-

telegrams, along with numerous other documents, must have been purposely left where the British would find them. But in that case one would have expected some report from the Staff Officer to be on the file, whereas the series is incomplete. Although at this stage one cannot rule out the possibility of Bose being still alive, and of these telegrams being part of a deception plan regarding himself, (particularly in view of his previous intentions of escaping to Russia), the general impression gained from the study of these documents and the talk with Isoda and my informant is that Bose did actually die as stated.

Sd. P.E.S.Finney.
Assistant Director,
Intelligence Bureau,Govt.of India.
Attached I.A.U. 7 Division
Bangkok.

AFTER

A copy of the original report is available in a declassified Ministry of Defence file which was seen by Sugata Bose. And yet he chose to trot out whatever the fraudulent reports of Shah Nawaz and Khosla said.

Another piece of 'evidence' dished out by Professor Bose pertained to journalist Harin Shah, who visited Taipei in 1946 and confirmed that Subhas had indeed died there. The centrepiece of Shah's evidence was a moving account given by nurse Tsan Pi Sha who had supposedly taken care of the 'dying' Indian leader.

Well, Shah was not an ordinary journalist. He used to be editor of the official journal of an organisation affiliated to the Congress party. His conduct in Taipei and thereafter was more like that of a government agent, rather than an impartial journalist. Sugata Bose forgot to tell his readers that Shah never detailed his findings in any newsreport in 1946. After ten years, he just popped in or was propped up when the Shah Nawaz Committee was formed.

To make his story appear credible in his tearjerker of a book titled *The gallant end of Netaji* Shah created at least two fictitious characters, one of which was nurse Tsan Pi Sha. *His Majesty's Opponent* just infused life into this figment of Shah's imagination.

In a secret file, there is a letter dated 23 May 1956 that Shah Nawaz wrote to AK Dar, the main man for his committee's inquiry in Japan, giving the names of some people he wanted to examine as witnesses. From the evidence of Dr Yoshimi—whose bona fides Sugata Bose doesn't question—Shah Nawaz named four nurses who were there at the hospital in August 1945. These names were then forwarded to the Japanese Foreign Ministry by Dar. There was no Tsan Pi Sha in any of these two lists. Even the subsequent British/Taiwanese inquiry failed to find any proof of her existence.

As item (3) in my letter of May 14th we have requested for the attendance of Japanese nurses who were on duty in the Nanmon Hospital, Taihoku, Taiwan when Netaji Subhas Chandra Bose was reportedly brought there. Dr. Yoshimi has now informed the Committee of the names of these nurses. The names as given are :-

    (a) Nakano,
    (b) Ohama,
    (c) Tomimoto, and
    (d) Nishimoto.

I would be grateful if you could kindly make arrangements for the persons listed above to meet the Commission at mutual convenience.

Yours sincerely,

(A.K.Dar)

Mr. Hisaji Hattori,
Chief of the 4th Section,
Asian Affairs Bureau,
Gaimusho, Tokyo.

Sugata Bose told his readers that the 'most compelling evidence' came from the testimony of interpreter Juichi Nakamura who talked to a badly-burnt Subhas Bose in Taipei. He cited the testimony of Dr Yoshimi, which said that Nakamura was a civil government official. But this wasn't a proper introduction. As Habibur Rahman identified him in his deposition before the committee, Nakamura was someone who 'belonged to intelligence or security service'. Now isn't that somewhat different from the innocuous sounding term 'civil government official'?

The Shah Nawaz's report—cited by Bose as if it's a holy scripture—claimed that Nakamura appeared before the commission on his own initiative on 30 May 1956, in response to a newspaper notice. But in a secret file, there is an 18 April 1956 letter in which TN Kaul is telling Ambassador BR Sen to request the Japanese foreign office to ensure the presence of Japanese witnesses. The attached list names Nakamura. The next we know is that this former intelligence officer travels 1,200 km to tender his evidence before the committee in Tokyo. Can we then rule out the possibility of his being propped up to support the official view?

Nakamura's evidence, as recorded by the Shah Nawaz Committee, says that when he reached the hospital, Dr Yoshimi identified a badly-burnt man to him as Chandra Bose. But Dr Yoshimi told the BBC for its documentary *Enemy of Empire* in the 1990s that he did not know who the burnt man was until Nakamura had told him so after the burnt man had died. On the other hand, Habibur Rahman told the committee that Subhas was barely conscious after he was brought to hospital and soon slipped into coma. And there you have Sugata Bose claiming in his book that Nakamura still managed to talk to Yoshimi's comatose patient. Which researcher in the world would describe such evidence as 'most compelling?' During a chat on the *Rediff.com*, Sugata was asked why there was so much 'secrecy surrounding Netaji'. He ducked the question by answering that 'we should pay less attention to myths and mysteries, and concentrate more on his life and work from which there is a lot to learn'.

Speaking to *The Economic Times*, Sugata pontificated: 'I think his life and work is more important and fascinating and it should be before the reading public, especially those belonging to the younger generation.' This rings a bell. In 1980 when Prime Minister Indira Gandhi launched the first volume of the *Collected works of Netaji* edited by Sisir Bose, she had said that Subhas's name was being 'misused for political purposes by some people' she wouldn't identify. She added that 'Netaji should be an inspiration to the younger generation', and complimented Sisir Bose for his compilation. The government-approved Khosla Commission report had already 'inspired' the youth of India by calling Subhas Bose a puppet of the Japanese!

Sugata crossed the line to imply that the Bose family agreed with the government view. In that list, he included his grandfather. He wrote that Sarat Bose had accepted 'with grief and fortitude' the news of his brother's death when he first heard it in prison.

PM feels Netaji's name being misused

Prime Minister Indira Gandhi said on Friday it was said 'that the name of Netaji Subhas Chandra Bose was used for political purposes by some people, reports UNI.

Such misuse of name would not do any good to any one, Mrs Gandhi said while releasing the first volume of Collected Works of Netaji.

Mrs Gandhi said Netaji has a very special place in the history of India and no body ever doubted his patriotism and emotional involvement in the freedom struggle.

Netaji should be an inspiration to the younger generation. His courage, perseverance and determination are examples for all time, she said.

Congratulating the Netaji Research Bureau, Calcutta, for bringing out the volume, she called for developing a sense of history. Netaji's awareness of the needs of the hour and his sense of history made what he was, she said.

The first volume of the 10-volume book in English contains Netaji's unfinished auto-biography, a collection of his letters and contemporary documents. It has been edited by his nephew, Dr Sisir K Bose.

How in the world could he possibly leave out what a wizened Sarat openly told the media afterwards is beyond me, because the whole Bose family knows about it:

> When the story of (of the air crash) came out, I [Sarat Bose] was in prison. I shall confess that as long as I was in detention, I felt upset. I had not had any materials then to enable me to judge whether the air crash story was true or not.

Sugata Bose spun an excuse that his grandfather died in February 1950 before convincing evidence was collected. It's a distortion of facts. Sarat Bose did not need to browse through the edited testimonies of crash survivors years later as Sugata Bose did; he heard it all from the horse's mouth there and then.

Sugata Bose is a famous historian; Sarat Bose was an ace lawyer. Sugata Bose cannot claim to have a better understanding of the event than his grandfather. Sarat Bose personally examined the most important witness to Subhas's 'death'—Habibur Rahman—and made this statement in late 1949:

> After I came out of the prison in 1945, I had the opportunity of talking to Colonel Habibur Rahman of the INA....the only conclusion I could come to was that he had orders from his Chief to keep his whereabouts a closely guarded secret.

In his book, Sugata Bose gave his late pediatrician father Dr Sisir Kumar Bose a larger-than-life image and implied that he was the sole inheritor of his father's legacy. That was quite natural for a son to do, but it was very conceited of him to project Sisir Bose's pro-air crash views as if they were some sort of last word on the issue. He wrote that after

Amiya with Subhas and Emilie in Badgastein in December 1937. Courtesy: Amiya Bose family

Sarat Bose's death, Sisir studied all the evidence, carried out what he calls 'investigations' in Japan and Taiwan and reached a conclusion. The narrative in Sugata's book precluded any references to Sisir's other siblings, especially elder brother Amiya Nath Bose.

Amiya also made his own enquiries about his uncle's disappearance. He dismissed the air crash theory like his father and all the siblings, except

Sisir. He did so publicly till his death in 1996. In fact, none of Sarat's children—except the one who joined the Congress party—believed in the air crash theory. For instance, brothers Ashoke, Amiya and Subrata wrote to Prime Minister VP Singh in May 1990 that

> during the lifetime of our youngest uncle, late Shailesh Chandra Bose, a statement signed by him and all sons of every one of Netaji's brothers was issued to the Press at Calcutta stating that the 'ashes' at Renkoji temple were not the 'ashes of Netaji'.

> finally decided that the story of Netaji's death in an air crash cannot be accepted as conclusive.
>
> We are firmly of the view that to bring the 'ashes' now lying in the Renkoji Temple in Tokyo to India as 'ashes' of Netaji Subhas Chandra Bose will be an act of sacrilege, which should not be allowed by the people and Government of India.
>
> With kind regards,
>
> Yours sincerely,
>
> (ASHOKE NATH BOSE)
>
> (AMIYA NATH BOSE)
>
> (SUBRATA BOSE)

In contrast to Amiya's frank demeanour, Sisir was not very forthcoming in making his case. When the Mukherjee Commission was set up, it was expected of him and the Harvard professor to file affidavits like the other family members to help the commission and the nation in overcoming the controversy. When Sisir did not, the commission summoned him. He refused to appear. He actually wrote this:

> I have no personal knowledge as to the issues referred to the commission. I am therefore not competent to depose in this matter.

The commission also summoned Sugata Bose, but he never turned up and nor did he ever file any affidavit detailing his case for Netaji's death in Taipei.

Sugata Bose opened the last chapter of his book by dramatising his grandaunt Emilie Schenkl's obvious reaction to the 1945 radio announcement of Subhas's death. Later he quoted from another letter to insinuate that she believed in Subhas's death in that air crash. Perhaps the motive behind erasing all the more dramatic happening of 1996 and misrepresenting Emilie's real views was that the professor did not want to embarrass Pranab Mukherjee, his late father's good friend.

The story goes back to 1995 when a group of Japanese war veterans, proud of their association with the INA, made an appeal that the Indian government should take 'Bose's ashes' to India. The demand was discussed by Prime Minister PV Narasimha Rao, Home Minister SB Chavan and Foreign Minister Pranab Mukherjee.

The Intelligence Bureau cautioned that 'if the ashes are brought to India, the people of West Bengal are likely to construe it as an imposition on them of the official version of Netaji's death'.

The Ministry of External Affairs, however, opined that 'the ashes should be brought back to India'. It was even ready with the outlines of a 'preparatory action', to create a 'consensus in favour of burying the controversy', under which 'respected public figures' could be 'discreetly encouraged to make statements, including in Parliament, requesting the Government to bring back the ashes'.

To sort the issue out, Prime Minister Rao asked the Home Minister to place the matter before the Cabinet.

```
                    TOP SECRET              IMMEDIATE
                                         COPY NO. 1
                    No.6/CM/95(iii)
              GOVERNMENT OF INDIA (BHARAT SARKAR)
          CABINET SECRETARIAT (MANTRIMANDAL SACHIVALAYA)

                    NEW DELHI, the 6th February, 1995.
                                    19 Magha, 1916 (S).

                    -----

        The following will constitute additional item on the agenda
    for the meeting of the Cabinet scheduled to be held at 1145
    hours, on Wednesday, the 8th February, 1995 in the Conference
    Room (No.155) South Block, New Delhi :-


            S U B J E C T S

    5.  Proposal to bring the mortal   MINISTER OF HOME AFFAIRS.
        remains of Netaji Subhash Chandra
        Bose from Japan to India.
        (Note dated 2.2.1995 (CD-92/95)
        from the Ministry of Home
        Affairs, attached).


                              (D.M. Rao)
                    Deputy Secretary to the Cabinet.
```

Document obtained in public interest

At the meeting on 8 February 1995, Home Secretary K Padmanabhaiah submitted a Top Secret backgrounder discussing the case. It even alluded to the machinations to bring around the Bose family to the government view. 'Netaji's wife and the only daughter...can best be approached through another nephew of Netaji, Dr Sisir Bose.'

It would, therefore, be necessary to take the members of Netaji's family into confidence in the first place by convincing them as to the genuineness of the ashes. It should then be easier to handle opposition from other quarters like the Forward Bloc. Netaji's wife and the only daughter are at present living in Angsburg, Germany. It is felt that they can best be approached through another nephew of Netaji, Dr.Sisir Bose. Shri Amia Nath Bose, the most vociferous sceptic of the air crash story, needs to be brought around by approaching at an appropriately high level. There is good chance that if reasonably approached, the family members may drop their opposition. The question of an appropriate memorial involving the mortal remains shall also have to be addressed in due course.

15. This issues with the approval of the Home Minister.

(K.PADMANABHAIAH)
HOME SECRETARY

F.No.I/12014/27/93-IS(D.III)
Ministry of Home Affairs

Document obtained in public interest

The Cabinet decided to stall for time and not bring the ashes to India. However, there was no stopping Pranab Mukherjee. So, off he went on a world-wide, never-before quest to exorcise the ghost of the Bose mystery. After meeting the Japanese Foreign Minister in Tokyo, he flew to Germany.

On 20 October 1995, from Augsburg an agitated Emilie Schenkl rang her grandnephew Surya, Germany-based eldest son of Amiya Nath Bose. She told Surya 'that Mr Pranab Mukherjee was coming...to convince her and Anita to give their approval [in writing] for bringing the so-called "ashes" of Netaji to India'. Ever since his arrival in Germany in 1973, Surya had heard his grandaunt telling him how she believed that 'Netaji was in the Soviet Union after 1945'.

According to Surya Kumar Bose, on October 21 'Anita and her husband, Dr Martin Pfaff had to take Mr Pranab Mukherjee out for lunch', as his grandaunt 'could not tolerate any discussion on the so-called "ashes" in her presence'. Emilie told Pranab Mukherjee that the Renkoji remains 'had nothing to do with Subhas'.

A decade later, Pranab Mukherjee was described in the Mukherjee Commission report as one of the seven witnesses who had testified before it in favour of the story of Subhas's death in Taiwan. In an ironical twist of fate, having returned to power in 2004, Pranab Mukherjee then sat in judgment on the commission report along with his other Cabinet colleagues.

Since the chances of minister Mukherjee taking an objective view of judge Mukherjee's report were bleak, there were murmurs of protest. Pranab was accused of trying to scuttle the commission's inquiry and that probably led to his facing 'mob fury in Kolkata' while his car was entering a hotel on 18 June 2006.

According to *Hindustan Times*, 'Mukherjee later said the report had already been placed in Parliament and "we wanted a discussion on the report but the Bharatiya Janata Party (BJP) stalled the debate"'. That's not true. On the other hand, then Lok Sabha Speaker Somnath Chatterjee, another Bengali luminary, invited scorn from the Forward Bloc that with his alleged help the 'Congress succeeded in putting to rest a debate on the subject', to quote a *Zee News* story.

Eleven

It's final—the mysterious Gumnami Baba of Faizabad was not Netaji. The DNA tests conducted by the Central Forensic Science Laboratory in Kolkata have laid all doubts to rest. Gumnami Baba's DNA samples do not match with either the parental or maternal genetic lineage of Netaji Subhas Chandra Bose.

—*The Times of India*, Kolkata edition,

1 September 2000

'Things aren't always what they seem!' is a dialogue from the movie *Tinker Tailor Soldier Spy* which depicts the hunt for a Russian mole in the highest echelons of MI6, the British Secret Service. It is an odd co-relation to make, but there are episodes in the Faizabad angle to the Bose mystery that compel one to think that it is perhaps just as well.

Time was when Justice Mukherjee Commission of Inquiry appeared to be inexorably moving towards an unimaginable conclusion. After considering all evidence on record, the feeling among the commission staffers was that the Faizabad angle was quite formidable. After visiting the dusty UP town in 2001 [picture] and having examined the witnesses and material evidence, that is Bhagwanji's belongings, Justice Mukherjee couldn't have ignored the angle for all the startling details it unfolded.

So the only logical step Mukherjee could now take was to locate Bhagwanji's writings and run them through handwriting experts and get hold of something that could yield his DNA for testing. Handwritings he got in plenty, both in English and Bangla. And while he was wondering if it would be possible to extract DNA from possible traces of saliva in Bhagwanji's smoking pipes, he came across seven teeth, assumed to be of Bhagwanji as they were found among his belongings.

The handwriting testing began against the backdrop of my obtaining a report on behalf of my then employer, *Hindustan Times*. B Lal Kapoor, a former Additional Director of the National Institute of Criminology and Forensic Sciences, Ministry of Home Affairs was approached as he was, I was told, the 'No 1 handwriting expert in India'.

During his service years, B Lal had honed his skills in several forensic labs in the US, the UK, Germany and Switzerland. Post-retirement, he was taken on the panels of several government departments and banks, such as the State Bank of India and Citi. When I met him, he was still getting cases from the police and being invited to give lectures to security officials and even judges on the aspects of handwriting testing.

Lal gave a positive report to *Hindustan Times*. After a story based on his report was front-paged, the commission hired him. Working on different and better samples, he now produced two detailed and far more convincing reports. Applying the fundamentals of the forensic testing of questioned documents outlined by AS Osborn and Wildon R Harrison, he found that the English samples picked up from Ram Bhawan (questioned documents) were 'written by the same person', i.e. Subhas Bose.

Regarding the Bangla handwritings, he wrote:

> The questioned Bengali writings are having time gap of few years, when compared with the date of execution of admitted Bengali writing…. Even having time gap the relevant questioned Bengali writings are showing characteristic similarities with natural variations and the collective occurrence of such similarities may not be found in the writings of two different persons as a matter of chance. The collective occurrence of significant similarities can only be explained by the fact that both the writings belong to one and the same person.

B Lal also highlighted that the writer of both admitted (Netaji's) and questioned (Bhagwanji's) writings was in the 'habit of giving a peculiar sign when making insertion of certain words'. This peculiar caret was described by him as having a 'very high identifying value'.

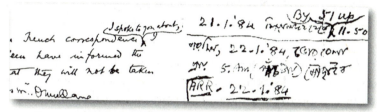

A specimen of Bose's writing in 1937; and a 1984 scribble by Bhagwanji (right)

The commission also obtained two more reports from the government. The government experts did not have the stature and experience of B Lal, and their subsequent conduct also did not inspire too much confidence in their findings. One report came from SK Mandal, senior scientific officer at the Forensic Science Laboratory, Kolkata. A look at his report was sufficient to convince one of its fraudulent nature. While giving a report, a handwriting expert is supposed to state reasons for drawing the conclusions. But Mandal's report had zilch. It simply said the writings were of two different persons.

The other one was signed by Amar Singh, Government Examiner of Questioned Documents, and ML Sharma, Deputy Government Examiner of Questioned Documents. 'We have carefully and thoroughly examined the original documents of this case in all aspects of handwriting identification and detection of forgery, with the scientific aids in the Government of India Laboratory at Shimla', they stated while explaining the reason for their opinion. They admitted that Bhagwanji's writings 'do not show any sign of imitation or forgery in them'. This was the only common ground between them and B Lal. In his report to the *Hindustan Times*, Lal had observed that Bhagwanji tried to conceal his identity by overwriting the strokes and writing in the capitals.

B Lal nevertheless emphasised that

> it is not possible for a writer to change his writing habit completely. Even in an effort to hide his identity, the writer is not able to leave his individual characteristics and other peculiarities found in his handwriting. There is such a

faithful reproduction of some peculiarities that even a gap of time to the extent of decades cannot hide them.

CARE   DAHYABHAI | CARE / SANTOSH / BHA

Left Netaji; right Bhagwanji

Lal's conclusion on this point was that he found 'no evidence…that the questioned writing has been made by a writer other than Shri Subhas Chandra Bose by imitating/copying the writing of Shri Subhas Chandra Bose'.

But if you believe the Government of India laboratory report, the resemblance was merely cosmetic.

> Both the handwritings in their pictorial appearance appear to bear a marked resemblance to each other at the first instance, which is due to similar style and class of writing. However, the analysis of the structures of the letters, the study of the 'master pattern' of the letters, in words as well as range of variations, on close observation, shows that the two writings are quite distinctive and different in their origin and are written by two different authors.

The report gave some details and at the end showcased a 'juxtaposition chart', highlighting the differences between the two handwritings. The chart had eight examples, five for English and three for Bangla, comparing both sets of writings and demonstrating the differences in ten alphabets in all.

That is not very impressive. B Lal's report was supported by 460 large-size photographs, accounting for each and every alphabetical letter appearing in the handwriting samples given to him. He also dwelt at length on the issue of 'natural variation' in handwriting.

> Every genuine writing has got natural variation since the human hand is not an exact reproducing machine, and it is very important to consider this natural variation for a correct conclusion regarding authorship of a writing. If natural variations are taken as differences, then there would be error in the identification.

His finding was that Bhagwanji's handwriting showed 'natural variations which are additional symptoms of genuineness'.

That the Central government experts were not confident of their report became clear to the commission staffers when they chose to ignore the commission's summons to appear before it in New Delhi on the same day when their former boss B Lal Kapoor was going to be examined. Amar Singh never turned up before the commission. ML Sharma went all the way to Kolkata from his office in Shimla to make the government's case. As Mandal was being examined, Sharma sneaked into the room and noted all the questions that he was also going to face. Later, armed with the prior knowledge of the questions he was going to face, Sharma started answering questions even before they were put to him.

The DNA test episode turned out to be even more curious. The Centre for DNA Fingerprinting and Diagnostics (CDFD) in Hyderabad had a go first. No one knows who the scientist-in-charge of the test was as the final report was signed by a junior technical officer only. This report said that two out of seven teeth made available to them were 'subjected to DNA isolation, and DNA fingerprinting profiles were prepared' and the same were then matched with the DNA obtained from blood samples given by Subhas Bose's relatives. The report was inconclusive as the teeth 'did not yield DNA suitable for complete analysis'.

For some strange reasons, the remaining five teeth were not used for meeting the desired concentration of DNA. And even as the report was given in a sealed cover to the commission, an impression was given over the phone that the DNA had matched.

The remaining five teeth were then handed over to Central Forensic Science Laboratory, Kolkata. Then a most suspicious thing happened. Bangla daily *Anandabazar Patrika*, which had had a history of scoffing at the entire Bose mystery, not to speak of the incredible Faizabad angle, published a report on 20 December 2003 saying that the DNA test was negative. 'That Gumnami Baba is by no means Netaji has been proved', the ABP report said. The commission regarded the report prejudicial 'to the progress of the inquiry' and complained to the Press Council of India.

Anandabazar Patrika contested this through their legal cell head, who told the Press Council that the story represented what was 'a scoop in journalistic parlance and they were satisfied about its genuineness'. It submitted that 'the information was substantiated by the official reports subsequently issued' in June 2004 when Justice Mukherjee had made all handwriting and DNA reports public.

The Press Council ruled in favour of *Anandabazar Patrika*: 'To say that the press should not publish any information till it is officially released would militate against the spirit of investigative journalism and even to an extent the purpose of journalism.'

Investigative journalism is a jolly good thing but can you investigate something that's yet to come into being? Yes, reports do get leaked out, findings of commissions are made known before they are made known officially. But only *after* they have been drafted or the conclusions have been reached. You cannot know the findings of a DNA test *before* it is completed.

It's an argument that no legal eagle can twist because the 'secret' DNA report was signed and sent to the commission by the CFSL director on 6 June 2004, a full six months after the *Anandabazar Patrika* got what they thought was a 'scoop'. As a matter of fact, in December 2003 the DNA test had not even started properly.

SECRET
CONFIDENTIAL

CENTRAL FORENSIC SCIENCE LABORATORY *(P – 1 of 15)*

Directorate of Forensic Science, MHA, Govt. of India, 30 Gorachand Road, Kolkata–14.

Ph:(033) 22641638, Fax:(033) 22649442, e-mail: cfslkolkata@indiatimes.com

No. CFSL/EE/04(G/I)-280   Dated the June   , 2004.

To
The Secretary
Justice Mukherjee Commission of Inquiry
for inquiry into the alleged disappearance of
Netaji Subhas Chandra Bose
'B' Block (Third Floor)
11/A Mirza Ghalib Street
Kolkata – 700 087.

Ref.: JMCI/EO/2002-2003/83(III)/371 dated December 22, 2003.

Sub.: **DNA profiling test of teeth allegedly found at the alleged residence of one Gumnami Baba at Faizabad, UP and samples of blood collected from two descendents on the father's side and three descendents on the mother's side of Netaji Subhas Chandra Bose to fix the identity of the person to whom the teeth belonged.**

This would mean that like Doctor Who of the BBC sci-fi series, the ABP reporter time travelled to June 2004, saw the outcome of the DNA test, came back and filed the story in December 2003. Or was it that the media-friendly director of CFSL Kolkata—who had all by himself carried out the test in violation of norms—reached a conclusion beforehand?

Some time before the Shah Nawaz Committee visited Japan, Calcutta newspaper *Amrita Bazar Patrika* carried an 'investigative' story titled 'How Netaji met with plane crash' with 'graphic details of Netaji's fateful journey from Saigon'. The story even carried a sketch showing the sitting arrangements of the passengers in the ill-fated plane. This was a major 'scoop' for those days.

But as one flips through a secret file, it emerges that the sketch used in the story was clearly a refurbished version of the one appearing in records supplied in confidence, by Japanese Foreign Ministry to the MEA. It was a tell-tale proof that someone either in Japan or India had leaked out information.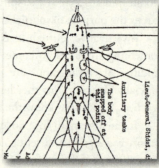

India it was, because a clipping of the newspaper article was pasted on the Press

Information Bureau sheet and kept in a secret file as a memento. Attached was a congratulatory note. 'With the compliments of AR Vyas, Dy Information Officer, EA Ministry' to the secretive NGO (Not to Go out of the Office) section of the MEA. TN Kaul also sent the clipping to Shah Nawaz, saying it would be 'of interest to you'. It was as though the government was gloating over a leak!

Bhagwanji may or may not have been Subhas Chandra Bose, but let no one talk about the DNA test 'proving' that he was not. Because the test was performed in a lab controlled by the Ministry of Home Affairs and the credibility of the Government of India over the Netaji death puzzle is zilch.

Amazingly enough, as early as 2000, the CFSL Kolkata was talking of a scientific 'breakthrough'—a sort of thing which rarely, if ever, happens in a third world country—that could lead to extracting of DNA from Renkoji temple ashes when the British, American, Japanese and other Indian experts had ruled out the possibility.

According to a *Times of India* report, the 'scientists here [at CFSL] claim to have hit upon a more sophisticated version of DNA testing, which, they said, could help them prove conclusively if the remains kept at the Renkoji temple in Japan are actually of Netaji Subhas Chandra Bose'. The director was quoted in the report as making a tall claim that 'recently we have mastered the technology and with

CFSL scientists claim breakthrough in DNA

New test could identify Netaji's ashes

By Saikat Ray

CALCUTTA: Scientists here claim to have hit upon a more sophisticated version of DNA testing, which, they said, could help them prove conclusively if the remains kept at the Renkoji temple in Japan are actually of Netaji Subhas Chandra Bose. Dr V.K. Kasyap, deputy director at the Central Forensic Science Laboratory, said that the CFSL achieved the breakthrough during the last six months after unsuccessful attempts to develop the technology since 1997.

The new "mitrocondial DNA test-

for a mitrocondial DNA testing," he added.

Kasyap, assistant director Rajni Trivedi and a team of scientists consisting Ranjan Dutta and Prabal Chatterjee inspired by encouraging results of mitrocondrial DNA testing produced in the US and the UK, started researching in CFSL, Calcutta, to develop the same kind of testing.

"Recently we have mastered the technology and with this breakthrough we are now able to do what forensic centres in Washington in US or Birmingham in UK are doing." Kasyap said.

this breakthrough, we are now able to do what forensic centres in Washington in US or Birmingham in UK are doing'.

The same director was to become incommunicado later on as the Mukherjee Commission repeatedly asked him if it was possible to lift latent fingerprints from Bhagwanji's belongings.

The process of DNA testing is scientific and beyond reproach. But man can err or pull wool over others' eyes or can become a victim of trickery. The credibility of DNA testing process in India has been called into question over matters that are nowhere as politically significant as the Netaji mystery. For example, in 2003 three police officers and two doctors were found guilty of 'fudging the DNA samples of five innocent civilians' killed in the Chattisinghpora massacre of 2000 in J&K. A September 2010 report in *Hyderabad journal* reported how a scientist at the Forensic Science Laboratory in the city was caught red-handed while accepting a bribe from a suspect in a rape case. The scientist said: 'The police usually tamper with DNA reports to help mighty culprits go scot-free'.

The Indian forensic labs are not like those in the US or Europe that one can take their word as final on sensitive issues.

Around 1999, the CFSL performed a DNA test on the remains presumed to be of Paul Wells, a British national kidnapped along with others by terrorists in J&K. According to a report published in the *Independent* of London, in January 2000 the J&K Police 'announced that scientists in the Central Forensic Science Laboratories in New Delhi and Calcutta had confirmed through DNA testing of samples of bones and other body parts that this was indeed the body of Mr Wells'.

To verify the claims made by the CFSL labs, the British carried out their own tests. The Foreign and Commonwealth Office later announced that 'British police forensic scientists had decided that the remains were neither those of Mr Wells nor of any of the other hostages'.

Out of a misplaced sense of patriotism, ordinary citizens like us may want to stand by 'our' report, but throughout the world everyone will go with the British report. Even our own ruling class, top bureaucrats, soldiers, intellectuals, journalists, everyone—

whose children's favourite destination for study, work and permanent domicile is more likely to be London or New York than Mumbai and New Delhi—won't give a fig to a report from an Indian lab when another one from the West is at hand. That's why every time there is some forensic test involved in some contentious matter in India, the parties involved try to seek opinion from labs in the US and Europe. That's the reason why in the Sunanda Pushkar case tests have been carried out in the UK and in the FBI lab in America.

In hindsight, the handing over of these teeth to government agencies was a mistake. But there was little that Justice Mukherjee could do in the face of general apathy with which the people and the media followed the progress of his inquiry. Unless an issue is being agitated in the media or has been politicised, no one really bothers.

In 2010, four years after his report had been dismissed, Justice Mukherjee burst out during an off-the-record talk while he was being interviewed by independent filmmaker Amlan Ghosh. All this was recorded and later a byte from it was shown on news channels. While his report had said that there was no 'clinching evidence' to show that Bhagwanji was Netaji, Justice Mukhejee could now be seen asserting that he was '100 per cent' sure that it was 'him' only. He said he couldn't prove his case because of impediments created in his path. He blasted the government in language he could not have used in his report and hinted at a forensic fraud.

Three years later, on 31 January 2013 to be precise, a new chapter was opened with the Lucknow Bench of the Allahabad High Court finding a link between Bhagwanji and Netaji. This became possible after Shakti Singh, son of the owner of Ram Bhawan and a Bhagwanji follower himself, approached the court.

Joining the new case with the unsettled case filed by Lalita Bose in 1986, Justices Devi Prasad Singh and Virendra Kumar Dixit surveyed the entire matter in their judgment, which referred to Sugata Bose's book as well as mine, *India's Biggest Cover-up*. The court accepted that there was some evidence linking Bhagwanji to Netaji. I came in for some praise as the court said in its order that my journalistic enquiry 'seems to be genuine and based on relevant material'.

> A little doubt with regard to survival of a national hero…casts a duty on the government to find out or explore the truth which does not seem to be difficult in view of recent scientific development. The efforts made and findings recorded by the author and with others extensive tour of various places with regard to survival or death of Netaji Subhas Chandra Bose including Gumnami Baba must be attended to by the Government of India with due sincerity to expose the truth.

More pertinently, the court observed:

> The articles/items of late Gumnami Baba raise reasonable curiosity for a probe to find out his identity. The celebration of the birthday of Netaji Subhas Chandra Bose on 23rd January every year, books, documents and material relating back to the period when the alleged death of Netaji took place in the plane crash, including the books with regard to war crimes and materials collected by Anuj Dhar in his two books as well as series of 17 articles published in *Northern India Patrika* from 20th December, 1985 to 23rd January, 1986 with regard to Gumnami Baba alias Bhagwan Ji prima facie makes out a case for a probe into his identity. The State and Central Governments should look into it to remove doubts with regard to Gumnami Baba by holding appropriate enquiry.

The court said it was a 'duty cast upon the [State] government to preserve the articles/household goods of such person at appropriate place/

museum scientifically, so that coming generation may not be divested from its right of access for research work or otherwise'.

In view of this, the court ordered that Bhagwanji's belonging 'may be kept scientifically, under the supervision of a qualified person (curator)' at a museum in either Faizabad or Ayodhya. Also, the State government was directed to appoint 'a committee consisting of a team of experts and higher officers, headed by a Retired Judge of High Court, to hold an enquiry with regard to the identity of late Gumnami Baba alias Bhagwanji'.

Given the complex nature of the matter and so many details it entailed, the High Court verdict was not covered by media across the country as it should have been, leaving people confused. There was virtually no reaction in Bengal but ripples moved across UP. Taking the lead in galvanising the public sentiment, five-term MLA Akhilesh Singh called a press conference in Lucknow in February, with Shakti Singh and myself in tow.

Rashtriya Sahara coverage of Akhilesh Singh's (left) press conference. The author is on right and Shakti Singh in the middle

On 14 March 2013, an adjournment notice was moved in the state assembly by about a dozen MLAs, including Akhilesh Singh of Peace Party, Anugrah Narain Singh of the Congress, Suresh Rana of the Bharatiya Janata Party, Mokhtar Ansari of the Quami Ekta Dal and Raghuraj Pratap Singh (Independent).

In the discussion to follow, leaders of all political parties sank their differences—a feat that one doesn't see too often in caste-riven Uttar Pradesh—and put across their views in a most dignified way. The Leader of Opposition, Swamy Prasad Maurya of the BSP, said Netaji was next only to Mahatma Gandhi in the freedom struggle and remarked that it was 'unfortunate for the country that the causes of Netaji's death have not been known'. As reported in *The Hindu*, 'Hukum Singh of BJP said the constitution of the commission should not be delayed'. Even Anugrah Narain Singh 'demanded the Government [should] constitute a commission' to settle the Bhagwanji mystery.

Twelve

If Bhagwanji was really Subhas Chandra Bose, why didn't he come out in the open? What was he really doing for all these years sitting behind a curtain? And, what did he say about the disappearance in 1945?

For the sake of argument, if it is accepted that Bhagwanji was Netaji indeed, these and many other questions would have to be taken up in right earnest. It would then be pertinent to postulate the following:

One, if Bhagwanji was really Netaji, there would have to be a very very big reason for him to go into hiding.

Two, there would have been no way that the Government did not become aware of the 'dead' Netaji's existence, considering the expertise India has in the field of intelligence.

Three, it would have been against Netaji's grain to just sit there and do nothing.

From what I have been able to collate and understand, the answers to all of the above are baffling.

Most clues about the secret life of Bhagwanji lie in his assorted utterances, jotted down by his closest followers, and letters written by him to them in confidence. A chunk from these was put together and published in the early 1970s in a book. There have been enlarged editions lately.

Titled after a famous Rabindranath Tagore song meaning, 'the great man comes', *Oi Mahamanab Asey* (Jayasree Publications, Kolkata) is unheard of even in Bengal. The reason for that being that it is written in quaint, hard to understand Bangla, interspersed with convoluted sentences in English. The massively incredible narrative goes haphazardly from one episode to another, without providing any context. *Oi Mahamanab Asey* is cryptic—just as Bhagwanji wanted it to be.

One has to read in between the lines, seek co-relations with something else to get a smattering of meaning. The book's writer, Charanik—who at one point in time was revolutionary Sunil Das—pieces together the life and times of the protagonist, variously called Mahakaal, Dead Man or other names denoting expressions to that effect.

My real identity is that I am a dust particle of Bengal. My false identity is Frankenstein, which I neither wanted nor deserved.

It is not for nothing that Ghost of the Dead has denied himself every worldly care and sacrificed unto utter nothingness, everything that this world—and flesh could offer.

Bhagwanji's notes found at Ram Bhawan were similar in tenor.

> He has died and turned into a ghost. …Very strange are you and your government that they constitute 'loaded-dice-commissions' over and over again just to know whether he is dead or not! You all are the reason behind this. *Populus Vult Decipi* - **You All People Wish To Be Fooled**. [Translated from Bangla, except the emphsised parts]

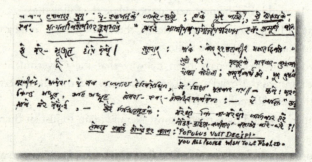

Bhagwanji repeatedly claimed that he had *undergone complete meta-morphosis* and was an altogether different person from what he used to be. And that the attempts to comprehend his present through his past would be futile.

With all your erudition and discernment, you simply cannot comprehend the state of metamorphosis of the Ghost of Mahakaal. How very complete and final!

His new life was a baffling amalgamation of spiritualism, mysticism, militarism and the paranormal. To the endless wonder of Charanik, Bhagwanji once wrote:

As human beings, we are, at all times, radiating energy, which is soaked and stored by items around us. Even our thoughts radiate an electrical field which leaves an imprint on objects in the form of energy. According to eminent Russian scientist Genady Sergeyev, every human being leaves an electrical imprint— energetical imprint—as well as an informational imprint on objects that he touches or is close to. Every object around us has magnetic characteristics of its molecules. It is then that it becomes a natural magnetic recorder. Even over a brief period, man can record the information of his entire life on a nearby object. By 'brief' I mean—in a split of a second.

While he claimed to have achieved 'a complete break with the past', Bhagwanji often lapsed into history, clearly identifying himself as Subhas Bose:

[Dead Man] has no rancour for Bapu though Bapu in his fight against him was so rattled that he gave up his Congress membership and also started a whispering campaign (against your Dead Man), and Congress thought otherwise. Your Dead Man has no rancour because Bapu at last turned a volte-face and preached fighting for freedom and honour (which was your right creed); and because hearing and becoming stimulated and emboldened by the radio exhortations of your Dead Man. He stoutly opposed partition and during the last fateful meeting, he wept like a child before them and sobbed out praying against partition but he was overridden roughshod. Also it has been kept a secret that your Dead Man went with Bapu's full blessings and concurrence of the inner committee. No, your Dead Man bore no rancour.

Bhagwanji's strange syntax had to do with caution, sounded to him by Leela Roy. 'The vocabulary you use, you cannot change and the vocabulary would lead to your identification. No other Bengali uses the words, idioms, etc. that you do', she wrote. He replied: 'Can you write 20/25 pages in diametrically opposite composition and send to me? I will see if I can change.'

So he took great care in anything that he wrote. He used capital letters while writing in English and Devnagari script for Bangla.

Bhagwanji did recall the 'INA' days, but not too often. He had mixed 'memories' about what had happened.

He was dismayed that even his home State failed to rise up, when the INA charged into the Indian boarder:

> *I had great hopes that Bengal would rise as one as soon as I crossed Burma. When the British commanders were about to seal the surrender letter from the Staff Command, four people defected. As a result, an order went to the Front – 'Do not surrender.'* [Translated from Bangla]

Bhagwanji's claim that the British Indian Army contemplated surrendering to the Indian National Army was backed by INA veteran Colonel Gurbaksh Singh Dhillon in his memoirs *From my Bones* (Aryan Book International), published in 1998.

> The 14th Army of the enemy was on the verge of surrender. ...It was at this crucial stage that two of our important officers, Major Prabhu Dayal and Major JBS Garewal, not being able to endure thrust and hunger any longer, went over to the enemy. ...It was from these two deserters that the enemy learnt that the INA and the Japanese were in a poor state in respect of food and ammunition. ...At such crucial juncture, orders went to the 14th British Indian Army to postpone their surrender.

Dhillon, a firm supporter of the air crash theory of Netaji's death with no known links with Bhagwanji, added that post-Independence both the INA traitors were given higher ranks in the Indian Army. While Garewal was murdered shortly afterwards, Prabhu Dayal became a brigadier and seemed to have led a luxurious life as other traitors did in free India.

Most pertinently, much before anyone had a clue about it, Bhagwanji told his followers that *the plane crash was a concoction*. Charanik actually narrates how, where and with whose help Dead Man escaped. The first step was parting from his associates. In the following passage, the allusion to 'Japanese general' is perhaps for General Isoda. 'Youngest general and adjutant' is clearly Habibur Rahman—who was just 32 in 1945.

> The Japanese general became restless—no more delay. Mahanayak now came to his generals. Everyone was anxious to know who would accompany him. Each person's expression spoke out that he was the sole appropriate candidate to be with him. But he who had to choose had already made his choice. He said...*my foreign friends have allowed only one extra seat. I am taking with me my youngest general and adjutant.* [Translated from Bangla]

Second step, 'Mahanayak' (the leader) never went to Taipei. He parted company from his fellow travellers, probably at Dalat, which was not too far from Saigon:

> He had to get down at a pre-determined place. Mahanayak now bade farewell to his trusted adjutant. He told his adjutant: *Remember my direction...I can't tell you everything in detail. But I have told everything to two of my very trusted*

Japanese generals. Get the directions from them and act accordingly. Mahanayak then left for an unknown destination. [Translated from Bangla]

Dead Man had nothing but praises for his adjutant [Rahman]. *Yes my adjutant was a complete man. Perhaps that is why he did not have any place in free India. At least I do not know of anyone who has followed orders with such unshaken dedication.* [Translated from Bangla]

In a note taken by Pabitra, Dead Man accused SA Ayer and Ramamurti of treachery—something that the *India Today* exposed in its special story, 'Who shrunk Netaji's fortune?' (25 May 2015), based on still-secret Ministry of External Affairs records.

> Minister Ayer was to follow the bomber with the treasure. But he went to Tokyo and handed over the treasure to Ramamurti. Disposed of some, encashed part of jewels with help of British military of Tokyo and Japanese foreign officials. JN knows it. Murti gave 'J' only small fraction of fabulous wealth. No treasure was burnt. It is a fabrication. Imperial Japanese Army, British men, India government and party men all involved. That is why no action was taken.

After spending some days in a small hotel near Saigon, Mahanayak headed to an 'unknown destination' in *bhalu-desh* (land of bears) with the help of *black society*. Soviet Russia was the land of bears and black society, the secretive Japanese Black Dragon Society, whose former head's son-in-law, Rash Bihari Bose had handed over the charge of the INA to Subhas.

Charanik goes on to put rhetorically something bearing an eerie match with a record, declassified in 1997. That Mahanayak had secretly visited Russia in December 1944.

> In Nov. 44 there was a general rumour in, Ye-U 'that S.C.Bose was preparing to leave for Moscow in order to place all information about the Indian Freedom Movement before the leaders of the U.S.S.R. It was also said that Col. S.A.Malik would follow S.C.Bose to Moscow. B766 heard these rumours from Lt. Subramaniam (ex-Azad Hind Dal, and then Adjutant of the Ye-U Rest Camp). In Dec. 44 Lt. Sadhu Singh of H.Q. 1 Div I.N.A., who was then acting as Q.M. of the Ye-U Rest Camp, informed B766 that S.C.Bose had left for Moscow, and was soon expected back in Tokyo.

The National Archives, New Delhi

Charanik also gave a description of the working of gulags before Aleksandr Solzhenitsyn's *The Gulag Archipelago* provided a ringside view to the rest of the world. He had got it from Bhagwanji's previous utterances.

> Does anyone know that Mahanayak went to the land of bears before his last trip? He met the leader of that country and made all arrangements. It is difficult to say where he stayed in that country or whether he was in a camp. Everything becomes clear when he talks about that huge snow-covered land and about events which he saw with his own eyes.

Concentration camps of central Siberia contain male and female labourers, farmers, craftsmen, authors, scientists and teachers—from 5 thousand to 25 thousand. Not one or two, there are almost 49 concentration camps. They are manufacturing ultramodern goods for daily use. These are transported to the retail outlets from the main city. Those who buy these do not know that they have been manufactured by their parents, brothers and sisters and other kin. If you came to know what goes on there, you would have run for your life. Driven by hunger, people have gone to the extent of eating their own skin. A new camp was being constructed; so the soldiers took 10,000 prisoners with them. But there was no hut there. Their duty was to install pillars by digging 12 feet holes in the ice. 'Keep your body warm by heavy work – anyone who does not follow this will freeze and die.' All this is not hearsay. Mahakaal has experienced all this. [Translated from Bangla]

Seen from Bhagwanji's perspective, Russia granted him asylum. He was hidden away in a camp somewhere in south central Siberia, in the vicinity of Lake Baikal. He was not a prisoner. There were occasions when he dined with the high and mighty and watched theatres. 'Stalin did not behave inimically towards me; my own people did', he said once. Bhagwanji claimed that at some point in time, Soviet Russia discovered his true worth after he was able to resolve some issue troubling them for long.

[Stalin] *tried something (to get done) in absolute secrecy (so that none should know that it was Russia's hands that did it)...he was a dismal failure. He tried once, twice,—no success. Then I came. Stalin, as a test, laid bare his intentions. I gave my thoughts over the whole thing. It was to be executed in a very vast area—about 1/5th or 1/6th of a very very vast land marks inhabited by 5 or 6 different races. To make long story short, I triggered off a mighty upheaval there, once; then, after a lapse—again, twice!*

When he left Soviet Russia in 1949 at the close of war crimes trials, Dead Man did not return to India because he felt—or was given this impression—that India was still not a free country and that under some hidden clause of the Transfer of Power, he was to be tried and handed over to the Anglo-Americans as a war criminal.

He alleged that Nehru compromised India's interests by making her part of the British Commonwealth of Nations after independence. *He shall always rave; spew and curse the English for hours and hours—but shall always act just the opposite,* he wrote when Nehru died in 1964. Worse, his allegations implied that India's long-term strategic interests were made subservient to those of the world powers and if the Dead Man were not to act, India would turn into a battleground for the cold war.

Nehru...has manipulated the whole thing in such a way that any miscalculated step...might make simple and innocent India and her people victim of the most horrible and undesirably hellish (game of) war!

Bhagwanji went on to claim that the day all the documents concerning the Transfer of Power in 1947 were made public, Indians would know why he had to go into hiding. While most Transfer of Power records are now in public domain and they do throw some light on Subhas's fate—that he perhaps did not perish in Taiwan and was probably in Soviet Russia—there are some more records that are still being held classified by the British government. In December 2012, the Foreign and Commonwealth Office in London turned down a Freedom of Information Act request filed by Chandrachur Ghose and this writer to disclose one file it was holding. The FCO said the file 'remains sensitive' and 'its release could compromise our relations with the countries concerned'. In India, the Ministry of External Affairs revealed during an RTI proceeding in August 2013 that records relating to India's joining the Commonwealth of Nations in 1949 were untraceable.

TN Kaul, former Ambassador to the USSR and Foreign Secretary, was to write in his memoirs, that even after independence Russians 'still looked upon India as a colony of Britain' and 'could not understand why we still wanted to remain in the Commonwealth, when we had suffered so much at the hands of British imperialism'. Russian journalist Valeriy Kashin recapitulated in 2012 that the transfer of power in India in 1947 was nothing more than a 'political farce' for Soviet Union. 'Out of 19 English major generals, 16 remained in India, and out of 280 brigadier generals, 260 would remain in support of the idea that India retained military and political allegiance with its former mother country.'

When it had come to the crunch, all vows of attaining *Purna Swaraj* (complete independence)—something that Gandhi was never in favour of—became a thing of the past. 'They got Independence in a begging bowl', was Bhagwanji's pet peeve. Subhas Bose never wanted India to remain in the Commonwealth. Writing in *London Review of Books* in 2012, British historian Perry Anderson observed:

> There was no overthrow of the Raj, but a transfer of power by it to Congress as its successor. The colonial bureaucracy and army were left intact, minus the colonisers. In the mid-1930s Nehru, denouncing the Indian civil service as 'neither Indian nor civil nor a service', declared it 'essential that the ICS and similar services disappear completely'. By 1947, pledges like these had faded away as completely as his promises that India would never become a dominion.

Winston Churchill, the most anti-Indian among the colonial British, gave a thumbs up to the Transfer of Power in 1947 only after being convinced by Lord Mountbatten. Kunwar Natwar Singh, arguably the greatest Nehruvian in our midst, was compelled to admit in an op-ed article in *The Hindu* that 'Nehru throughout the freedom movement was vigorously opposed to independent

India having anything to do with the British Commonwealth' and that 'there is little doubt that the Mountbattens talked him into changing his mind'.

Mountbatten even wanted the Union Jack on the upper canton of the Indian Tricolour—a proposition to which Gandhi, Nehru and Patel were amenable. Gandhi actually panned those who were opposed to it. 'But what is wrong with having the Union Jack in a corner of our flag? If harm has been done to us by the British, it has not been done by their flag and we must also take note of the virtues of the British. They are voluntarily withdrawing from India, leaving power in our hands', he said at his Prayer Meeting of 19 July 1947.

Bhagwanji, reflecting disapprovingly in 1963, stated that Gandhi, Patel, Nehru and others always compromised, whereas 'he' never did. *It is death to compromise on principles.*

In the early 1970s, Mountbatten described to writers Larry Collins and Dominque Lapierre how he had ensured that India remained a part of the Commonwealth even after the Transfer of Power.

> They would keep the same uniform [in the armed forces], merely putting the three lions on their shoulder instead of the actual crown...they would keep the white ensign with the red cross of St George, just as in the Navy.... They must owe some common allegiance to the King....

And allegiance to the King India did pay beyond Independence. George VI signed the letters of credence and appointment of Indian ambassadors after August 1947. Even Natwar Singh saw too much of 'Raj phraseology' in Nehru-George VI correspondence.

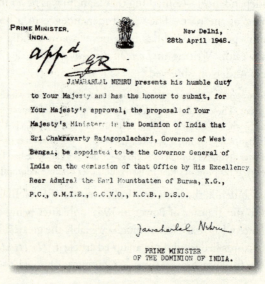

PRIME MINISTER.
INDIA.   New Delhi,
                                                 28th April 1948.

app^d GR

JAWAHARLAL NEHRU presents his humble duty
to Your Majesty and has the honour to submit, for
Your Majesty's approval, the proposal of Your
Majesty's Ministers in the Dominion of India that
Sri Chakravarty Rajagopalachari, Governor of West
Bengal, be appointed to be the Governor General of
India on the demission of that Office by His Excellency
Rear Admiral the Earl Mountbatten of Burma, K.G.,
P.C., G.M.I.E., G.C.V.O., K.C.B., D.S.O.

Jawaharlal Nehru

PRIME MINISTER
OF THE DOMINION OF INDIA.

The 'free' India government was as hostile towards Subhas Bose as it was before 1947. The chiefs of the Indian Air Force and the Navy were still British and their Indian subordinates were more British than them. Indians did not head the Indian Army, Air Force and Navy until 1949, 1955 and 1958.

In March 1948 Nehru told Parliament that the INA men would have no place in the Indian Army. 'To reinstate them would lead to many complications, both practical and psychological, and the unity of the army might be affected', *The Times* of London reported him as announcing.

INDIAN NATIONAL ARMY

LONG CONTROVERSY ENDED

FROM OUR OWN CORRESPONDENT

DELHI, MARCH 29

Pandit Nehru, speaking in the Dominion Parliament to-day, said that officers, and other ranks of the Indian National Army, which was formed mainly of prisoners of war who traitorously elected to fight with the Japanese after capture in the Burma campaign, would not be allowed to rejoin the Indian Army. To reinstate them would lead to many complications both practical and psychological, and the unity of the army might be affected. However, the order for dismissal of all I.N.A. men passed by the previous Government would be superseded by an order for their discharge from the army.

In 1949, the Army Headquarters issued a circular against displaying the picture of Subhas Bose 'at permanent places, in canteens, quarters, etc'. The same HQ continued to insist for decades that the history of the INA should not be published, as doing so would affect the 'morale of the soldiers'.

So much so that free India's national security structure did not undergo any change. 'The framework Lord Ismay formulated and Lord Mountbatten recommended was accepted by a national leadership unfamiliar with the intricacies of national security management. There has been very little change over the past 52 years', the Kargil Committee report of 1999 flatly accepted.

In the intelligence arena, British suzerainty continued till the 1960s. 'An unwritten agreement during the Transfer of Power in 1947 was the secret positioning of a security liaison officer (SLO) in New Delhi as MI5's representative', wrote V Balachandran, former Special Secretary of R&AW,

in *The Times of India* on 12 April 2015. Astringent details had previously appeared in the authorised history of MI5 by Prof by Christopher Andrew. *The Defence of the Realm* (2010) revealed on the basis of the official records that in March 1947 deputy head of MI5 Guy Liddell 'obtained the agreement of the government of Jawaharlal Nehru for an MI5 security liaison officer (SLO) to be stationed in New Delhi after the end of British rule'. The first SLO was Lieutenant Colonel Kenneth Bourne, who was supplied with information pertaining to Netaji by the Intelligence Bureau. The IB, according to Balachandran and Prof Andrew, played a second fiddle to MI5.

Former IB and police officers of the Raj era, like Bourne, were stationed in New Delhi as SLOs. All the Indian IB chiefs, beginning with Sanjeevi Pillai, made their obeisance to the MI5 bosses in London. Details given in *The Defence of the Realm* show that DIBs had opened their hearts and archives to MI5. Walter Bell, the SLO in 1952, described IB boss BN Mullik as 'the fount of all knowledge that I wanted'. Following a request by Mullik, an MI5 officer was sent to India in 1957 so that IB's counter-intelligence operations against the Soviet Union could be improved upon. Humbled by the 'help' the IB had received from MI5, Mullik told his counterpart Roger Hollis that he never felt that he was 'dealing with any organisation which was not my own'.

'When the last SLO left India in the late 1960s, they did so not at India's behest, but as consequence of swinging cuts forced on the Security Service [MI5]', wrote domain expert Paul McGarr in the *Journal of Imperial and Commonwealth History* in 2010. The then IB Director, SP Verma, wrote to his counterpart in London that he didn't know 'how he'd manage without a British SLO', added Balachandran in his TOI article.

As an Anglophile of a sort, I do think that joining the Commonwealth, and all that it entailed, was and is for India's overall good. But who am I, and how does my view count here? Dead Man did not like the state of affairs in India in 1949. Claiming that it *may well require God's own intelligence to rescue Mother India from this diabolic plot,* rather than returning home, he went over to China on a covert mission to help his Soviet benefactors in return for their generosity in giving him a shelter. Another incredible claim of Bhagwanji was that he met Mao Tse Tung several times, 1949 onwards. They discussed a whole range of issues: from Mao's dead son and the fallen Queen of Jhansi to the clash between India and China. 'The land belongs to you', Mao admitted to Dead Man while discussing Aksai Chin in J&K.

Oi Mahamanab Asey reads:

What kind of a ruler must he be who has no idea of his own boundaries? He invites disaster by leaving his frontiers unmanned. The unmanned frontier beckons the foreign powers,'come hither, here I am, yours for the taking, conquer me and fill me up'. I hope I do not have to remind you that when we took that thirty-three thousand square miles of your territory and built a six-lane highway through it, the highest leadership in your country had no inkling of it! He came to know of it after six years, that too from traders. To cover up his own bungling, he stood up in the parliament and said, 'No one goes there, cannot go or cannot live there because not a blade of grass grows there'. In other words, it makes no difference to us if we lose the whole area. And all your members of parliament applauded him. [Translated from Bangla]

Mao told Dead Man that as long as he lived, China would not commit another aggression after 1962, notwithstanding intermittent warlike rhetoric. But Dead Man was worried that the 'four-lane highway', the huge warehouses along with it and a railroad across the Amdo province of Tibet, would ultimately extend right up to Lhasa. Future was to prove Dead Man right.

He was proven right in another instance too. Much before the world came to know about the secret Dixia Cheng (underground city) of Beijing—a network of massive tunnels built as shelter during air raids or even nuclear strikes—Bhagwanji talked about seeing *a whole city in the deep underground with all modern amenities*. He said it could not be destroyed even with ten atom bombs.

Whatever they were, Bhagwanji's utterances weren't hallucinatory patchworks. A journalist who otherwise believed that Bose died in Russia once shared with me what he had heard from a R&AW officer that: There was some information about 'Bose' being in China in 1949—doing some backchannel mediation between the Russians and the Chinese. I can even tell you that several members of the Bose family are aware of the Chinese angle to the mystery' but prefer not to talk about it publicly.

I don't know how much truth it holds, but there is definitely a Chinese angle to the Bose mystery. All those who believe that Bose died in Russia also know of it as well, but refrain from alluding to it for an obvious reason. If Netaji was in China in 1949 and afterwards, he was certainly out of the USSR—alive.

For the background, you must know that our hostility for the Chinese communist leadership—not the Chinese people—started in late 1950s when the dragon devoured Tibet and turned to our lands. Before that almost all of our top leaders shared warm vibes with China. Bose even wrote an article in *Modern Review,* where he denounced Japan's assault on China.

Records declassified in 1997 show that with the end of the Second World War in sight, Bose weighed his options. On 21 March 1946, INA's Chief of Staff, General JK Bhonsle, was interrogated at Red Fort on the subject of 'last plans of SC Bose'. Bhonsle told his interrogator: 'Bose had also decided that in case the Japanese Govt did not agree to taking up his case with Russia, he himself would try to get to Shanghai and from there, try to contact the Russians through the Chinese Communists'.

Azad Hind Government minister Debnath Das told the Khosla Commission that one of the escape plans for Bose was to go 'to Yunan, the headquarters of Mao Tse Tung, who would help him carry on his campaign against the British'. He even had Ho Chi Minh on his mind. Anand Mohan Sahay was actually sent to Hanoi and he forged a life-long friendship with the Vietnamese statesman.

In 1949, rumours began doing the rounds in India and elsewhere that Subhas Bose was in China. So much so that when the pro-Soviet Bombay tabloid *The Blitz* carried a sensational news headlined, 'British report Bose alive in Red continent' on 26 March 1949, the American Consul there transmitted its text to the Secretary of State under the subject 'Ghost of Subhas Chandra Bose'.

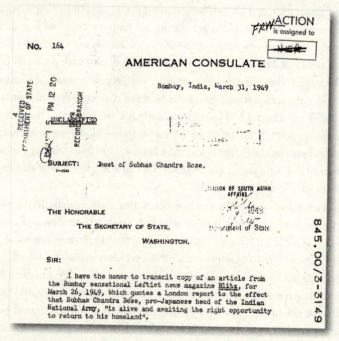

The Blitz story had made a string of claims:

The British government is rumoured to be very much perturbed over confidential information that has come into its possession, quite recently, that Netaji...is alive....This sensational news...was originally transmitted to the British Foreign Office from the British embassy in Turkey and is reported to have been confirmed since from Anglo-American secret agents in the East.

It is not known whether the news of the living Bose is based upon positive evidence of his whereabouts—suspected to be in Red China or Soviet Russia, or upon what is described as the 'negative' evidence of the failure of the best brains of the Anglo-American security services to dig up slightest evidence in confirmation of the story of Bose's death....

Anglo-American sources, haunted by the bogey of the Red Peril, seem to see the hand of Bose behind every Communist offensive in South East Asia and the Far East.

> **APR 12 1949**
>
> Enclosure to Despatch no.164, dated March 31, 1949, from William Witman II, American Consul, Bombay, India, entitled: "Ghost of Subhas Chandra Bose".
>
> Copy - db
>
> **BLITZ** - March 26, 1949
>
> **SUBHAS MYSTERY DEEPENS**
>
> **British Report Bose Alive in Red Continent**
>
> - From **Blitz's** London Correspondent -
>
> London: The British Government is rumoured to be very much perturbed over confidential information that has come into its possession, quite recently, that Netaji Subhas Chandra Bose, the great Indian revolutionary leader and head of the famous INA resistance movement, is alive and awaiting the right opportunity to return to his homeland.

Forward Bloc general Secretary RS Ruiker told the media in July 1949 that Bose, 'who is presumed to be in Red China, may come back to India provided the ban on his entry into the country is withdrawn'. According to IB memo No: 12586 TP. 605 dated 30 July 1949, located at the National Archives by Sai Manish of the *Daily News and Analysis*, Amiya Bose received a letter from Chinese national Chou Hsiang Kuang. 'Amiya in previous letters to Kuang had asked him to help find out if Subhas Bose was somewhere in China', the *DNA* reported on 19 April 2015. Kuang had no proper clue.

Then a bombshell was dropped by Sarat Chandra Bose. No one can dispute that if Subhas were alive and in a position to communicate after 1945, the one person he would have reached out to would be his *mejda*. This very Sarat Bose made a public declaration which fitted well with the Dead

Man's narrative. On 7 October 1949, his paper *The Nation,* ran a full page story. You've got to see it to believe it.

'Netaji in Red China', read the headline in *The Nation* on 7 October 1949. It goes without saying that a person of Sarat's stature and intelligence would not have published this in such a manner, without being sure about it. The story quoted him claiming 'that the Government of India were in possession of definite information that Netaji Subhas Chandra Bose was in Red China of Mao Tse Tung'. When asked why Subhas was 'not coming to India', Sarat Bose replied, 'I don't think the time is ripe for his coming back home'.

A shocker of such magnitude couldn't have been ignored, but New Delhi tried to downplay it. The Ministry of External Affairs dismissed Sarat Bose's claim with a terse denial. Soon the news travelled to the West. On 28 November 1949, German news agency *Interpress* released a story titled 'Babu Bose: Mann Hinter Den Fronten' (Mr Bose: The man behind the front), which too said that Bose was in China. Even the Americans, who had nothing to do with Bose, couldn't help noticing the story. The February 1954 issue of *National Republic* carried an essay, 'Jawaharlal Nehru and the Red threat to India'. Its author, Elliot Erikson, wrote:

> There is a strong possibility that Bose is alive. At the end of the war, when the Japanese front collapsed in Burma, Bose, if he showed himself, ran great risk of being prosecuted as an international war criminal. If Bose is still held prisoner in Communist China, he could be sprung as the leader of a Red 'liberation' of India from capitalism. The most strongly anti-Communist

Congress leaders admit that if such an event happened, Indian resistance to China would collapse immediately.

In 1956 came another shocker. Close Subhas Bose associate Muthurama-lingam Thevar, whose statue now stands in the Parliament House precincts in New Delhi as a tribute to his eminence, told newspapers such as *Hindustan Standard* that he had secretly visited China on Sarat Bose's instruction.

Thevar said that towards the end of 1949, when Sarat Chandra Bose was ailing, he went down to Calcutta to meet Bose. He saw Bose on December 7 and stayed with him for ten days. They had consultations on the matter as Bose apprehended that he was going to die. After these talks, Thevar said, he left India incognito on December 17. He crossed the Burma border and entered China, where he stayed almost the whole of 1950. He met Netaji in January but where, he would not divulge. He returned to India in October 1950. He said that the Government of India knew that he had visited China but if it doubted that he could prove that he had been to China.

Wednesday, April 4, 1956

STORY OF MEETING NETAJI LAST FEBRUARY

REPORTED STAY NOW IN CHINA

From Our Delhi Office

APRIL 3.—Sri Muthuramalinga Thevar, member of the Madras Legislative Assembly and a Forward Bloc leader, told a Press conference in New Delhi on Tuesday that he would furnish conclusive proof that Netaji Subhas Chandra Bose was alive if the Inquiry Committee appointed by the Government of India to go into this question was reconstituted.

HE said that he was prepared to tell the Committee as much as it was possible in the circumstances, provided he was convinced that the Committee would be able to resist outside influence.

His suggestion was that Dr. Radhabinod Pal, the eminent Jurist, be appointed Chairman of the Committee.

Sri Thevar who claims to have been a member of the 8-man War Council formed by Netaji before his mysterious disappearance from India said that he might tell the Prime Minister also about Netaji if he was sympathetic.

I cannot believe that the Chinese attention was never drawn to numerous claims about Subhas's presence in their country. Priyadarsi Mukherji, professor in Chinese & Sinological Studies Centre at the Jawaharlal Nehru University, thinks that the Chinese are holding some records about Bose. In January 2011, Mukherji met Professor Wang Bangwei, director of the Indian Studies Centre, Peking University and asked him about the possibility of Bose's contacts with Mao after 1949.

Professor Wang did not directly answer my query but said that both Bose
and Mao had the same objective of achieving liberation of their countries by
armed struggle, so it was natural for them to be close. On being asked about
documents on Netaji in the Research Cell of the Chinese Communist Party
(CPC), Wang categorically said that it is impossible for a foreigner like me to
get access to it. Even many Chinese can't get access either.

So, could all of this mean that this Bhagwanji was a communist?

No, he was a Rightist to the core. Actually, some of the things Bhagwanji
talked about would gladden the hearts of those who go by the RSS school
of thought. If Hinduism became extinct, he propounded, India would be
reduced to being just a land mass. 'Egypt is at present only a geographical
land mass. It is an object of archeological interest only'. He said ancient
Indian wisdom was an *ocean of unbounded energy*. He admired Jews for their
unswerving faith in their religion and scripture.

> They have kept their ancient culture as it is. 2000 years of **buffeting**
> has destroyed their everything but their **faith in their religion, faith in their
> destiny, faith in Old Testament** is **intact**. This is why they **have implicit
> confidence in their faith. Could you achieve anything** if you do not have this
> perspective? What sustains a man? **It is faith**, do you understand? [Translated
> from Bangla, except the highlighted portions]

On the other hand, Communism came into repeated denunciation
from Bhagwanji. *Oi Mahamanab Asey* further reads:

> A race which cannot bind itself to its history and culture cannot ever
> win. This is the **axiomatic truth**. This is the state of the communists. They
> are like a **flash in the pan**, glare for two days and will then evaporate. **This
> creed is carrying its death in its own cell.** [Translated from Bangla, except
> the highlighted portions]

He even said he did not he see any future for this *Godless greedy creed*.
He prophesied at the peak of the USSR's power—that 'three quarters of
the house of cards that Stalin had built has been destroyed, the rest will be
destroyed in front of you'. *Communism shall die at the place of its birth*, he
put it in English. But he also said: *In international dealings there is no eternal
friend or foe*. In a letter written in early 1963, Bhagwanji wrote that Russia
desired to see Communism take over India *in peaceful constitutional manner;*
whereas China wanted that it *engulfs India in anyway*. Bhagwanji even
claimed that his activities helped frustrate these designs. He joined covert
Soviet operations to essentially further India's long-term strategic interests.

The rumours about Bose and China peaked during the 1962 war and
were noted by the Intelligence Bureau. As a matter of fact, a former Delhi
Congress chief Jagdish Kodesia told something startling to the Khosla

Commission regarding Lal Bahadur Shastri. He testified that during the 1962 war he heard at Shastri's house that 'information during Chinese aggression did come that Netaji was living'.

Jagdish Kodesia is seen in this combo image with Nehru in 1958
and Shastri on the day he took over as PM

Several times during his on-oath deposition, Kodesia linked the Bose mystery to the controversy surrounding Prime Minister Lal Bahadur Shastri's sudden death. He stated that 'Shastriji was one person' who did not believe in Netaji's death in the plane crash. 'When he became Home Minister...he wanted to know the truth whether Subhas Bose was alive or not.'

> After the death of Pandit Nehru, Shastriji became the Prime Minister. When we were returning after the cremation of Panditji, Shastriji said after seeing the huge crowds: 'Could you imagine that this type of crowd would collect spontaneously if it were declared that Netaji is coming to Delhi on such and such date?' I said: 'I do not think there will be a single man, woman or child sitting in the house, they will all come to greet him.' He smiled at me, though the occasion was sad.

Kodesia, going by the record of his deposition before the commission, added:

```
     One thing is there that Shastri definitely
wanted that there should be another inquiry
Commission. If he would have lived longer, he
must have seen to that and you, Sir, would have
```

Further spine-chilling comments and observations regarding the controversial death of Shastriji in Tashkent on 11 January 1966 were made in 2015 by his sons Anil and Sunil Shastri and maternal grandsons Sanjay and Siddharth Nath Singh. They recalled Shastri's last call from Tashkent to his family that he was not perturbed at all by the criticism over the Tashkent Treaty and was 'going to announce something big upon his landing in India'. From what they could make out, the family members think that Shastriji had Netaji in mind.

'There is a possibility that he wanted to tell the people of India something about Netaji on his return. He was aware of Netaji and we cannot rule out that it had some link with Babuji's mysterious death', Sunil Shastri told *The Sunday Guardian* on 11 July 2015.

On that fateful day in Tashkent, Shastri looked agile and healthy, though he had suffered a minor heart attack in 1964. Following the signing of the agreement with General Ayub Khan at 4 pm and a public reception at 8 pm, he reached the villa where he was staying. There, he had a light meal prepared by Jan Mohammad, personal cook of TN Kaul, the Indian Ambassador to Moscow. At about 11.30 pm, Shastri had a glass of milk. When his personal staff took leave of him, he was fine.

At 1:25 am, the Prime Minister was awakened by severe coughing. He himself walked out to tell his personal staff to summon his personal doctor, RN Chugh, from another room in the villa. The doctor arrived to find Shastri in his death throes as a result of symptoms of a heart attack. Dr Chugh made frantic efforts, but in vain. Then he started crying, saying that Shastri 'did not give him enough time'.

At about 4 am, Ahmed Sattarov, the Russian butler attached to Shastri, was rudely woken up. The butler recalled his nightmare in an interview with Russian journalist Anton Vereshchagin for the *Russia and India Report* on 2 October 2013:

> Early in the morning, I was woken by an officer of the Ninth Directorate of the KGB (who guarded members of the Politburo and the government), from whom I learned about the death of Lal Bahadur Shastri. The officer said that they suspected, the Indian Prime Minister had been poisoned. They handcuffed me and three other head waiters, of which I was senior, and loaded us into a Chaika automobile. We four had served the most senior officials, and so we immediately came under suspicion.

> They brought us to a small town called Bulmen, which is about 30 km from the city, locked us in the basement of a three-story mansion, and stationed a guard. After a while, they brought the Indian chef who had cooked the Indian dishes for the banquet. We thought that it must have been that man who poisoned Shastri. We were so nervous that the hair on the temple of one of my colleagues turned gray before our eyes, and ever since, I stutter.

When Shastri's body was brought home, his mother spotted bluish patches on her son. *Mere bitwa ko jahar de diya!* (My son has been poisoned!) she cried out. In a letter to President R Venkataraman in August 1990, Kodesia wrote that apart from 'patches in various colours', the body bore 'a cut at the back of the neck and a cut at the stomach, where sticking plaster had been pasted'.

'The cut at the neck was pouring blood and the sheets, pillows and the clothes used by him were all soaked in blood.'

On 16 February 1966, several MPs led by HV Kamath, JB Kriplani, Prakash Vir Shastri and Madhu Limaye raised the issue in Parliament. However, the government response did not satisfy the lawmakers. Subsequently, it was in 1970 that the issue could be discussed at length. Inspired by the success of the Opposition MPs in compelling the government to probe Bose's death afresh, Shastri's well wishers and family members demanded an enquiry. In April 1970, Rajya Sabha MP and Shastri's childhood friend, TN Singh, claimed that a relative's demand for an autopsy to rule out poisoning charges was rejected by acting Prime Minister Gulzari Lal Nanda.

On 18 December 1970, the Ministry of Home Affairs laid a statement of facts before the Lok Sabha. It fairly responded to many of the charges and included copies of the medical reports issued in 1966 and 1970. The 11 January 1966 medical report, signed by Dr Chugh and many Russian doctors, stated that in view of Shastri's medical history and the symptoms that manifested before he passed away 'it can be considered that death occurred because of an acute attack of infarktmiocarda'. A November 1970 statement issued by Soviet doctors detailed the process of embalming, which had led to the body turning bluish. The Indian government, however, rejected TN Singh's claim that the Shastri family had sought a post mortem because 'there is no record of any suggestion having been made' and Nanda had 'no recollection of anyone having spoken to him about a post mortem examination'.

Some MPs accused the then government of giving a 'one-sided' version on the last day of the session to ward off any serious discussion. Prakash Vir Shastri wanted the government to clarify, whether a security officer named GC Dutt had disapproved of the arrangements made by Ambassador Kaul and if he was taken off the duty a day before the PM died.

In 1996, CP Srivastava, one of Shastri's former aides, discussed the outcome of his personal enquiry in his book *Lal Bahadur Shastri: A life of truth in politics*. Because he was not present at the moment of the Prime Minister's death, Srivastava detailed the accounts of the staff members.

He also consulted a leading British doctor, who opined that while without a postmortem it could be not said with cent per cent accuracy that there were no chances of poisoning, all available details indicated that the death was natural and followed a heart attack. Finally, Srivastava recalled having a word with the Home Secretary in around 1966. LP Singh told him that the issue of postmortem had come up during his discussion with Ambassador Kaul, but was ruled out in view of the report of Dr Chugh and the Russian doctors.

I played a role in the matter by making some general enquiries from the PMO and MEA under the RTI. The PMO told me that it possessed only one classified document relating to the former PM's death, and that there was no record of any destruction or loss of any document related to the tragedy.

The MEA informed me on 1 July 2009 that the concerned division had no information on the subject matter. It was quite strange because the sudden death of the Prime Minister must have thrown the Indian Embassy in Moscow in a tizzy. Ambassador Kaul must have scrambled to inform Delhi of the tragedy. A flurry of telephone calls and telegrams over the tragic development would have ensued for sure. The ministry would have gone on an overdrive to find out the circumstances leading to the PM's death. The ambassador must have been asked to send blow-by-blow reports, and he must have done that. The Russians too would have felt obliged to tell the Indians about their handling of the matter. And as the charges of foul play emerged, the Government of India, through the Ministry of External of Affairs (and also the IB, which was then responsible for foreign intelligence), must have tried to get to the bottom of the story. So how could the concerned division in the ministry have no records, I wondered?

The MEA further stated that the only main record available with the Indian Embassy in Moscow was the report of joint medical investigation conducted by Dr Chugh and the Russian doctors. The ministry confirmed that no post-mortem was carried out in Moscow. I also got to know from the Delhi Police, through another RTI reply, that no post-mortem was conducted in India as well.

On 21 July, I filed another application seeking copies of the entire correspondence between the MEA and the embassy and between the embassy and the Soviet Foreign Ministry over the issue. I requested the Ministry to clearly state in case no such records were extant. In its belated response, the MEA refused to release the information, pleading that doing so would harm national interest. I was even denied a copy of Dr Chugh's report, even though it was a public document.

It was only after the intervention of Chief Information Commissioner Sadananad Mishra that the MEA in August 2011 supplied me copies of Dr Chugh's medical report and a copy of the statement made by the External Affairs Minister in the Rajya Sabha.

The issue about the sole secret record held by the PMO was also fairly settled by Commissioner Mishra in June 2011. After hearing the PMO's and my views, he summoned the classified record to decide whether or not it could be made public. The record was shown to him and he ruled that the PMO was right in keeping it classified, for its disclosure would indeed harm India's relations with a friendly nation.

Later I learnt that this record cited an intelligence report blaming the United States, probably the CIA, for spreading a 'canard' that Shastri's death was not natural. To me, this version looked more like a conspiracy theory because available information did not indicate any such thing. On the other hand, I came across a declassified memorandum, written to US President Richard Nixon by his National Security Adviser Henry Kissinger, proving that America sensed no foul play and saw no Russian hand. The following excerpt from this 1972 document must be read keeping in mind the abominable aversion Nixon, and even Kissinger, had for India and Indira Gandhi at that time. And still, in this Top Secret backgrounder about Russian premier A Kosygin, Kissinger wrote that 'the sudden fatal heart attack of Indian Prime Minister Shastri at Tashkent has never been traced, by any one, to the effect of his personal encounters with Kosygin'.

For Shastriji's family and others, the needle of suspicion points towards an inside hand. On 2 October 2012 in a CNN-IBN programme hosted by Karan Thapar, veteran journalist Kuldip Nayar, who was in Tashkent on that fateful day as Shastri's advisor, stated that his suspicions were aroused some time after the tragedy when a Member of Parliament raked up the charges of poisoning and TN Kaul, by then the Foreign Secretary, 'rang me up to issue a statement' against it.

'He badgered me literally 4-5 times.'

Like the Shastri family members, Nayar too went on to express grave suspicions about the fate of Dr Chugh and Shastri's personal assistant Ram Nath, just before a committee of Parliament was to look into the matter. Chugh, his wife and two sons were run over by a truck in 1977. Only his daughter survived—crippled.

Thirteen

From whatever I can make out from Bhagwanji's puzzling claims, in his 'life after death', Dead Man became involved in Soviet covert operations to undermine the American hegemony in South East Asia and elsewhere with the larger aim to ensure that India was not caught in bloody proxy wars between the free and communist worlds. The trigger for him choosing the path came about in the year India became free. Bhagwanji accused Nehru of having sacrificed India's long-term interests to those of the Anglo-Americans. He claimed that a big change in Indian leaders' attitude came after they were released from prisons in 1945, following their arrest at the inception of the stillborn Quit India movement of 1942.

Because of his covert activities, unpublicised role in international events, and not as much due to war criminal tag of the second world war, Bhagwanji thought he was regarded as 'enemy no 1' by the world powers. In his estimate, if he emerged, people of India would have suffered as there would have been economic sanctions and other instances of arm-twisting to ensure his capture, which would have been opposed tooth-and-nail by his supporters in India.

There are scattered leads in support of some of the incredible things that Bhagwanji said he did. But only a comprehensive declassification of files and a proper inquiry can bring out the truth. In the wake of Justice Mukherjee's statement that Bhagwanji was Netaji and the Allahabad High Court's order suggesting a judicial inquiry to ascertain his identity, it should be abundantly clear to anyone that to wish away the Bhagwanji episode, no matter how implausible it appears on the face of it, would be a big mistake.

Whoever Bhagwanji was must be ascertained, so as to settle the Netaji mystery. The truth is closer than it was ever before.

The lead that warrants our closest attention concerns Bhagwanji's imagination defying claim—that he had been involved in the efforts to drive the American forces away from SE Asia, especially Vietnam. For argument's sake, if there's any truth in this staggering scenario, and if Bhagwanji was indeed Bose, then this would have been reason enough to make his reappearance rather risky in those days of intense Cold War rivalries. Viewed in this assumed context, Bhagwanji's claim that India would face international wrath by way of economic sanctions and even armed intervention if his location was disclosed rings somewhat credible.

Chomping a cigar, Bhagwanji once said that 'about 50-60 wars have been fought in the world since WWII, but America has not been able to win even a single one of them'. He deliberately pronounced 'single' as 'thingle'—mocking someone he did not like. 'Churchill could not pronounce 'S'; I am alive to tell you this.'

In a similar tone, he claimed that on his advice, Ho Chi Minh dumped free cocaine and opium in south Vietnam. *The Americans have consumed at least a thousand tons till now—avidly. Change my name if the greatest power of the present world can win north Vietnam even in thousand years.* [Translated from Bangla]

He went to the extent of claiming that when the Vietnamese and Americans met for truce talks, on the former's side there used to be Ho Chi Minh's *pride of nine generals and a shadow behind them.*

'That shadow has caused many upheavals in the world in the last few decades', Charanik chipped in with a hyperbolic claim.

But how could this be? What is the guarantee that Bhagwanji was not having a fragile grip on reality? Was this man even mentally sound?

'Superhuman' is the word Bhagwanji's leading followers in Faizabad and Ayodhya usually use for him. Of them, Dr RP Mishra, nearly 93 now, used to be a plastic surgeon and his colleague Dr BN Rai an anesthetic. Dr Priyabrat Banerjee, who died rather young in 2012, was a homeopath, like his father

Dr TC Banerjee, who had an easy access to Bhagwanji. Dr DS Tomar is a known homeopath of the Ayodhya town.

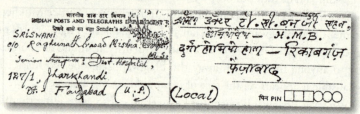

It was around 1966 when Bhagwanji told Sunil Krishna Gupta and others about the dumping of drugs in south Vietnam, where the American forces were. At this time, it was not known or at least not understood well that the drugs menace would become one of the reasons the US forces would quit the region. It was only in 1971 that US President Richard Nixon's deputy assistant for domestic affairs informed him that up to 20 per cent of US soldiers were heroin addicts. According to the 2010 book *The politics of Cocaine* by William L Marcy Jorrit Kamminga, high-ranking US officials 'believed that Chinese communist and Soviet-North Vietnamese operators had flooded South Vietnam with heroin, facilitating the escalation of use by US soldiers'.

Now the question is, how could a holy man located in a remote part of India have possibly known about it in advance? There certainly are many dots which need to be connected in this whole matter:

- Every news story or report concerning Subhas Bose used to reach Bhagwanji. Among them was a typed copy of a 15 May 1970 report published in a certain 'Evening Post' newspaper. The purported report was about the 'Asian and Pacific Conference on Cambodia' being held in Jakarta. One of the participants, former US Defence Secretary Clark M Clifford, was quoted saying something about the existence of a certain 'missing WWII general' in the Viet Cong army. According to the typed copy, Clifford refused to disclose the identity of the general. This said, it is to be noted that some of the typed stories sent to Bhagwanji were found to have been fabricated by their senders.

- But this is a matter of record that in late 1971, Balraj Trikha, a leading Supreme Court advocate who represented a party before the Khosla Commission, saw someone who he thought was 'Subhas Bose' at a South Vietnamese airport. He reported it to the media. But when Justice Khosla summoned him to appear before him, he just vanished. Thereafter Khosla called Prem Bhatia, then Indian

High Commissioner in Singapore, to state on oath what Trikha had told him. Now, Bhatia was too wise a man to have lent an ear to such a fantastic claim, considering that he was a legendary journalist. The trust set in his memory afterwards would have Manmohan Singh for a trustee among other luminaries.

- This very Prem Bhatia testified before the Khosla Commission that he met Trikha at the High Commission, heard his claim that he had seen someone dead for twenty-five years and yet thought it prudent to invite Trikha for a dinner. At no point did Bhatia, a man of outstanding intelligence, experience and eminence, tell Trikha to consult a psychiatrist. On the contrary, 'taken aback' by Trikha's statement, which he 'mentioned to more than one person', he brought it to the commission's notice through a confidential letter to his friend, Justice Khosla.

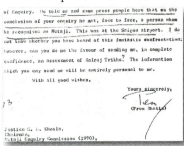

Nehru Memorial Museum and Library, New Delhi

- In 1994, a Calcutta newspaper correspondent happened to visit Vietnam to cover the visit of Prime Minister Narasimha Rao. The correspondent had no interest in the Netaji mystery, but at a gathering she met a Vietnamese Foreign Ministry official who passed on to her a lead on the condition of anonymity. He said that Vietnam was holding some material which could shed some light on the disappearance of Subhas Bose. The official said, he had tried to speak with the Indian embassy officials but they showed no interest in their documentation.

- The journalist filed her story, and it was carried by her employer newspaper, *The Telegraph,* part of the *Anandabazar Patrika* group. Since the paper has supported the air crash theory, there was no way it could have lend credence to the Bhagwanji angle which was virtually non-existent in 1994. But here is how the published story read:

'...There is accessible material here on Netaji's stay in Saigon in 1945.... However, the Indian government is reluctant to pursue this lead, which is likely to help us unearth some exceedingly interesting material on Netaji's disappearance since it will re-open the entire issue', said a highly placed source. ...Material on Netaji is also believed to have been accessed by the government here, while collecting archival material on both the World War II and the Vietnam War period.

- It is a matter of common knowledge that the Vietnam War began years after Subhas Bose's supposed death, so the very existence of some archival material concerning Netaji from that period would be quite intriguing on the face of it. The correspondent did not depose before the Mukherjee Commission despite repeated summons.

- Pictures taken during the plenary session of the Paris peace talks in January 1969 show eight senior Vietnamese officials, some of them ex-generals, facing the American delegation. There, moving around with the journalists and other officials, is a bespectacled, bearded man with some resemblance to Subhas Bose. The resemblance is apparent in all the images taken from different sources, including movie reels.

- The images show that this man is of medium height and has fat around his waist. A close-up shot shows bags under his eyes. But could the bearded man be 72—which Bhagwanji was said to be in 1969? That's possible, if one discounts thick black hair on the back of his head. According to his followers, by the mid-1960s,  there was considerable loss of hair on Bhagwanji's head compared to when they last saw 'him' in 1939-1940. He had grayed, put on more weight around the waist but his face was not wrinkled. One follower, who had seen Bose several times before 1940, caught a glimpse of Bhagwanji and found him to be 'more radiant than before'. The followers also said that Bhagwanji not only took interest in makeup tools and accessories, on occasion, he altered his facial features to avoid attention as he ventured out.

- So, who could this man be? My efforts to ascertain his identity from Vietnam history experts in America and Vietnam did not yield any results. No one could identify him. The Vietnamese Foreign Ministry did not respond to my email. The Diplomatic Academy of Vietnam directed me to the Historical Research Department in the ministry, which never responded.

Against this backdrop, it is important to recall that Justice MK Mukherjee had noted in his report that 'a reliable piece of documentary evidence, in support of the ocular version of the witnesses referred to earlier, could have been furnished if photographs of Bhagawanji/Gumnami Baba were taken by those persons who claimed to have interacted with him face-to-face on a number of occasions since 1963 and an opportunity given to this Commission to compare the same with the admitted photographs of Netaji'.

The Allahabad High Court underlined the above in its judgment of 31st January, adding that

> there appears to be **no room for doubt that there was substantial oral and documentary evidence** which prima facie makes out a case for scientific investigation with regard to the identity of late Gumnami Baba. [Emphasis mine]

A scientific way to go forward would be to run the images of the bearded man through a facial-mapping expert. In India, facial mapping tests are routinely carried out by the security agencies to identify people. And in some countries, most notably Great Britain, opinions of facial mapping experts are accepted as evidence in conjunction with other proofs.

Neil Millar, a facial mapping expert who was earlier with the British military, analysed the pictures of the bearded man and Bose. His initial observations were:

Netaji; the bearded man

- The (ear) lobe appears similar... the lobes [appear] to be large in structure.
- The nose has some similarities such as the general shape of the nose tip.
- The top lip has a 'cupids bow' which I would suggest is very similar in its appearance to the verified images [of Subhas Chandra Bose].
- I also noted some similarity in angular appearance in the right eyebrow and the structural appearance of the right orbit.

Because of the high costs and other factors, a proper forensic facial mapping test of the pictures of the bearded man could not be organised by me. However, Abhay Oberoi, who co-runs a film production house in Bangalore and is an amateur facial analyst, stepped in and carried out a most fascinating exercise:

> On the left [see next page] is a computerized imagery of Subhas Bose. With the help of facial recognition software, this face has been modelled to show how he would have looked at the age of 70, keeping his basic features intact.

> On the right is a computerized imagery of the bearded man at Paris. His features are made distinct for clear comparison with the imagery of Subhas Bose, after removing the beard and spectacles. Due to less clarity in this imagery, the comparison is not as good as I'd have desired. In any case, similarities and dissimilarities in both the faces are being listed out.

As we can see clearly, both the faces have a similar structure; they are round in shape.

1. We can also see that the far end of eyebrows are similar and bend at quite a similar angle in both the faces. The layout of the eyebrows is also relatively the same.

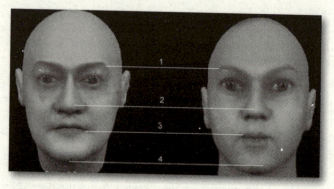

2. Again, when we compare the noses, we see a distinctive similarity in the apex of the nose. Ala of the nose does not show much similarity, but that could be because of the different angle from which the photographs were taken. The root (from the frontal bone) and bridge (from the nasal bone) also depict little similarity. However, the upper lateral cartilages do not show any kind of similarity and are significantly different.

3. There are no significant similarities in the lip structure. However, the outer pattern does seem to be a little identical. The area near cupid's bow of the upper lip tubercle are quite similar. But we don't see any similarities in the lower lip area. The lower vermilion border is quite distinct in both the faces. Also, commissure of the lips shows little similarity.

4. The area near the chin shows little similarity. The mental protuberance in both the faces shows significant similarity. However, anterior portion of the mandible in both the faces does not show any such similarity.

After analysing both the pictures carefully, and also studying their computer-generated imagery by facial recognition tools, I can conclude that there are many similarities in the facial structures and features of Subhas Bose and the bearded man at the Paris conference. The comparison would have been more exact if the pictures of the bearded man were clearer.

I would say that these faces are about 50 to 60% similar, even though the pictures of the bearded man were taken more than two decades after Bose was last seen. The opinion of a prosthetic make-up artist consulted by me is that the bearded man is probably wearing make-up. He observes that his beard is almost disproportionate to his face. It can only be possible if he has a little goitre around his neck, and this seems highly unlikely to me in view of what has been shown to me thus far.

As far as this analysis goes, there is a high possibility that what we are seeing is a dead man walking over here.

AFP Photo (with Netaji's picture in inset for comparison)

And if that is going to be the case, the big question would be how can a person who claimed to have wreaked such havoc elsewhere was sitting quietly in India?

None of the Bhagwanji's faithfuls believe that he was sitting and merely preaching. They give jaw dropping examples.

Bhagwanji claimed that it was around the Dalai Lama's arrival in India in 1959 that New Delhi got wind of his existence.

A follower once took a note of Bhagwanji's incredible words:

The Dalai Lama never really wanted to come to India. At one point of time, he had asked for fifty thousand rifles with adequate ammunition but the Indian government did not oblige him. Had it helped him, history might have taken a different turn. China could have been thwarted. America was also afraid to help from that far. As long as the British were in India, there was a pact that India will help Tibet in case of danger. That opportunity could have been utilised by Nehru's government but it did not do so. He wanted to please China. Dalai Lama wanted to go to Bhutan.

It was I who persuaded him to go to India. I persuaded him and convinced him that the Indian public was 100% for him. The Indian population was so much sympathetic to him that if he was not accepted in India, they would hound Nehru out. I further convinced him by saying that Nehru was my friend (at one time he actually was). Then the Dalai Lama relented and agreed to come to India.

It was when he was a week's journey from the Indian border that the Chinese found out that he was heading for India. China prepared to bomb from the air. The huge group of 2000 men, with mules and palanquins were moving together.

That is when a celestial event occurred. The caravan was covered from the skies by a mist. It was impossible to have an aerial view of the group for any bomber aircraft. The mist cleared up only after the Dalai Lama had safely crossed over into India. [Translated from Bangla]

Shedding further light on his 'role' in the escape, Bhagwanji claimed that disapproving the Chinese designs on Tibet, he approached the Dalai Lama under the *nom de guerre* of 'General Death' or 'General Shiva'. I personally am not able to make sense of it all. There is no way I can reach the Dalai Lama for verification. And even if I did and raised the issue with folded hands, I don't expect His Holiness to dwell on the secrets of his extraordinary life. Also, if Bhagwanji's word is taken on the face value, how would one reconcile it with the official version that the only outside helping hand to the Lama was of the CIA?

Lowell Thomas, Jr (92), is a man who has been a part of history. Along with his father Lowell Thomas, he was the last westerner to reach Lhasa before the 1949 Chinese invasion. In 2005, the Dalai Lama bestowed on him the International Campaign for Tibet's Light of Truth Award. Thomas's 1961 book *The Dalai Lama* throws some light on an event which probably occurred around 1955, and involved 'a spokesman for the Khamba tribesmen'.

> He called himself General Siva, a threatening title, for Siva is the god of destruction in the Hindu religion. We may call him General Death as the nearest English equivalent.

According to Thomas's book, General Siva was of some help to the Living Buddha. But who was this General Death?

'A total mystery to me', Thomas, a former Lt Governor of Alaska, wrote to me when I emailed him several years ago.

The year of Bhagwanji's 'return' to India is important because barely a year later, from nowhere, the Shaulmari Sadhu legend cropped up. Dead Man said that around 1959 the government of ours came to know that he was either in China or in the vicinity of India. Since he had no desire to get in touch with Prime Minister Nehru or his government, Bhagwanji claimed he created the 'parallel bluff' of Shaulmari to make the Intelligence Bureau chase a mirage. 'If you go to Shaulmari, you will find letters in this faquir's handwriting', he said on one occasion. He said he used to 'choke with laughter' over 'the game of Shaulmari' as it played out. Because he was not Netaji, Saradanand himself did not emerge to proclaim in front of a big crowd who he really was and end the controversy. If he had, Bhagwanji reasoned, the 'combine' (a loose term by which Bhagwanji meant Nehru and the Americans) would have been 'free to concentrate' in one direction, in search of the 'real' person. He said he couldn't lower his guard because any 'carelessness' on his part would 'give the key of the puzzle' to the combine. 'Then this ghost that is sitting on their shoulders would be removed by the ghostbusters.'

From available Bhagwanji notes, it appears that he believed that Soviet Russia was *extremely grateful* towards him for the things he had done for them, but apprehensive that he might tilt towards the Chinese, who began contacting him through the Russians initially but eventually these contacts became unilateral. At the same time, Bhagwanji kept it secret from the Chinese that he sympathaised with the Tibetans, that he did not approve of Communism and that he despised anything which was against Indian interests.

In one letter, Bhagwanji tried to elucidate his aims as he balanced himself between the big powers and the larger interests of India:

(a) China must not be provided with valid reason to force Khrushchev's hands—to give China the bombs (which China has not); (b) China must not be provided with a 'so called' valid reason to force Khrushchev to use his bombs in China's defence; (c) Khrushchev must not be given a valid reason to back up China fully; (d) Khrushchev must not be given the chance to fight USA (for and over India). If world situation needs it, let the two of them fight it out elsewhere.

While he secretly came back to India in 1955 or 1956, Bhagwanji would often quietly slip out of the country. Where would he go? One place he alluded to was a *very vast region (not excluding portions of the Himalayas)* where he enjoyed *completely unhindered freedom*, thanks to the Russians.

The concerned governments considered those regions as 'dead', useless for any and all persons. Now Dead Man has a carte blanche over the whole.

The area was in the Pamirs between China and Russia, where *some extremely important and vital secret base* had been built by Stalin.

One wonders if Bhagwanji was referring to the region near about the Pedak corridor, a reference about which I came across in the National Archives at Kew in London.

"Intelligence Digest". Edited by Kenneth de Courcy.
16th Year. No. 181. March 1954.

A Corridor to Afghanistan.

Peking has also let Russia have the 100-mile Padak corridor, connecting China with Afghanistan over the Pamirs. That part of China linking with Russia, Afghanistan, and Kashmir, has never been clearly demarcated; but China, as the historical protector of the region, had virtual control.

In the years preceding the India-China war of 1962, the Gandhians had been castigating the Nehru government for making marginal increase in defence expenditure. JB Kripalani, who had sided with Gandhi against Bose in 1939, pontificated in Parliament in 1958 that 'in a non-violent India, the last thing the Government would contemplate would be an increase in the military budget, but I am sorry to say, and I think it would disturb the soul of the Father of the Nation....'

Left to Nehru and Kripalani, the Indian Army might as well have been disbanded in 1947 as per the wishes of the Apostle of non-violence. The following absurdity is attributed to the former: 'Our policy is *ahimsa*. We foresee no military threats. Scrap the army! The police are good enough to meet our security needs.'

The Chinese blow took out Gandhian considerations from India's national security calculus. Suddenly, the lawmakers and the man on the street alike wished Netaji was there.

And in a mindboggling realisation of the ultimate 'what if' scenario, 'Netaji' was there! In his letters written soon after the war, Bhagwanji, fulminating at India's humiliation, outlined his take:

What India needs is, not cursing the enemy, but, matching him in his own skill squarely and beat him at his own game.

China is a past master in war strategy, craftiness, war-diplomacy, state craft, all sorts of war and their execution, most shrewd calculations, etc. They have been so, for thousands of years. Their becoming Communists does not mean that they have lost their heritage.

Describing the Chinese as *100% correct students of Maharshi Kautilya*, Bhagwanji characterised himself *a military seer*. He even went on to lament that it was 'greatest misfortune of India' that she did not have another Chanakya. *No military seer for the last two thousand years! No national military thinking for the last thousand years!*

The world respects-venerates-fears only the strong. Be strong and preach! The world shall hear and accept with admiration and growing respect. Be weak and preach: The world shall know you to be a real despicable-coward-hypocrite, fit only to be patted-and-booted and enslaved!

As Bhagwanji saw it in 1962, India's handing of the Chinese invasion was a disaster.

Any conquering race given opportunity (in this case, open invitation), shall embark on a conquering venture; this is cold truth. China rightly knows Jawaharlal Nehru to be a totally unworthy-of-taking-serious-notice of person.

It is a fact (proven to the hilt) that Nehru is absolutely no match for China in any sphere.

It is sheer hypocrisy and utterly stupid to bemoan and bewail one's weakness—unpreparedness. It is simply not done. It is all in the game of war and fighting that you must vanquish your enemy through his unpreparedness, what then strategies mean?!

The 'military seer' had a piece of advice for the *mentors and policy makers of India*:

If there is one principle of war that can be condensed into a single word, it is concentration. It implies concentration of strength against weakness. And for any real value, it needs to be explained that the concentration of strength against weakness depends on the dispersion of your opponents' strength, which in turn, is produced by a distribution of your own that gives appearance…of dispersion… that is your dispersion, his dispersion, your concentration—suchis the sequence, and each is a sequel. … True concentration is the fruit of calculated dispersion.

Those who shall complain that all this is not easy reading should be gently reminded that war is no easy business. …Basically, the approach is simple: The enemy must be made to disperse his forces under pressure and should be kept in the dark about the point or points where a concentrated attack will be made to bring about disorganisation. To ensure success, two major problems must be solved – disorganisation and exploitation. One precedes and one follows the actual blow, which in composition is a simple act. You cannot hit the enemy with effect unless you have first created the opportunity; you cannot make the effect decisive unless you exploit the second opportunity that comes before he can recover.… You must, somehow, wrest the initiative from the invader and aim at bringing about disorganisation of his forces in some vital sector on the front line, as well as on his home front. The more you make it clear that you shall fight only at the place of his choosing and disperse your forces at his dictation, the more you shall place yourself at a disadvantage. You have to harry the enemy on all fronts, including home front.

In one of his letters, Bhagwanji even outlined the 'unalterable principles' of war. Of these 'the two significant Dont's' were:

Don't lunge whilst your opponent can parry. The experience of history shows that no effective stroke is possible until the enemy's power of resistance or evasion is paralysed. Hence no commander should launch a real attack upon enemy in position until he is satisfied that such a paralysis has developed.

Don't renew an attack along the same line or form.

In fact, from what he said, it appears that the 1962 shocker made Bhagwanji so desperate that he even tried to come out, sending out a signal to Nehru. His version, as incredible as most of what he said, was as follows:

- In the wake of a previous Chinese assault, the Army [Indian] prepared a Top Secret expert report on how to prevent an enemy from the other side of the Himalayas by taking affordable counter measures at key places.

- The report was leaked; it reached Pakistan, and from Pakistan to China. Some factions on the Chinese side became overenthusiastic and advanced the invasion of 1962. They used exactly the same routes as were described in the report.

- It was precisely at that time that the Dead Man rushed out twice, and secured a unilateral halt, using his influence with the Chinese. In his words: *It is not for nothing that an old man, in the course of the recent months went out of India twice, braving all the fatal hazards to his life and frail body. The result is before you. As I have told you, war is not an emotional business. It is a cold calculated affair.*

- Thereafter, Dead Man persuaded the Chinese to make an extraordinary proposal to India, which would have served Indian interest. It was not agreed to. The Dead Man had a message sent, purportedly from China, to Nehru: *I want to return.* There was no response.

- More attempts were made through *a mutual foreign friend* but Nehru *remained mum.* Then attempts were made through someone in India. But Nehru would not budge and a sympathetic Lal Bahadur Shastri was silenced.

Bhagwanji claimed to practice *the elementary rules of strategy* he preached. Four years later, when India faced danger from the Pakistani side, he again turned restless. He took great offense to disparaging description of the Indian Army in certain quarters, especially in Pakistan, against the backdrop of the 1962 rout.

He said, with much indignation, that Pakistani dictator Ayub Khan had the temerity to tell Prime Minister Lal Bahadur Shastri in London: 'I can walk over to Delhi any hour I want to, you know?' In Pakistan, Ayub, as per Bhagwanji, contemptuously said, 'These *dhotiwala* Hindus...what do they know of fighting...they only know how to lose and run from a fight. Now we'll simply kick them and take Delhi and Kashmir with ease. The Chinese crossed hundreds of miles and took thousands of Indian troops captive. Heaven knows how many were killed. Indian troops could not even take a dead Chinese soldier.'

Bhagwanji's rejoineder: Whatever was said about cowardice, 'was true only for Indian politicians and not the Indian Army'.

He claimed that then he sent PM Shastri some 'clues' on how to handle Pakistan, and it was only after some time that Shastri understood.

The result according to Bhagwanji was:

Lahore was completely evacuated by the civilians, Pakistan military were fleeing Lahore like squirrels. It was a matter of punching-and-taking! ...Sialkot, Muzzafarabad and that 1/3rd of Kashmir were a matter of one week.

'Seven more days, and there would have been no Kashmir problem', he said.

'When Lal Bahadur and Ayub Khan first met each other in a separate room after the war, Ayub said to Shastri in Urdu. *Ab to raham karo, jo ho gaya so ho gaya.*' Translated, it reads: Please forgive us at least now, whatever has happened has happened.

Bhagwanji did not want Shastri to go to Taskhent. *Invite them on Indian soil.*

To the best of my understanding, Bhagwanji's exact whereabouts became known to the Government of India at the highest level in the days of Indira Gandhi. I have no reason to doubt the word of followers that Chaudhury Charan Singh started visiting him frequently from the late 1960s onwards. The would-be UP Chief Minister, Union Home Minister and Prime Minister remained in the good books of Bhagwanji for long, but not forever. H praised Singh's ideas and efforts about improving India's agrarian output.

But that's not to say that Bhagwanji had been 'sheltered' by the authorities. Nothing that I know indicates that. My hunch is that since they knew that he was not going to go public, the authorities just let him be. But they kept in touch with him. Ram Bhawan was and is located at walking distance from the local top cop's residence and office. Just behind Bhagwanji's room was the fencing of the HQ of the Gorkha Regiment of the Indian Army. According to the locals, there was a transmitter in the room. Every day around 6 pm, Bhagwanji would be on it, talking in English. But Bhagwanji was always wary of the authorities.

You have raised this Frankenstein and now feelers are being sent to him. It is too late.

According to a local source, before India and Pakistan went to war in 1971, Prime Minister Indira Gandhi visited Bhagwanji in Basti. I asked a follower in Kolkata why did he 'help' her, when he so much disliked her father and was not particularly fond of her. 'He did not help her, he helped the country', the follower snapped. Going by Bhagwanji's words, his hidden intervention came about with the full knowledge of the then Army chief, and would-be Field Marshal, Sam Maneckshaw.

In fact, a follower claimed that in the dead of night, Bhagwanji would join Maneckshaw in a secret place to take stock of the war. He claimed that bombing of the Governor House in Dhaka one day before Pakistan surrendered was at Bhagwanji's instance.

But wouldn't the then R&AW chief, RN Kao, know of Bhagwanji if that were the case? Bhagwanji mentioned Kao's name once—so far as I know—when hardly anyone was aware of it. It was on the day Indira was assassinated. 'No one should ever hurt a woman', said Bhagwanji, bristling in anger. Pounding his hand on a desk in front of him he rued that his repeated instructions to Kao to increase Indira's security were overlooked. In 1984, Kao was the Prime Minister's security advisor.

If I were you I would also scoff at these claims, but the believers take them as truth. Sunil Das, the publisher of *Oi Mahamanab Asey*, recalled before the Khosla Commission on 6 September 1972 that in 1965 Leela Roy had forewarned her close associates about the influx of a large number of refugees from east Pakistan. 'In March 1971, Indo-Pak conflict came about... Whether this was a hint sent to her or whether it was a divine disclosure, I do not know', Das told the commission.

What Das did not tell the commission was that months before the 1971 war started, Bhagwanji asserted that 'free Bangladesh will be established due to the secret moves of a particular great chess player' and that 'after some time, history will record that this area was known for a short time as east Pakistan'. He even said that after freedom in the east, 'the other side—Pakistan, Balochistan—will turn volatile'. *Oi Mahamanaba Aasey* has many astounding passages relating to Bangladesh:

> One voice, very well known, was heard from the free autonomous radio station. The announcer said, 'You will now hear a voice which you have always known'. That voice was heavy and heart-touching. It said: 'I have gone around many countries in the world with a rifle on my shoulders. I was in Germany and Japan and have roamed around in many places in Southeast Asia. For the last nine months I was with you and even now I am with you.'

> Why do we hear in the southern, eastern, western and northern areas of Bangladesh the same story that there is someone, some secret power! He is behind everything, even the inspirer of our imprisoned leader! [Translated from Bangla]

Hidden truth or hallucinatory patchwork, I really don't know what to make of all this. Bhagwanji's two closest followers in Naimisharanya and Basti, Srikant Sharma and Durga Prasad Pandey, both said that during that period former revolutionary Amal Roy involved himself in running of a clandestine radio on India-east Pakistan border at the instruction of Bhagwanji, who knew of the developments 'before they were reported on the All India Radio'.

I also heard claims that certain Bangladeshi fighters of those times alluded to the guiding hand of a great figure during the war, but I never saw any of the contemporary press reports people said they had seen. What I find quite interesting is that Bengali godman Sitaram Omkarnath Thakur is said to have played some role in the war. Omkarnath, who had some sort of a connection with Bhagwanji, 'directly imparted his spiritual power to the freedom struggle'—states a website dedicated to him. It further claims that a general had made a statement that 'the commander-in-chief of this war was indeed Thakur!' This general, I learnt from an article titled 'India's secret war in Bangladesh' published in *The Hindu* on 26 December 2011, was Omkarnath's follower Sujan Singh Uban. The writer of the article was Praveen Swami, currently National Editor (Strategic and International Affairs) of the *Indian Express*.

In 1971, the Uban-headed and R&AW-controlled Special Frontier Force had carried out military offensives in the Chittagong Hill Tracts. According to Swami, who is too sophisticated a person to take any interest in the holy-man angle to the Bose mystery on the face of it, Uban 'later said, he had received a year's advance warning of the task that lay ahead from the Bengali mystic, Baba Omkarnath'.

In a letter written to Bhagwanji in January 1981, it was mentioned that 'Sri Sitaram Omkarnath Thakur has hinted that he is in contact with Netaji Subhas Chandra Bose'. In a letter to another follower, Bhagwanji dissected the semantics of names used in the Ramayan and disapproved of Omkarnath's approach in his translation of the epic. Also located in Ram Bhawan was a newspaper story about secret visits of some special person, not Omkarnath, to then east Pakistan. I don't have the details of this news item, but I do have a clipping from the *Anandabazar Patirka*, where Sheikh Mujibur Rahman himself is quoted as saying on 17 January 1972 that 'the fact that Bangladesh has become a reality proves that Netaji is alive'.

'It's just a general statement. Only someone with a fragile grip on reality can think along the lines the Bhagwanji's followers do', you might rejoin.

I actually browsed through declassified US records of the 1970s—as far as it was possible for me to—and found only one reference to Subhas Bose. A derisive, stray comment made in a State Department telegram originating from the US Embassy in Dacca on 3 January 1975. Referring to the reported shooting of one political leader, the embassy telegram said that unless his body was displayed, 'there will soon grow up stories that he still lives, *a la* Subhas Chandra Bose'.

This would mean that the rumour that Bose was still alive was current in Bangaldesh too in that period.

It is somewhat perplexing that records pertaining to the 1971 were illegally destroyed. On 9 May 2010, *The Times of India* ran the following front page story by award winning journalist Josy Joseph.

Bangladesh war files destroyed by Army
True Story Of 1971 Is Lost Forever

Josy Joseph | TNN

New Delhi: The history of the 1971 India-Pakistan war will never be fully written. Most official records of the war that led to the liberation of Bangladesh have been destroyed. The destroyed files include those on the creation of the Mukti Bahini — the Bangladesh freedom fighters — all appreciation and assessments made by the army during the war period, the orders issued to fighting formations, and other sensitive operational details.

Authoritative army sources said all records of the period, held at the Eastern Command in Kolkata, were destroyed immediately after the 1971 war. This has remained secret until now.

According to at least two former chiefs of the Eastern Command and other senior army officers TOI spoke to, the destruction may have been deliberate.

They say the destruction may have happened when Lt General Jagjit Singh Aurora, the Indian army's commanding officer on the east-

General A A K Niazi (centre) signs the surrender documents in Dhaka on December 16, 1971. Lt General Aurora is on the left

The Missing Files
▶ Include those on the creation of the Mukti Bahini and sensitive operational details
▶ The files were probably shredded when Lt General Jagjit Singh Aurora, hero of the war, was heading the Eastern Command
▶ Army headquarters may have some records but the picture can never be complete

were part of the operations   er in August 1974 I asked to

'The destroyed files include those on the creation of the Mukti Bahini —the Bangladesh freedom fighters—all appreciation and assessments made by the Army during the war period, the orders issued to fighting formations, and other sensitive operational details', the TOI report said.

On July 27, Defence Minister AK Antony made a terse statement in Parliament that 'no official records pertaining to the 1971 war that are available with the Defence Ministry have been destroyed'. Qualified as this statement was, it in a way did not clarify the TOI scoop sourced to 'authoritative Army sources' that 'all records of the period, held at the Eastern Command in Kolkota, were destroyed immediately after the 1971 war'.

Come to think of it, actually there is no disputing the fact that Subhas's memories were summoned as a psychological boost during the Bangladesh liberation war. Going by Yatindra Bhatnagar's book *Bangla Desh: Birth of a Nation* Bose's classmate at Cambridge and later ICS officer CC Desai, who used to be India's envoy to different countries including Pakistan before becoming an MP, saw shades of his friend in Sheikh Mujibur Rahman's tactics. Mujib's 'directives immediately before Yahya troops struck, may be well compared with Netaji's thesis of anti-imperialist struggle and Samveda propounded by him in 1933'. Mukti Vahini's war cry 'Joi Bangla' was inspired by 'Jai Hind'. So, Mujib's statement had to be a metaphoric expression, or he was misquoted. Certainly nothing more than that!

But if you flipped through *Oi Mahamanaba Aasey* and, for a moment, believed in the contents as Bhagwanji's followers did, you would be tempted to think of Mujib's statement as a Freudian slip. Because Charanik claimed that 'in the three decades between 1945 and 1975, one man has attained a divine power, much above all physical powers, which is beyond comprehension of mind and senses'. [Translated from Bangla]

If it is of any help, here's how Bhagwanji, a practitioner of *Tantrasadhana*, put it in English: *You cannot comprehend to what end your Mahakaal is working and with what powers. Your imagination will be awed, your brain will reel if even by chance you could come to know even a fractional part of his present activities.*

But why, despite such 'powers' did he remain in hiding? What was he afraid of? Is it not cowardly for someone who talks so big, not to have the courage to come out?

Cowardice is not the right word. Whatever it is, it is an entangled issue involving interrelated conundrums, for which there are no quick and simple answers.

The era of fighting a thing out on the prowess of men is gone. Do you know? Can you comprehend what shall happen if 'A' or 'H' bombs were dropped on India?!

'Let me be where I am. My coming out is not in India's interest', Bhagwanji would summarise.

Fourteen

For more than fourteen years now, I have been making unrelenting efforts to crack the Netaji mystery. While this 'obsession' for truth, as most would characterise it, has brought me into some sort of prominence in certain circles, it has done irreparable damage to my life. At that, I have been supporting the incredible Faizabad angle to the mystery, which, in the view of many well-wishers, has 'spoilt' my otherwise 'good work'. And yet I continue to be at it—decades after the clout around Subhas Bose dissipated even in his home State of Bengal.

Many have asked me what is the reason that I refuse to give up, and how did I get pulled into the Netaji mystery case in the first place? Answers to the both are the same. Years ago, simply by fluke, I stumbled upon what I was told was 'India's best-kept secret'. As a journalist it then became impossible for me to let go of it, because I saw in it the prospects of my becoming instrumental in exposing it and finding a place in history. Who wouldn't relish such prospects? Don't people chase big dreams all their lives?

My grandfather was a King's Commissioned Officer (Junior Commissioned Officer in today's terminology) in the British Indian Army. He happened to be on the Kohima front, facing the INA-Japanese offensive. From what I heard, my grandfather and others in the army were told that they would take on the Japanese. But when they reached the front in Kohima, they heard Indians shouting through loudspeakers on the other side, asking why they were fighting against their own brothers. There was some sort of commotion on my grandfather's side. Some refused to fight. Then my grandfather and two others went missing-in-action. As he somehow survived in the jungle, my grandfather was presumed dead back home. My grandmother turned a widow for a brief period. Then my grandfather came back from the dead. But that experience made him, a loyal defender of the British Raj, pro-Subhas Chandra Bose. That was my tenuous personal connect with Netaji prior to 2000.

What happened to me thereafter is interesting enough to be turned into a movie. In 2000, I got involved in the Netaji mystery case professionally as a journalist. At *HindustanTimes.com*, my colleague Shali Ittaman came up with the idea of conducting a journalistic enquiry and made me a part of it. Our CEO, Sanjay Trehan, was very supportive of the probe from the word go. After reading the government-approved inquiries report and coming to know of the views of those who appeared credible on the face of it, I initially thought the Taipei air crash theory was true. Then, digging further, I began having doubts and the Russian angle began troubling me. I distinctly remember the day when a visitor from UP said something about Gumnami Baba and the revulsion I felt. The very question of lending an ear to such an outrageous suggestion did not arise.

And then one day, I discovered something so startling that my life was never the same again. A source with a direct access to a highest-level contact in the government told me, strictly on condition of anonymity, that the Prime Minister of India had in his possession an ultra-secret file which held the key to unraveling the Bose mystery.

Quoting the highest-level contact, this secret source revealed that the government was keeping the facts under wraps from the people of India, for fear of triggering a 'political earthquake' at home—apart from causing complications at the foreign front, even at this distant time.

According to the highest-level contact, not only did our government hold precise records about what became of Netaji, the records recorded that he was very much alive much after his alleged death in a reported plane crash in Taipei. The government's public backing of the air crash theory was an 'eyewash' and that the 'whole matter was so complicated that it would not be understood by the people'. 'He never died, he went to Russia.'

Thus far, it sort of fitted well into the picture. But subsequent words from the highest-level contact took my breath and sleep away: 'He was a mastermind. We were in touch with him till 1985.' That is, after Russia, Netaji was in India.

I felt as if I was living a plot from a John Le Carré novel.

From that very moment I felt that that exposing the truth about Netaji, now that I had come to know of it, was a cause worth fighting for. I regarded the revelation a godsend opportunity for a journalist of no consequence like me—someone who had been a non-achiever in life till that point in time.

I have no qualms in admitting that prior to 2001 I was not a devout Netaji admirer. I have never made secret of seeking personal recognition and glory as the motivating factor making me chase this story. I am not a monk. But yes, I do have a conscience. Would you not have done what I have if you were in my place? Isn't this exactly how your favourite journalist lives by?

And because of this backdrop, I have always been without prejudice. It is the exposition of truth which will bring laurels to me. My life hinges on the truth about Netaji—whatever it is. Therefore, I always pursued the matter objectively. I was lucky that I could access far, far more information about this matter than anyone else had done before. Because of that I could dwell far deeper into this than anyone else.

Fifteen-odd years after suffering from sleepless nights having heard out the source, the further I go, the clearer, the highest-level contact's information appears to me. The file in the PM's personal custody and the Faizabad angle loom so large that I am now beginning to think that I am almost there.

And if I ever got there, it would surely not be solely because of my own efforts. In my quest for truth, I have had support of those who have the deepest admiration for Netaji. They came out of their way to help with no consideration of personal aggrandisement on their part.

Today, we are fellow travelers in this journey. We are aiming at doing what previous generations could not: Crack India's longest-running mystery. This is our 'Mission Netaji'.

What Mission Netaji has achieved thus far is of the stuff movies are made of. We have revived a 'dead' issue in a country that is not particularly known for a sense of history. After the rejection of the Mukherjee Commission report by the Manmohan Singh government, the Netaji mystery again became a lost cause. We figured out that since the matter was unlikely to impress the media and our thinkers, we could spotlight it indirectly by underlining the dark secrecy around it. State secrecy was a larger issue no one could have run from.

Luckily for us, by the time we got our acts together, the Right to Information Act, 2005 had elevated India into a select group of nations giving their public an unfettered right to seek information from government. Of course, to respond or not was the government's prerogative within the ambit of the Act.

Our first go proved to be a milestone in the Freedom of Information movement in India.

This was the story on the Home Ministry. Of the MHA holding something like 70, 000 classified pages and the fear that the release of some Top Secret records would unleash law and order problem across India.

The Times of India (Kolkata) frontpaged this story on Mission Netaji on 18 Sept 2006

Subsequent to this RTI case, several more such cases were filed by the Mission Netaji members and their results highlighted in media. Sample the following:

- In 2009, RTI request by Chandrachur Ghose for a copy of the history of the INA complied at the behest of the Ministry of Defence way back in 1950 was turned down. Even a favourable directive from the Central Information Commission could not persuade the MoD to release the report and it took a stay on the RTI application in the Delhi High Court.

- In August 2013, the Prime Minister's Office turned down an appeal from Ghose to reconsider its decision not to release three files about the 'widow and daughter of Shri Subhash Chandra Bose'. The PMO Director upheld the previous decision of the office to deny Ghose these secret files,

Chandrachur Ghose is seen in this grab from *Times Now*

because their release would 'prejudicially affect relations with foreign countries'. An appeal made before the then Chief Information Commissioner Rajiv Mathur, former IB chief, also met the same fate. Yet another application by Chandrachur was turned down by the PMO in 2015.

- In August 2006, the Ministry of External Affairs—which is currently holding 29 secret files concerning Netaji—refused to part with its correspondence with the Soviet and Russian governments over Bose's alleged presence in the erstwhile USSR. MEA's reasoning was: 'It involves relations with a foreign state.' The MEA's roundabout response to my question 'whether the MEA sought information from the Russians by issuing mere note verbales, or some serious efforts were ever made from a higher level', only confirmed that the Ministry had not.

- In 2006, I asked the Prime Minister's Office to provide me a list of records, the Research and Analysis Wing was holding on or about Netaji. The PMO forwarded my request to the agency as I had emphasised in my request that the R&AW was directly under the Prime Minister. In response, Deputy Secretary PN Ranjit Kumar made a sweeping statement that 'R&AW does not have any information pertaining to Netaji'. He added: 'It might be added that we are under no obligation to provide this information under the Right to Information (RTI) Act, 2005.'

- But this statement was not truthful. Because in 2001, the then Home Secretary, Kamal Pande, had filed an affidavit before the Mukherjee Commission. This affidavit listed out several Top Secret/Secret records about Netaji, whose disclosure was likely to 'evoke wide-spread reactions' and harm India's 'relations with friendly countries'. Among the records listed by Pande, one originated from the R&AW. It was an Under Office note of 1994 vintage dealing with certain articles published in a Russian journal on the basis of classified KGB records.

2

9. 1-81/n	No.I/12014/27/93-IS(D.III)	Notes of Ministry of Home Affairs containing pages 1 to 81 on controversy regarding Netaji's death and bringing his ashes to India from Japan.
10. 7-18/c	No.I/12014/27/93-IS(D.III)	Draft note for Cabinet on bringing the mortal remains of Netaji back to India.

(KAMAL PANDE)
Home Secretary
Government of India
New Delhi.

- Even as our own government stonewalled our attempts to access information about Netaji, we were somewhat lucky, even if symbolically, with the Central Intelligence Agency (CIA). During the inquiry of the Mukherjee Commission, the MEA had refused to do anything about obtained secret records from the US, saying that 'classified documents of the US Government can be requisitioned under the US Freedom of Information Act only by giving specific details of the documents; and…this is a tardy and complicated process'. The biggest complication was the lack of intention. A little later, I located two classified CIA records sitting in Delhi, with the help of Sarat Bose's granddaughter Madhuri Bose-Gaylard. Using the Freedom of Information Act (FOIA), I sought copies of these two records. The agency turned the request down because the release was likely to harm US interests. I appealed that they should be released for the sake of Bose's admirers world over, including in America, with necessary censorship of the names of agents and the method employed to collect information. The arguments that do not cut ice with our government were accepted by the CIA. The two records were duly released, and they showed that in 1950 rumours were in circulation at high levels in India that Subhas was alive, and probably in the USSR. In January 2014, the agency dispatched copies of four declassified records from its database in response to a subsequent FOIA application filed by NRI Abhishek Bose of Maryland. According to the last of these documents, in February 1964 the CIA was told about the 'possible return' of Subhas Bose. 'There now exists a strong possibility that Bose is leading the rebellious group undermining the current Nehru government.'

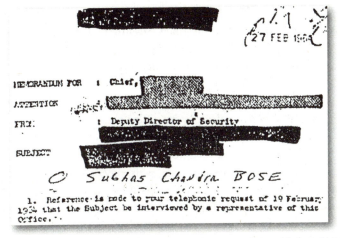

- In 2006, I requested the PMO to let me have a list of classified files about Netaji it was holding. It would take two years and an order from the Central Information Commission for the PMO to provide me a truncated list of 31 classified files. In 2015, Sreejith Panickar managed to secure a detailed list of 36 files, of which 20 were about Netaji's disappearance.

S.N.	File No.	Subject	Classification
1.	23(156)/51-PM	Disposal of properties of Indian National Army in the far East	S
2.	2(658)/53-PMS	Jankinath Bhavan at Cuttack, birthplace of Shri Subhas Chandra Bose – acquisition by the Orissa Government of – use of the building as a hospital by the Netaji Subhas Seva Sadan	S
3.	2(64)/56-66-PM(V.1)	Death of Shri Subhash Chandra Bose -Appointment of an inquiry committee to go into the circumstances of the death	S
4.	2(64)/56-66-PM(V.2)	Death of Shri Subhash Chandra Bose -Appointment of an inquiry committee to go into the circumstances of the death	S
5.	2(64)/56-67-PM(V.3)	Death of Shri Subhash Chandra Bose -Appointment of an inquiry committee to go into the circumstances of the death	S
6.	2(64)/56-68-PM(V.4)	Death of Shri Subhash Chandra Bose -Appointment of an inquiry committee to go into the circumstances of the death	S
7.	2(64)/56-70-PM(V.5)	Death of Netaji Subhash Chandra Bose -Appointment of an inquiry committee to go into the circumstances of the death	S
8.	2/67/56-71-PM (V.1)	Widow and daughter of Shri Subhash Chandra Bose Miscellaneous correspondence with and about	TS
9.	2(67)/56-71-PM (V.2)	Widow and daughter of Shri Subhash Chandra Bose Miscellaneous correspondence with and about	S

- The PMO further informed Sreejith that five more files about Netaji were so highly secretive that even their names cannot be divulged. Intriguingly, a file dealing with the funeral of Netaji's widow in Germany in 1996, was classified as 'Confidential'. One file concerning the abortive bid to confer Bharat Ratna on Netaji in 1992 was stamped 'Secret'. Also classified as 'Secret' was a file dealing with the 'disposal of properties of INA in Far East'.

Any record containing classified information is given one of the three security markings to commensurate with the damage its unauthorised disclosure will cause to India's interests. When it is determined that the damage could be exceptionally grave', the file is stamped 'Top Secret'. So what could possibly be 'Top Secret' about Netaji in this age and time?

Tormented by this very question, members of the Netaji's family threw their weight behind Mission Netaji. Things began rolling in 2012 with the release of my book *India's biggest Cover-up*. The book laid out, for the first time, a methodical approach to ending the Bose mystery by way of declassification and other related steps. This was the consummation of Mission Netaji's strategy— to re-brand the Netaji mystery as a matter of transparency—a larger issue which no right-thinking person could sidestep.

Outline of an action plan was chalked out in November 2012 at Kolkata. This was at a function organised by Netaji's niece Chitra Ghosh, daughter of Sarat Bose, to felicitate this writer. Around two dozen members of the Netaji's family from all over the world assembled on the occasion.

At the meeting, Mission Netaji members impressed upon the Bose family members that the only realistic chance of getting the files declassified lay with a powerful leader who would not co-exist with the Congress party and was a nationalist to the core. Only one man fitted the description—then Gujarat Chief Minister Narendra Modi. Some members of the Bose family reacted sharply to this suggestion, as they felt— perhaps due to their long association with the Left Front in Bengal—that Modi was 'communal' and so they were not ready to approach him.

Chitra Ghosh

Since the family wouldn't agree to write to Modi at that moment, it was agreed to approach Mamata Banerjee. So, a letter was sent to the West Bengal Chief Minister by Netaji's nephew, DN Bose on behalf of the Bose family. Banerjee was requested to ask Prime Minister Manmohan Singh to declassify all secret Netaji-related files. The letter said that she was being approached because the family members thought that 'it will be most appropriate that this demand for declassification should be made' by the Chief Minister of West Bengal.

Side by side, the family members also tried to seek an appointment with the Chief Minister so as to press the demand in person.

Further attempts by the writer to access details about seventy-or-so classified files on or about Netaji being held by the WB government under the RTI act did not succeed as the authorities did not give any clear information, except that the bulk of the files were in the custody of the Secret Cell of the Home Department being run by the Chief Minister herself.

Finding no alternative, Mission Netaji and the family members and admirers of Netaji began organising marches and press conferences to sensitise the people about the need for declassification. Cousins Chandra Kumar Bose and Abhijit Ray, both grandsons of Sarat Bose, played a most prominent role in building up the momentum.

At the same time, I used social media, especially Facebook, to spread the word about the need to crack the case by way of declassification. With a view to reach out worldwide audience of different outlooks and sustain their interest over a period of time, I couched my daily messages in a variety of ways. To relieve the monotony, I even took resort to satire and dark humour. In early 2013, one of the spoofs created by me reached Narendra Modi's table, who looked at it and smiled. It was a make-believe *Washington Post* front page where I imagined Modi, the new Indian Prime Minister, ordering declassification of the Bose files.

Facebook spoof titled 'Future is here' dated 11 December 2012

In the fullness of time was done what had been unthinkable earlier. A matter which was discussed in local community halls began to be thrashed out internationally. Before 3,000 plus receptive students and teachers at the Jaypee University of Information Technology in Solan, Himachal Pradesh, I gave a TED Talk on the Netaji mystery. For hours in IIT, Kanpur the students and professors remained attentive as I ran them through the case details.

Meanwhile, thanks to our activities in Kolkata, the local BJP unit under Rahul Sinha started supporting the declassification demand. Sinha did a good thing by writing a letter to party president Rajnath Singh about the need to flag the Netaji issue.

Eventually the Bose family came around to the idea of reaching out to Narendra Modi. In April 2013, Bose family spokesperson Chandra Kumar Bose met the then Gujarat Chief Minister, courtesy his friend Rahul Sinha. Chandra handed over to the Gujarat CM a letter approved by two dozen children and grandchildren of Netaji's brothers Sudhir, Sunil, Sarat and Suresh.

In the letter—drafted by Chandrachur Ghose and myself—the kin underlined the reason why the Chief Minister of Gujarat was being approached over the declassification issue:

> Netaji belonged to the entire nation, so we extend our appeal to you for your kind support in demanding from the Prime Minister that the Central Government must release in the public domain, all records to help unravel the mystery about his fate and bring a closure to the issue. It goes without saying that as long the Government of India continues to sit on secret records about Netaji's fate, it would not be able to take up the issue of secret records held by foreign governments.

> ...We are constrained to bring it to your notice because the Central Government's approach in this has been rather hostile. The report of the Mukherjee Commission, for instance, was dismissed by the UPA government without assigning any reason in the Action Taken Report tabled in Parliament. Such arbitrary dismissal of a report, concerning the fate of a man who was one of chief architects of the independence, reeked of deep-rooted aversion in the hearts of the members of the political party which never treated Netaji fairly.

Modi was attentive throughout his meeting with Chandra Bose, and he promised to do something. He expressed as much subsequently in private talks as more feelers were sent to him and Rajnath Singh from our side. On a promising note, after giving me considerable attention, Swami Ramdev assured me in August  2013 that he would take up the demand for declassification with the higher ups.

Throughout 2014, Mission Netaji and the Bose family, led by Chandra Bose and Abhijit Ray, continued to press for the release of the files. I made power point presentations in various parts of the country. In September-October, Jayanta Dutta Majumdar from Hong Kong worked out a visit for me to the island and subsequently to Singapore, where Diptasya Jash took over. Thus, Mission Netaji began shoring up support for our cause outside India.

SINDA auditorium, Little India, Singapore

As a result of many such lobbying efforts by us and the Bose family, the word went around. On 23 January 2014, then BJP president Rajnath Singh flew to Netaji's birthplace in Cuttack to make a solemn promise there that if the BJP was voted to power in the General Elections, the party would try and resolve the Netaji issue.

Courtesy: PTI

The message was hammered on Twitter by Singh on the same day.

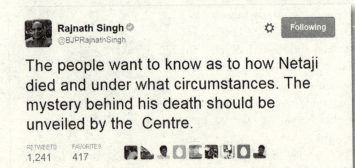

Rajnath Singh ✓
@BJPRajnathSingh

The people want to know as to how Netaji died and under what circumstances. The mystery behind his death should be unveiled by the Centre.

RETWEETS   FAVORITES
1,241   417

10:23 AM - 23 Jan 2014

As it happened, Rajnath Singh became the Minister of Home Affairs, the man officially in charge of the matters relating to the Bose mystery. But after coming to power, the BJP continued with the previous Congress line.

On day one of his taking over as Prime Minister, Narendra Modi's office received a letter from Mission Netaji seeking steps to resolve the mystery. We emphasised the need for declassification and drew the PM's attention to the Allahabad High Court's order regarding Bhagwanji. After considerable delay, we received a routine response from a section officer at the PMO intimating that our letter had been forwarded to the Home Ministry. It was what would have happened in the days of Congress.

I heard from a source that a review of the Bose files was undertaken by the Home Ministry soon after the BJP took over. The conclusions arrived at were the same as those before. Consequently, Rajnath Singh's evasive statements in Parliament as well as in private, began reflecting the new government's status quoist attitude.

We did not take all this kindly. On 23 January 2015, a mega rally was organised by Akhilesh Singh, the Rai Barelli MLA, in his home town. TMC Rajya Sabha Member Sukhendu Sekhar Ray, whose father had links to Netaji, Akhilesh Singh and I addressed a mammoth crowd of several lakhs—the biggest ever assembled in a rally organised in the name of Netaji and that too, in Congress supermo Sonia Gandhi's parliamentary constituency.

Rashtriya Sahara

On more than one occasion, Sukhendu Sekhar Ray—the only parlia-mentarian to be consistently raising the demand for declassification—tried to elicit a favourble response from the Home Minister, but couldn't. Feigning ignorance about a matter about which he must have figured out a lot after taking over, Singh began beating about the bush.

Finally, on 17 December 2014, he fielded his junior minister Haribhai Parathibhai Chaudhary in Rajya Sabha to respond to Ray's pointed questions. Chaudhary responded in the negative to Ray's query, whether the government was considering declassifying the Bose files.

Worse, the Home Ministry gave a misleading response to Ray's basic question—exactly 'how many files relating to…Bose are lying with government?' The MHA gave figures for only PMO (58); National Archives (4) and MEA (29), leaving out other ministries (including the MHA itself) and departments and, above all, the intelligence agencies. The Intelligence Bureau, for instance, has at least 77 files on or about Bose, going by their secret affidavit filed before the Mukherjee Commission. Isn't the IB part of Government of India? So why did the Home Ministry, which controls it, not give figure of its Netaji-related files in Parliament?

Even as it concealed the actual number of Bose files, the Ministry tried to take credit for something Mission Netaji was responsible for, as it was the fallout of the 5 July 2007 Central Information Commission full Bench decision favouring us. 'Files relating to both the [Khosla and Mukherjee] commissions have been sent by Ministry of Home Affairs to the National Archives of India (NAI) on 01.10.2012 for permanent retention', read the statement made by the Minister. What it did not say was that while some of the released files were formerly classified, most of them were of an 'unclassified' nature—routine papers of the Mukherjee and Khosla commissions, which were unlikely to interest anyone other than a handful of researchers. The valuable oral record of depositions by various witnesses before the Khosla Commission had earlier been obtained under the RTI act by Chandrachur from the Ministry after considerable efforts, and after spending his hard-earned money.

From the media's perspective, the main highlight of the Home Ministry's statement, was Rajnath Singh's tweet, that '2 Top Secret files have been declassified'.

Here too, there was more than that met the eye. The two formerly-secret files sent to the National Archives, were about the INA treasure. The one from the Ministry of External Affairs detailed how the burnt INA treasure, weighing about 11 kg or so, was brought to India in 1952 in a manner that could have easily inspired a plot in a Sean Connery James Bond flick in the 1960s. The original file had 67 pages, but what was sent to the archives had around 50. Which would mean the file was sanitised before being released in the public domain.

The other PMO file said on its cover that it was about Netaji's death. But inside there were only 6 pages concerning the re-opening of the INA treasure box in 1978 following Subramanian Swamy's sensational allegation that the treasure worth Rs 20 crore in that year containing 'gold and diamond ornaments' had been handed over to Jawaharlal Nehru. 'All these ornaments were subsequently melted in Allahabad and credited to Mr Jawaharlal Nehru's personal account', Swamy had charged. There was nothing in the two files to support Swamy's specific charge concerning Nehru, though much of what he said tallied with the official records.

In contrast to what was given out in a section of media, all the files sent to the National Archives had been declassified by the Manmohan Singh government, following the 2007 Central Information Commission directive in the RTI case involving Mission Netaji.

I was the first one to check many of the declassified records at the National Archives, thanks to the helpful staff. Junior and middle-level government officials on the whole treat Netaji with reverence, which the top bosses have denied him for decades. At the National Archives in Delhi in December 2014, I stumbled upon the copies of two West Bengal Intelligence Branch files detailing how Netaji's nephews, Amiya Nath Bose (father of Chandra Kumar Bose) and his younger brother Sisir Bose (father of Prof Sugata Bose), were snooped on for more than two decades by local sleuths at the behest of the Intelligence Bureau in New Delhi.

It was obvious that these Intelligence Branch papers had made it to the archive as a result of some oversight because their originals remained locked up in Kolkata. Even then, the Bengal government was not ready to share a list of the files held by it, leave alone sharing the full contents of the local intelligence files. But 'errors' do happen sometimes in large-scale declassification drives, involving the handling of thousands of documents. It happened a few years back in the US as copies of some sensitive CIA records concerning the 1971 India-Pakistan war were released by the State Department, even as the originals were regarded as secret at the agency.

All the same, thanks to the 'mistake' on the part of the MHA, events reminiscent of the Watergate scandal-era America came to my mind as I browsed through the papers at the archives.

Freedom fighters in their own right, Amiya and Sisir, one a barrister and another a famous paediatrician, died never knowing that files carrying their names had been kept by Director, Intelligence Branch, West Bengal.

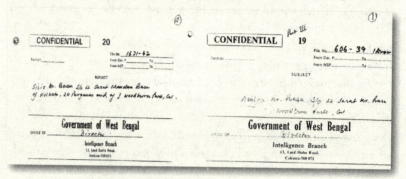

The files had been updated at regular intervals from the late 1940s to the 1960s—the heydays of democrats Jawaharlal Nehru and Dr BC Roy, chief minister of West Bengal from 1948 to 1962—as the brothers were subjected to continuance surveillance in what was India's most liberal city back then.

More shockingly, evidence coming from London showed that the fruit of the illegal surveillance mounted on Amiya at least was shared by the Intelligence Bureau with our former masters, who had been secretly allowed to maintain an MI5 office in New Delhi. Loyalty surely knows no bounds. This IB record (picture) originated from an MI5 file declassified in London in late 2014.

Back in Kolkata, the reports appended in the files were so meticulous, so neat and clean, and professionally

The National Archives, Kew

worked out as to be compared with reports generated by the MI5 or MI6 or even the CIA at that time. Put another way, when the *bhadraloks* in Bengal were regaled by the exploits of fictitious Byomkesh Bakshi out to crack petty crimes, real-life Intelligence Branch officers were performing feats that would have given the CIA agents a run for their money.

Just savour, for instance, the language and sophisticated appearance of the report dated 17 May 1948. SP Sinha, Esq, Dy Commissioner of Police, Security Control to HN Sircar, DIG, IB, CID: 'Would you please let me know if there is anything adverse on record in your office regarding the undermentioned person who has applied for passport facilities to UK, France, Switzerland, Turkey for the purpose of...'

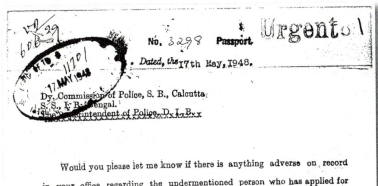

The National Archives, New Delhi

The copy of the response that 'there is no objection' was duly forwarded to RN Kao, Esq, Assistant Director, Intelligence Bureau. Yes, it was the legendary spook Rameshwar Nath Kao, R&AW's founder chief. His name figured in another 'Very Secret' record of an interception of Amiya's letter to Sisir in November 1949.

Copy forwarded to:-

1) R.N. Kao Esq., I.P.,
   Assistant Director(S), Intelligence Bureau,
   Ministry of Home Affairs, Govt. of India,
   New Delhi-3,

2) Sri B. Banarji, I.P.,
   Special Superintendent of Police, I.
   Intelligence Branch, West Bengal,

for information.

DEPUTY COMMISSIONER OF POLICE,
SPECIAL BRANCH, CALCUTTA.

Also coming in the picture was Kao's colleague in IB—MML Hooja, who became the Director, Intelligence Bureau in the late 1960s. Evidently, the shining lights of IB had been kept in the loop over such a seemingly innocuous matter involving two non-entities.

Appended in the Intelligence Branch files were numerous hand written records of telephone messages regarding the movements of Amiya.

'Amiya Nath Bose (SRP) arrived Howrah R/S ... on Puri Express at about 7.35.'

'Amiya Nath Bose left Sealdah Station....'

'Shri Amiya Nath Bose left Dum Dum airport by 1 AC line No 1 today.'

'Shri Amiya Nath Bose arrived here to-day from Bagdodara....'

'Shri Amiya Bose MP (FB) left Howrah R/S for Delhi to night (25.7.68) at 19.45 hrs by 1 UP Howrah Delhi Kalka Mail....'

The copy of a security control officer's report dated 6.10.57 seen here was a typed one:

A report dated 23 October 57 noted that Amiya 'has probably gone to Tokyo to collect materials for Netaji Research Bureau started at Netaji Bhawan'.

The National Archives, New Delhi

The file on Sisir Bose contained a fine example of the national intelligence grid in the good old days. This showed that surveillance on the Bose family members was not limited to Bengal.

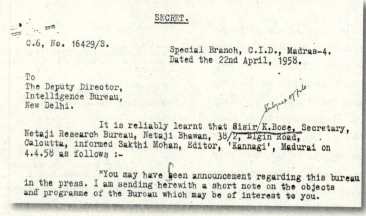

The National Archives, New Delhi

In fact, so thorough was the interception that letters from Emilie Schenkl to Sisir and his brothers' acquaintances in Japan, Europe and America— like historian and Netaji biographer Leonard Gordon—were opened, read, copied and kept on file. All of the letters that Sarat Bose sent to Amiya from abroad were read. A 1955 note by the intelligence department, on an intercept described Emilie as the 'alleged wife' of Bose, rather than widow. It was a giveaway that for the sleuths, Subhas Bose was still living.

Comment

    The addressee is evidently the alleged wife of Sri SUBHAS CHANDRA BOSE.

The National Archives, New Delhi

Some of the contents weren't to the likings of the spies. Writing to his aunt Emilie on 14 July 1955, Sisir, who had not yet been won over by the Congress party, made a snide remark: 'If you were in India today, you will get the feeling that in India's struggle, two men mattered—Gandhi and Nehru. The rest were just extras.'

And what Amiya wrote to an acquaintance in Germany on 7 December 1958 must have caused heartburns. 'Gandhi was not a saint', he wrote to Carl Vincent Krogmann, German banker, industrialist and former Nazi Party politician. 'He was an astute politician', Amiya wrote.

> Gandhi's theory of non-violence has practically no influence in India today. If India is attacked, she will be defended by her Army…Gandhi's movement of 'non-violent non-cooperation' did not bring independence to India. The movement he started in August 1942 was smashed by the British Government in a few months…the immediate cause of British withdrawal was the INA trial held in Red Fort.

A Top Secret report prepared towards the end of the 1960s betrayed the hostility of the sleuths, as if they were living in the Raj era: 'The subject [Sisir] took part in the reception which was accorded to Major General Chaterji of INA on his arrival…he delivered speeches praising Major General Chaterji for his selfless services to the country as a prominent leader of the INA and also demanded his release. He used to visit the office of the INA Relief Committee at Bowbazar.'

The report further recorded that in November 1965, Sisir visited Taipei and 'met Mr Sih Shon Heng, Director of European Dept, Ministry of Foreign Affairs and had discussions with him on a "very important subject"'.

Of course, Netaji figured heavily in the correspondence. The focus was him. What else would his family discuss? But what was the interest of the authorities in knowing what they did? An intercepted letter of Sisir revealed that he had written the following to Tatsue Hayashida in Tokyo on 17 August 1965:

'The Netaji Enquiry Committee (of 1956 that was set up by Nehru under public pressure) made a great mistake by not visiting Formosa and holding an investigation on the spot. This weakness of the investigation is obvious…'

> A secret information disclosed that Dr. SISIR K.BOSE, Exe cutive Director of this Bureau, Netaji Bhawan, Calcutta-20 requested TATSUO HAYASHIDA, T.Hayashida & Co., 26 21st Street, 3-Chome Harneshi, Fukuska, Japan to enlighten him on the following points in connection with NETAJI's death :-
>
> (1) When and by whom, was he informed of NETAJI's death :-
> (2) Did he see NETAJI in hospital?
> (3) Did he see NETAJI's dead body?
> (4) When was the cremation held and was he present at the Cremation?
> (5) Was he present at theCrematorium when the ashes were collected and what was the nature of the last remains which were put in the box now preserved at the Renkoji Temple in Tokyo?
>
> It was mentioned that the Netaji Enquiry Committee made a great mistake by not visiting Formosa and holding an investigation on the spot. Moreover there was no judicial person on the said Committee,
>
> FM.3028/65. R-1/43.

The National Archives, New Delhi

The remark had been underlined in the document, signifying its importance. Sisir hadn't joined the Congress party at this time around, and so his views about Netaji's disappearance were much like the rest of his family members.

That is why, Sisir's informing Hayashida (who was working on Netaji's biography) that as per a report 'the present Government in Formosa have documents in their possession showing that an air crash of the same description occurred in October 1944, but no such air crash took place in August 1945 (in which Bose had allegedly died)', was underlined. According to a Top Secret note prepared in 1968, when Jyoti Basu was West Bengal's home minister, the State committee of the Forward Bloc (the party Netaji had established) was miffed with Amiya because the 'subject

(Amiya) has been carrying on concerted propaganda…that the party has virtually become the stooge of the communists'.

In other words, spying on Amiya continued even after Basu, later regarded by Amiya's children as their well wisher, came to power and Amiya had become a Member of Parliament. On 12 June 1968 another report revealed that Amiya and Sisir had attended 'the meeting of the all Indian Jan Sangh leaders…on the proposed formation of a third front in West Bengal composed of non-Congress and anti-Communist forces'.

But why were the authorities so interested in knowing what the brothers did or were up to, especially with regard to Subhas Bose?

Intelligence agencies do not perform tasks of ghostbusters. They are not interested in dead people but those living, as their tasks pertain to tackling the present and future threats. In keeping an eye on the Bose brothers, who did not possess any significant political clout, the sleuths were actually keeping a tab on anything and everything related to Subhas Bose. Why would they do that unless they disbelieved the story of his death?

Wanting to get to the bottom of the spying saga, I filed an RTI application with the Intelligence Bureau. In addition to information relating to spying on the Bose family members, I sought copies of the following files, whose details I had managed to gather:

File Number	Subject	Contents
17/DG/83	Netaji Subhas Chandra Bose	A note on Hemandra Nath Pandit, journalist, Calcutta. He made a request to examine the contents of two suitcases of Subhas Chandra Bose
I/INA/D/60	INA personnel- General file	Correspondence with MEA on Netaji Research Bureau, Aims and objectives
25/DG/70	INA	Note on the issue 'Whether Netaji Subhas Bose is still alive or not' comments and views of different political parties
15/D/87(13)	Enquiry related to Subhas Chandra Bose	Regarding exploitation of Netaji's name by political leaders and others
I/INA/D/61(1)V	Papers released by a former JD	Notes on statements of general public on Netaji's death, formation of Shah Nawaz Committee

However, the IB curtly turned down my request, saying that it was exempted under the RTI from giving any information. Ignored was my submission that under clause 24(1) of the RTI Act, the exemption was not applicable in cases of 'allegations of corruption and human rights violations'.

Before that happened, Sandeep Unnithan's brilliant exposé on the spying case had made it to the cover of *India Today*. And thereafter, the issue was splashed across the media. For the first time in the history of India, the Netaji mystery matter became a top issue. It was all over print, electronic and social media.Sarat Bose's grandchildren Surya Kumar Bose, who met the Prime Minister in Germany, Abhijit Ray, Chandra Kumar Bose, and to an extent this writer, were thrown into national spotlight. Also joining the fray were leading commentators on strategic and security affairs, Major General (Retd) GD Bakshi and Colonel (Retd) RSN Singh, formerly of the R&AW.

I got the opportunity to take the Netaji mystery matter to the people of India through the discussions in the studios of *Aaj Tak, Headlines Today, NewsX, IBN7, India TV, NDTV* and *News24* among others. I also helped many correspondents to file stories, by providing contents and contacts. Because everyone wanted to do a show at the same time, I missed the chances to be on several shows anchored by top journalists. But I couldn't have missed for anything in the world being on 'The Newshour', India's most watched news show hosted by India's No 1 TV journalist. Arnab Goswami was good enough to describe me as the 'one man army' before an audience spanning 90-odd countries.

As a direct result of it all, government emissaries went into a damage control mode and started sending feelers to the Bose family. An idea was floated to take a select group to the Prime Minister for a meeting so that the declassification matter could be addressed. The Bose family was then approached to give a list of people to be included in that group.

At this point, certain members of the Bose family were so overwhelmed by the attention coming their way that they started objecting to including my name, and that of Chandrachur, in that list. They started to say that only the Bose family members should meet the PM. The consideration of gaining political mileage out of this sudden celebrityhood also lurked in the air. In one swoop, they forgot their own repeated statements that Netaji belonged to the entire country not just to his blood relatives. They also forgot that the attention coming their way was because of Mission Netaji. The very people who were once not even willing to approach 'communal' Modi now began vying for a photo opportunity, exclusively for them.

Anyhow, thanks to such massive boost by mainstream media, Mission Netaji's relevance increased manifold. A process was set in motion, which continues as of this writing. Its final consummation, we expect, would result in taking the demand for declassification of the Netaji files to such levels that the Government of India will find it impossible to ignore it.

Already, the demand is permeating across and outside India. On the foreign front, the Netaji Subhas Foundation, UK has taken the lead. In June 2015, the foundation's head Suhas Khale invited me give a series of lectures across the UK. Of these, the ones at the YMCA hall in London, Cambridge University and London Business School were sort of high point as even a year ago it was unimaginable to think that the Netaji mystery matter would be discussed at such exalted places. Thanks to Mrinal Chaudhury, a former Mayor of the London Borrow of Harrow and part of the foundation, I was feted by the current Mayor at a public function. This was the first time I was felicitated by any government authority anywhere. By the time I left the UK for India, Anirban Mukhopadhya, who had coordinated and worked out the UK programmes on behalf of the foundation, had been thinking of another 'INA', the International Netaji Association. In a good sign, my American tour kicks off in October 2015, thanks to NRIs Abhishek Bose, Saurav Das and Sudip Mukhopadhyay.

Within India, people are becoming increasingly interested in Mission Netaji. In Vadodara, Anand, Kashi, Lucknow, Silchar, Bangalore, Pune people turned up in good numbers and everywhere, the enthusiasm and feelings were the same. The media coverage was fabulous in Gujarat, in particular.

In Kashi, OP Kejeriwal, former information commissioner, historian and director of the Nehru Memorial Library, became first top-run historian to see merits in the Bhagwanji matter. In Silchar, thousands gathered to listen to Chandra Bose. In Bangalore, our talks were hosted by the Mythic Society.

The thrust in Lucknow, organised and executed by logician Adheer Som, proved to be more successful. Several members of the ruling Samajwadi Party, including personal friends of Chief Minister Akhilesh Yadav, attended a presentation made by Adheer and myself. Thanks to the interest shown by the influential lot present and wonderful coverage in *The Times of India* Lucknow edition and other media, the Chief Minister took note of the development.

On July 14, the *Times* reported that the UP government had decided to comply with the first part of the Allahabad High Court's 31 January 2013 order—to transfer Bhagwanji's belongings to a museum.

Fifteen

Some 528 years after he fell in the battle of Bosworth, Richard III was raised from his grave by archaeologists. The remains of the last English king to die in a battlefield were recovered in Leicester. The media the world over reported it in February 2013.

The quest for finding Richard's long-lost remains began twelve years earlier with screenwriter Philippa Langley reading a book. Wondering over Richard's fate, she then made it the mission of her life to locate his remains as her tribute to the much-maligned monarch.

Richard's non-descript grave was originally located near a church which got dismantled in the middle ages. It was last reported to be in the garden of a mansion that came up in the same area. This too had been demolished in the 1870s. By dint of intuition and hard work—devoted to researching, networking and raising funds—Langley found herself standing next to a car park.

A few months on, archaeologists were digging around the same spot and before long the skeleton of a man evidently killed in a battlefield was uncovered. The DNA obtained from the bones was then tested with the sample provided by a direct descendent of Richard's sister, a Canadian carpenter based in London. It matched. And the story broke.

So, why can't such a simple straightforward approach be applied to the Netaji mystery? Why can't we try DNA and other scientific tests on the presumptive remains of Netaji kept in Tokyo's Renkoji temple? Why can't our government heed the Allahabad High Court's order and find out the truth about Bhagwanji 'which does not seem to be difficult in view of recent scientific development?'

Anyone you meet has his own preset ideas, beliefs and notions regarding the fate of Subhas Bose. There is no problem with that. But when one's own thinking takes precedence over facts, it becomes a problem. 'I believe this' and 'I don't believe in that' as the focal of the discourse has kept the Netaji mystery more or less exactly where it was decades ago, despite there being great advancement in our understanding of it in recent years.

We are not living in the days of Jawaharlal Nehru or Indira Gandhi when things could be shoved under the carpet with considerable ease. The Modi government won't come in the way should the people demonstrate their determination to get the truth out. It's all about bringing a change in our mindset; media would just follow and other obstacles will be neutralised.

Obstructing the path to the truth are people masquerading as public-spirited personalities. They have, for last several decades, hoodwinked, confused and misled people, leading to the creation of a retrogressive environment in which the controversy surrounding the fate of one of the greatest Indians ever has just perpetuated rather than getting solved.

When the Mukherjee Commission was set up in 1999, leading historians and academics went hammer and tongs against its appointment without caring for the fact that it had happened not because of some whim of the then Atal Behari Vajpayee government, but because of an order from the Calcutta High Court.

Nowhere else in the world would you find academics speaking the language that was employed back then. Historian Salil Ghosh reckoned the new probe to be a 'sheer waste of time and money'. 'Government is playing a game to please the Bengali lobby', he theorised. 'At the end of the enquiry, the public should have the right to know about the money and time wasted', Ghosh told the *Indian Express*.

'Why don't we accept that the man is dead and that he died more than 50 years back?' Jawaharlal Nehru University's Harbans Mukhia asked. In Mukhia's progressive worldview 'the whole controversy stemmed from the "old-folk mentality" that great men do not die'. He prejudged the new inquiry as 'waste of time', and so did Delhi University historian Sumit Sarkar, who actually remarked that the 'subject is so boring and unimportant that I do not even feel like reacting to it'.

If Netaji mystery is boring, what is interesting? Research projects cleared by the Indian Council for Historical Research?

It is baffling that the setting up of the new commission was booed by the bulk of intellectuals and leading English newspapers of Bengal. The matter described as 'very sensitive and important' by the Internal Security Division director in a confidential April 2000 letter to a future head of R&AW, India's external intelligence agency, was rubbished by editorial writers. One contention that was repeatedly made pertained to the 'wastage of public money'.

It is noteworthy that every time something is making headlines in the media for its sensational or sleaze value, heaven and hell are moved for the sake of truth and justice. Recall the Bhanwari Devi murder case of 2012. This was about a woman who had disappeared after her extra-marital affair with a local minister became public knowledge. An inquiry was carried out in right earnest. The CBI sleuths actually went all over Rajasthan with a fine tooth comb and managed to dig out from a remote village, pieces of bones thought to be hers. These bones were then sent all the way to the United States, so that the FBI could find out if these indeed were of the missing woman.

Isn't it rather strange that when it comes to ascertaining the truth about Subhas Chandra Bose's fate, some people turn philosophical? 'What is the use of it now? What difference will it make? Why waste money? We are such a poor country! Let's care for the living rather than worry about someone dead. Let's forget about it all! No matter what you do, he is not going to come back alive now!'

But, pardon me, was the FBI going to bring Bhanwari Devi back to life? A question was asked a few years ago in Parliament by Daggubati Purandeswari, who later rose to become a minister in the Manmohan Singh government and has now joined the BJP. I don't know what made her put the bizarre question about the amount of money spent on the Mukherjee Commission's foreign visits. The UPA Government was ready with the details: UK, Rs 313,760; Japan, Rs 439,635; Taiwan, Rs 147,288; Russia, Rs 201,761.

Some will say this million odd rupees is a lot of money for a nation whose hunger and debt-ridden farmers commit suicide routinely. But that's not too much money when you consider the real wasteful expenditure of public money! I never came across anything to show that Purandeswari ever talked about massive scams to the tune of billions of rupees, especially in her home State. Or that she supported Swami Ramdev in his quest to bring black money home from foreign banks. To get into a cost-benefit analysis over the Netaji mystery is to sidestep the basic issue. Even a court case involving petty theft incurs costs many times over than the cost of stolen items. But that doesn't mean we will stop following the procedures. Justice has to be done no matter what the cost is. According to the figure released by the Delhi High Court in February 2015, the 12-year-old Nitish Katara murder case cost the State exchequer Rs 5.86 crore.

No one in their right senses would suggest that wheel of justice should be stopped from turning because it takes a lot of money to run it even as farmers are committing suicide. And has anyone suggested let's not inquire into the death of someone because inquiry won't bring them back to life? Please do excuse me if you find this a bit irreverent; I am merely giving my reaction to what many people opine privately. 'What is the use of inquiring about Netaji's fate? He is not coming back to us!' This abhorring approach has always been a big hurdle in cracking the mystery. There is nothing novel about this argument; it was being parroted in the 1950s and 1960s, when the case could have been cracked with relative ease.

Writing in 1965, Satyanarayan Sinha, someone who had raised his voice then, recalled how he had to confront the oft-repeated query: What is the use of your reviving Netaji affairs if he is not returning to us in any case?

Although I don't share many of his views, I find myself in complete accord with Sinha's counter statement that 'such questions amount to an expression of betrayal' of Bose. 'Posterity will never forgive us for such criminal negligence of a national hero of the highest order'.

Of course, many years have passed since Sinha said this, but don't some cases take a very long time to resolve? Do we brush them under the carpet? In October 2010, *The Times of India* reported how '40 years later', an ex-IG was found guilty of gunning down a Naxal in a fake encounter case. This case involving a former Inspector General of Police in Kerala 'took a decisive turn' when a cop admitted to having shot the Naxal 28 years earlier on the orders of the DIG in question. 'Following this, human rights activists sought reopening of the case....'

OutlookIndia.com further reported the judge's observations as he delivered the verdict:

> Truth by its very nature does not yield to be kept hidden for ever. Truth, which has been hitherto hidden as covered by the glitter of golden plate, has by now, though belatedly, been discovered. Truth triumphs; truth alone. ....The offence of custodial murder, be it of an extremist, terrorist or Naxalite, in the hands of the police whose duty is to produce him before a court for trial, does not get wiped off merely by efflux of time, be it decades... cannot be justified in a society like ours....

In no compassionate society would the issue of such magnitude and consequence as that of the fate of 'Prince among the Patriots', as Gandhiji called Netaji in 1942, be forgotten just because a few decades have gone by.

The United States continues to make efforts to locate the remains of its soldiers lost decades ago. *The Washington Post* reported on 6 June 2012 how 'India agreed...to allow American military teams to search the Himalayan mountains for the remains of hundreds of US service members who went missing during World War II'. US Defense Secretary Leon Panetta was reported as saying that 'this is a humanitarian gesture by a government with whom we share so many values'. 'The ability to return heroes to their loved ones is something that America deeply, deeply appreciates.'

What you will not appreciate is that in March 2002, the Ministry of External Affairs turned down the Mukherjee Commission's request to seek classified records regarding Netaji's fate from the US government, saying that such records 'can be requisitioned under the US Freedom of Information Act only by giving specific details of the documents; and...this is a tardy and complicated process'.

The biggest complication was lack of intention. A little later, sitting in Delhi, I located two classified Central Intelligence Agency (CIA) records. I was eventually able to secure their release from the agency, which accepted appeal made in the name of Netaji's admirers world over, including those in America.

In 2012, some Japanese dead soldiers were exhumed from their graves in India for repatriation to their homeland. Researchers have continued to dig into the causes of Napolean's death—whether he was poisoned or not—and new findings about how Egyptian pharaohs died thousands of years ago have made news the world over, including in India. And yet we have researchers and journalists, historians and politicians telling us in India that there is no need to discuss the Bose issue, which is 'boring and unimportant'.

British writer William Dalrymple rightly said that 'Indians feel that freedom of speech is for journalism' only. 'But freedom of speech is not only about present, it should permeate into all layers of life. You should be able to talk about Shivaji and his poor administration, and Subhas Bose and debate whether he is still alive', he told *The Hindu* on 6 November 2006.

The 'posterity' Satyanarayan Sinha referred to is 'us'. Our generation is best placed to settle the matter that those before us could not. And those who will come after us would have little or no connect with the past relevant to this issue. So if we fail to act now, the next chance might come in the shape of some momentous moment—some gracious act of declassification by a foreign country—in the distant future. And I am not sure how many of us would be there to witness that moment of truth.

The reasons for settling the controversy about Netaji's fate aren't limited to the principles of justice and transparency. It is also about the gratitude that people of India should be displaying for a man, but for whom they would not have attained freedom from the colonial rule.

The official propaganda so far has been that independence came about solely due to the non-violence movement led by Mahatma Gandhi. It has been immortalised in a famous 1950s Bollywood song—*De di hame aazadi bina khadag bina dhal. Sabarmati ke sant tune kar diya kamaal.* Speaking on Doordarshan on 23 January 2015 Major General GD Bakshi (Retd) observed that this idea constituted a gross insult to those freedom fighters who did not subscribe to Gandhi's fetish for ahimsa.

While there is no denying that Gandhiji did wonders for the freedom struggle, from all accounts available now it stands established that—borrowing a term from the cricket arena—'the man of the match' of the Indian freedom struggle was Subhas Bose.

'Mass movements by the Congress between 1920 when Gandhi arrived on the scene and 1947 were niggardly, and hardly upset the British', wrote former R&AW official Colonel RSN Singh on Sify.com on 24 April 2015.

In 1942, Gandhi launched the Quit India movement. The view from Bose's side was that it was his suggestion in 1939 to serve a six-month's ultimatum on the British government which was accepted by Gandhi in totality in his Quit India resolution of August 1942. Prior to this, Gandhi was, as Bose himself stated repeatedly, most reluctant to launch a movement. This is what he wrote in his book *Indian Struggle*.

> On 6 September (1939), Mahatma Gandhi, after meeting the Viceroy, Lord Linlithgow, issued a press statement saying that in spite of the differences between India and Britain on the question of Indian independence, India should cooperate with Britain in her hour of danger. This statement came as a bombshell to the Indian people, who since 1927 had been taught by the Congress leaders to regard the next war as a unique opportunity for winning freedom.

All the same, the Quit India movement was launched in good earnest. Bose praised Gandhi's stirring speech as he launched it. But, the movement 'failed to galvanise India', reasoned Colonel Singh, for 'those arrayed against it included the Viceroy's Council (majority Indians), Jinnah (Muslim League), Communist Party of India (who supported only when Russia entered war), and the Princely States'.

> Immediately, the entire top leadership of Congress was taken into custody. Leaderless and rudderless, the movement died in a year's time, but the Congress leaders remained in prison till the rest of the war. This served

the interest of the British and as well as the reputation, prestige and political prestige of Congress leaders.

Putting it more bluntly was late author-journalist Khushwant Singh. He said the movement was 'crushed within three weeks'. Singh was far from being an admirer of Bose.

'It was during this period, when the Congress leaders were ineffective, that Subhas Chandra Bose was exerting himself for India's independence', Colonel Singh wrote.

The failure of 1942 gave such a blow to the Congress party that the All Indian Congress Committee, which met in September 1945, saw no hope for independence at that time. 'Neither the end of the War nor the change of Government in Britain appears to have resulted in any real change in British policy towards India', an AICC resolution noted. Such was the level of frustration that according to then Congress president Abul Kalam Azad, 'the majority, including Gandhiji...held that we must devote ourselves to exclusive construction work. They believed that there was not much hope on the political plane'.

Throwing light on the dull Indian political scene at that time, British historian Michael Edwardes wrote: 'The mass of the people was once again indifferent. There was nothing to hand to which popular indignation could be excited, no Jallianwalla Bagh nor anything remotely resembling it.'

Congress leaders had no political programme at hand to infuse new life in the dormant freedom struggle. Before they could take up the case for the general amnesty of those imprisoned since 1942, the authorities released all of them, depriving the Congress of an issue it could agitate about.

This was the backdrop against which the Congress geared up to go to the general elections in the winter of 1945-1946, as announced by the new Labour Government as a precursor to reaching an agreement about the question of India's freedom. The British were insisting on substantial agreement between the Congress and the Muslim League before considering giving independence. The World War had greatly affected the British capacity to rule India further.

The Congress election manifesto would go on to articulate that 'in this elections, petty issues do not count nor do individual or sectarian cries— only one thing counts: the freedom and independence of our motherland'.

The 'sectarian' jibe was against the Muslim League, bent on partitioning India on religious lines. The Congress was all for secularism in contradiction of League's claim that it alone had the right to represent the Muslims of India.

At that time that the Red Fort trials commenced against the INA soldiers—Hindus, Sikhs and Muslims.

It made all the sense for the Congress party to make the best of this opportunity, handed out on a platter. By September, the censorship had been lifted and the

INA saga was becoming known to the people of India for the first time. The nationalist press had also dismissed the war time propaganda that the INA-Japanese win would have made India a colony of Japan.

Thanks to records declassified by the UK Government, we now have an inside view of why Congress leaders came around to backing Netaji's INA, even though violence had no place in their world. Mahatma Gandhi was still of the opinion that India 'shall be able to win freedom only through the principles the Congress has adopted for the past 30 years'.

On 23 October 1945, Brigadier TW Boyace of Military Intelligence sent a damning secret report to the Secretary of State for India in London. To understand the Congress gameplan, the MI had used a mole of theirs. Capt Hari Badhwar had first joined the INA, then switched sides and finally gave evidence against the INA men during the Red Fort trials.

Sourcing his information to Asaf Ali, a leading Congress Working Committee member, Capt Badhwar reported that before taking a stand on the INA issue, the Congress high command had sent Ali out on a recce mission to gauge public feeling. He travelled across India and discovered that people were overwhelmingly in support of the INA. 'This inflamed feeling forced Congress to take the line it did', Badhwar told his handler.

In his free-wheeling talks with Badhwar, Asaf Ali, free India's first Ambassador to the United States, offered the information that 'Congress leaders had realised that those who joined the INA were far from innocent', and that's why Nehru always made it a point to refer to them as 'misguided men', even in his public speeches. Ali was positive that as and when Congress came to power, they 'would have no hesitation in removing all INA (men) from the Services and even in putting some of them on trial'.

Badhwar, who would led a comfortable life in free India as a General, asked Ali why couldn't the Congress 'repudiate their championship of the INA' when they knew 'the true facts?' Asaf Ali had replied that 'they dare not take this line as they would lose much ground in the country'.

Boyace's comment at the end of his note was: 'In other words, the present policy [to back the INA] is one of political expediency.'

These facts belie the fantasy interpretation of history, fed to us over the decades by loyal Congressmen and their cronies in historical and intellectual circles. PR Dasmunshi wrote in *The Pioneer* in January 2006 that 'Pandit Nehru, notwithstanding his political differences with Netaji, saluted the historical march of the INA and came forward to defend it...as a lawyer in the Red Fort trials'. In August that year, while defending his rejection of the Mukherjee Commission report, his Cabinet colleague Shivraj Patil proclaimed in Parliament that Nehru had 'donned the black coat and gown and went to the Red Fort to defend' the INA men.

Netaji's nephew Dwijendra Nath Bose, during his appearance before the Khosla Commission in August 1972, gave an angry rejoinder. He accused Gandhi and other Congress leaders of 'rubbing their noses on the floor' before the British and washing their hands off the Quit India movement after it turned violent. 'This is not our movement. This is all violence going on. You have put us in jail before the movement was started', Dwijendra taunted.

Dwijindra, who had been tortured in jail during the freedom movement, was not impressed with the argument that Nehru had set aside all past acrimony to defend the INA soldiers during the Red Fort trials.

Do you understand the word *namavali*, which means the words 'Hare Krishna Hare Rama' are printed on clothing worn by Brahmins? So, Panditji thought it proper to wear that *namavali* of INA to cross the river of election.

Several records in the Transfer of Power series released in the 1970s by the British government show that the Congress leadership's defence of the INA was motivated by a desire to excel in the elections of 1946. Commander-in-Chief of British Indian armed forces, General Claude Auchinleck wrote to Field Marshal Viscount Wavell on 24 November 1945 that 'the present INA trials are agitating all sections of Indian public opinion deeply and have also provided the Congress with an excellent election cry'. Similarly, Wavell was informed by Sir M Hallett of the United Provinces on 19 November 1945 that 'the publicity on this subject (INA trials) has been a useful gift to political parties, especially the Congress, in their electioneering campaign'. The Governor of present-day Uttar Pradesh wrote to the Viceroy the same month that those hitting the streets were actually suggesting that 'Bose is rapidly usurping the place held by Gandhi in popular esteem'.

It was the 'failed' INA military onslaught and the Red Fort trials of 1945-46, and not the 'peaceful' Quit India movement which majorly impacted the British decision to quit India. The colonial British regarded Bose as their sworn enemy. No top Congressman of the 'peace loving' variant fell in that category. Major General FS Tucker, GOC Eastern Command, thought Bose was a 'plump Bengali' of 'over-weening personal ambition' and like everyone else, demanded a 'condign punishment for the INA'.

But in the face of public anger and much in their own interest, the colonial rulers had to backtrack. India was sitting on a tinderbox. Viceroy Wavell received a letter from the United Province in November 1945. It read that

> handwritten leaflets are said to have been found in a hotel that if any INA soldier were killed, Britishers would be murdered. These may be rather petty matters, but they do show which way the wind is blowing.

No one knew India's internal situation better in those days than the Director, Intelligence Bureau. Sir Norman Smith noted in a secret report of November 1945, which was declassified in the 1970s: 'The situation in respect of the Indian National Army is one which warrants disquiet. There has seldom been a matter which has attracted so much Indian public interest and, it is safe to say, sympathy... the threat to the security of the Indian Army is one which it would be unwise to ignore.'

On 12 February 1946, Commander-in-Chief General Claude Auchinleck was forced to explain to his top military commanders through a 'Strictly Personal and Secret' letter the reasons why the military had to let the INA 'war criminals' and 'traitors' get off the hook:

> Having considered all the evidence and appreciated to the best of my ability the general trend of Indian public opinion, and of the feeling in the Indian Army, I have no doubt at all that to have confirmed the sentence of imprisonment solely on the charge of 'waging war against the King' would have had disastrous results, in that it would have probably precipitated a violent outbreak throughout the country, and have created active and widespread disaffection in the Army, especially amongst the Indian officers and the more highly educated rank and file.

The nationalist fervour in the country had reached such levels by that time as to drown differences between the Hindus and the Muslims. Violence had broken out in many States. *The New York Times* reported on 17 February 1946:

> In spite of the uncompromising struggle between the two factions, last week for the first time since 1921, Moslems and Hindus together staged street protests and riot against the British in Calcutta, Bombay and New Delhi. The catalytic agent in this case was the Indian National Army, organized by a Japanese collaborator named Subhas Chandra Bose....

An editorial in *The Times of India* further elaborated this on 26 February:

> As a result of the extravagant glorification of the INA following the Red
> Fort trials in Delhi, there was released throughout India a flood of comment
> which had inevitable sequel in mutinies and alarming outbreaks of civil
> violence in Calcutta, Bombay, Delhi and elsewhere....

At the same time in London, a number of perceptive British MPs met
Prime Minister Clement Attlee to give their frank reading of the situation.
'There are two alternative ways of meeting this common desire (a) that we
should arrange to get out, (b) that we should wait to be driven out. In regard
to (b), the loyalty of the Indian Army is open to question; the INA have
become national heroes...'

In the words of KK Ghosh, who was the first to write an authoritative
and comprehensive account of the INA in 1960s, 'the revolutionary
condition in the country created by the INA trial contributed largely to the
naval mutiny', which proved to be the last straw that broke the camel's back.
The mutiny, Ghosh added, 'frightened Congress leadership' and that's why
the party 'withdrew its support' to it.

All those who had a ringside view of the situation agreed that the INA
played a pivotal role in making India free. In a no-holds-barred interview in
February 1955 with BBC's Francis Watson, Bhimrao Ambedkar wondered,
'I don't know how Mr Attlee suddenly agreed to give India independence'.

'That is a secret that he will disclose in his autobiography. None expected
that he would do that', he added.

In October 1956, two months before Ambedkar passed away, Clement
Attlee himself disclosed in a confidential private talk that very secret. It
would take two decades before PB Chakravarty, Chief Justice of Calcutta
High Court and acting Governor of West Bengal, would muster courage to
tell the public what the former British PM had told him in the Governor's
mansion in Kolkata in 1956:

> Toward the end of our discussion I asked Attlee what was the extent
> of Gandhi's influence upon the British decision to quit India. Hearing this
> question, Attlee's lips became twisted in a sarcastic smile as he slowly chewed
> out the word, 'm-i-n-i-m-a-l'!

Babasaheb would not have been surprised with Sir Attlee's admission
that Bose's struggle had to do with his decision to free India for he had
foreseen it. He told the BBC that from his 'own analysis' he had concluded
what convinced the Labour party to take the decision to free India:

> The national army that was raised by Subhas Chandra Bose. The British
> had been ruling the country in the firm belief that whatever may happen in

the country or whatever the politicians do, they will never be able to change the loyalty of soldiers. That was one prop on which they were carrying on the administration. And that was completely dashed to pieces.

British historian Michael Edwardes would put it dramatically in his 1964 book *The Last Years of British India:*

> It slowly dawned upon the government of India that the backbone of the British rule, the Indian Army, might now no longer be trustworthy. The ghost of Subhas Bose, like Hamlet's father, walked the battlements of the Red Fort (where the INA soldiers were being tried), and his suddenly amplified figure overawed the conference that was to lead to Independence.

Some thirty years after independence, Lt Gen SK Sinha came out with another inside story in an op-ed article in the *Statesman* newspaper. The would-be Assam and J&K Governor, as a young captain along with fellow Lt Col Sam Manekshaw and Maj Yahya Khan,were the only natives posted to the hitherto exclusively British Directorate of Military Operations in 1946.

'The real impact of the INA was felt more after the war than during the war', Sinha agreed, adding: 'There was considerable sympathy for the INA within the Army. ...I am convinced that well over 90 per cent of officers at that time felt along those lines.'

> In 1946, I accidentally came across a very interesting document... prepared by the Director of Military Intelligence. It was classified document marked 'Top Secret. Not for Indian Eyes.' ...The paper referred to the INA, the mutinies at Bombay and Jabalpur and also to the 'adverse' effect on the Indian officers and men of the humiliating defeats inflicted by the Japanese on the white nations in the early days of the war. The conclusion reached was that the Indian Army could no longer be relied upon to remain a loyal instrument for maintaining British rule over India.

Lastly, this is as official as it gets. In striking contrast to the interpretations of all those who cannot see beyond the Gandhi-Nehru combine, National Security Advisor and former legendary IB chief Ajit Doval, probably the best person to make such an assessment, echoed the same view as others in a talk which is freely available on YouTube.

'The British understood that the revolt in the Indian Army was something that they couldn't handle', summarised Doval, son of an Army officer himself.

Sixteen

In March 2015, Markendya Katju, former Supreme Court judge and ex-chairman of the Press Council of India, created a controversy by his irreverent comments against Netaji. 'Subhas Chandra Bose was a Japanese agent', he blustered.

As for his reasons for alleging so, he marshaled the following argument:

> If the Japanese had been victorious against the British, do you seriously think they would have granted independence to India? No, they would have made India a Japanese colony, and ruthlessly exploited and looted it.

Justice Katju's rant was symptomatic of fairly widespread misconceptions many Indians came to conceive as a result of psy-war unleashed by the colonial British during the Second World War. Such was its impact that even top leaders fell for it. On 15 May 1942, Mahatma Gandhi was reported to have said that while he appreciated that Bose 'risked so much for us', 'but if he means to set up a Government in India under the Japanese, he will be resisted by us'. Nehru, on the other hand, made several infuriating statements publicly.

At a press conference in New Delhi on 12 April 1942, Nehru said, 'It is a slave's sentiment, a slave's way of thinking to imagine that to get rid of one person who is dominating us, we can expect another person to help us and not dominate later. Free man ought not to think that way'. Nehru also said he 'would oppose and fight Subhas Bose to death'.

> **"WE SHALL FACE ALL DANGERS AS MEN"**
>
> **Nehru's Stirring Speech At Calcutta Meeting**
>
> NO CHOICE BETWEEN IMPERIALISM, FASCISM OR NAZISM
>
> People Asked To Follow The Example Of China
>
> " LET us be brave and take courage from the example of China and face any aggressor or any fascist who thinks in terms of subjecting India or dictating India," observed Pandit Jawaharlal Nehru while addressing a vast gathering at Sraddhananda Park, Calcutta, yesterday evening (Friday).
> They had always been saying, Pandit Nehru pointed out, that they did not want either British Imperialism, Fascism or Nazism. Let them not commit the error that they had fallen into in the past, by thinking that they could ask for the aid of any other Power outside. Therein lay danger; therein lay peril; and if any of them thought in those terms, it was not any kind of courage, it was a sign of cowardice.
>
> Hindustan Standard

And because in free India hardly anyone did anything to counter this propaganda, its ill-effects continue to this date. Perpetuation of such falsehood has a bearing on the Bose mystery issue as it attempts at tarnishing Netaji's unmatched contributions in making India free and, therefore, weakening the demand to settle the issue of his fate.

In a sense, for those opposed to Netaji, there is only one stick to beat his legacy with. Finding faults with his 'collaborating' with the evil Axis powers—Nazi Germany and Imperial Japan.

Such instances of criticism and sniggering are usually come from those who think that they are conscience-keepers of the world and that India, the nation of Buddha, Gandhi and Nehru, is somehow morally superior to the other nations of the world. The approach is pretty simple: Go and occupy a high moral ground, and then take selective pot-shots from up there.

We must not apply a different yardstick when it comes to Netaji, who was not an ambassador for world peace like India's first Prime Minister. Nehru's desire to get a Nobel Peace Prize was nevertheless not fulfilled despite all that he did for world peace. Bose was merely the leader of an oppressed nation whose first, foremost and the only priority in those days was to shake off the colonial rule before pretending to shed tears on the woes of people elsewhere on the globe.

But if one is going to view Netaji's activities through morality's tinted glasses, it would be hypocritical not to put under scanner how India has followed the Apostle of Peace since 1947.

On 16 November 2014, Prime Minister Narendra Modi unveiled Mahatma Gandhi's statue in Brisbane, Australia. According to a report carried in *The Economic Times*, 'exhorting the world to heed Mahatma Gandhi's advice to tackle terrorism,' the PM said at the venue that 'Mahatma's teachings of non-violence and love are as relevant in our times as it was during his lifetime'.

Inspired by long-standing well-propagated worldview of our government that India stands dedicated to peace, I did some reading. It turned out that there are relevant passages in the *Mahatma Gandhi Collected Works*—the most authoritative and exhaustive collection of Gandhi's writings compiled and published by our government. As with numerous other issues, Gandhiji did have a clear idea how free India's national security doctrine should be. For instance, he opined in 1932 that 'India's defence lies in the cultivation of friendly relations with her neighbours and her ability to resist, through nonviolent non-cooperation, her exploitation by any nation. The first act of a National Government should be to disband this menace (Indian Army)....' In November 1947 Gandhiji had said: 'Peace in Asia depends on India and China. These two countries are large. And if they build their edifices on the foundation of *ahimsa* they will become known among the great countries of the world.'

The same month, his attention was drawn to the following statement of Major General KM Cariappa: 'Non-violence is of no use under the present circumstances in India, and only a strong army can make India one of the greatest nations in the world.'

Gandhiji's response to this was:

> I make bold to say that in this age of the atom bomb, unadulterated non-violence is the only force that can confound all the tricks put together of violence. ...Generals greater than General Cariappa have been wise and humble enough frankly to make the admission that they can have no right to speak of the possibilities of the force of ahimsa.

In January 1949, Cariappa was appointed as the first Indian Commander-in-Chief of the Indian Army. It was General (later Field Marshal) Cariappa who had led the Indian forces during the Indo-Pakistan War of 1947. His statement in 1947 was made during that war and in its context.

As it happened, on 3 December 1947 Cariappa had met Gandhiji to seek his counsel. 'Pakistan will not heed my word, but if you, the Generals of the army of the Indian Union listen to me and help me, I shall believe we have truly gained freedom in a non-violent way', he was told.

Cariappa then made this pointed query: 'Pakistan has no use for non-violence. How then can we win their hearts and prove the efficacy of ahimsa?'

Gandhiji replied:

> Violence can only be overcome through non-violence. This is as clear to me as the proposition that two and two make four. But for this one must have faith. **Even a weapon like atom bomb when used against non-violence will prove ineffective.** ...And if Pakistan does not stop violence, the violent killings can still be stopped if Hindus in the Union have faith in non-violence.
> [Emphasis mine]

Baffled, the General began to fumble for words.

'If we have to have an army at all...it must be a good...Tell me, please, how I can put this over, ie. the spirit of non-violence to the troops?'

'I am still groping in the dark for the answer', Gandhiji said, claiming that 'even Lord Wavell and Lord Mountbatten, both veteran professional soldiers, had expressed their implicit faith in the value of non-violence'.

> They both hoped that our ideologies of non-violence and pacifism would be understood by the peoples of the world and practised by all in solving international disputes.

On 18 January 1948, before taking over charge of the Delhi and East Punjab Command executing operations in J&K, Cariappa again met Gandhiji. He was blessed with these words: 'I hope you will succeed in solving the Kashmir problem non-violently.'

While the majority of peace loving people of India under the leadership of Congress leaders understood and imbibed these high ideals, hotheads and renegades such as Subhas Chandra Bose held an opposite view. Writing to his elder brother Sarat in 1940, Subhas expressed his outrage over Gandhi's fetish for ahimsa even in the realm of national security. 'Gandhism will land free India in a ditch—if free India is sought to be rebuilt on Gandhian, non-violent principles. India will then be offering a standing invitation to all predatory powers', he asserted presciently.

Perhaps wanting to make free India on hallowed non-violent principles, Prime Minister Jawaharlal Nehru is said to have harboured a pathological dislike for the armed forces. What such an attitude on his part eventually led to was succinctly summed up by Major General Bakshi in *The Sunday Guradian* on 15 November 2014: '[Nehru] set about emasculating the military leadership, starving the military of resources and set in train the tragic events that would bring about the humiliation of 1962.'

Seen from the Gandhian periscope, in the last few decades, especially after 1962, India has done everything that Gandhiji abhorred. We continue to resort to violence to settle disputes with Pakistan, and we have amassed a massive stockpile of nuclear weapons. For most Indians, the catchphrase 'Buddha is smiling' denotes the blasting of our first nuclear device in 1974. Sitting under Mahatma Gandhi's portrait in the South Block, our successive defence ministers have turned India into the biggest importer of weapons in the world.

If indeed we want to preach to the world that it should heed 'Mahatma's teachings of non-violence and love', we should demonstrate it by practicing it first. Gandhiji used to set examples for others to follow. If indeed 'non-violence is the greatest force at the disposal of mankind' and that 'it is mightier than the mightiest weapon of destruction devised by the ingenuity of man', as Gandhi said, why can't free India employ it against those inimical to her? Has there ever been a dearth of Gandhiji's true followers in free India? Why did we then go nuclear? Why did we not follow the model of Japan Self-Defense Forces for our armed forces and set an ideal for the rest of the world to follow? Why is India itching to join the United Nation Security Council, when we can teach the entire world about the potency of ahimsa in resolving all sorts of crises?

In our imperfect world, pontificating sanctimoniously about how things should be suits only saints and preachers. When politicians venture out to say something along those lines, it is mostly for the purpose of making headlines.

A German pointed out to me that before he joined the Axis, Bose had opposed Nehru's idea that the European Jews could be given sanctuary in India. I submitted that most Indians of that time couldn't think of anything else except their own emancipation. Bose was as much humane and enlightened as any other Cambridge alumni like him. Between 1933 and 1939, for example, he had for friends Kitty and Alex, a sensitive, newly-married Jewish couple in Berlin. Before they met, Kitty had heard an American priest in Berlin calling Bose a 'traitor to the British government'. But in their first meeting, he came across to her as a 'mystic, a spiritual man'. In their last meeting, he told her to 'leave this country soon'.

The couple went to the US and from her Massachusetts home, Kitty Kurti wrote her tribute for 'Netaji'. She reminisced in her 1965 book *Subhas Chandra Bose As I Knew Him* about the various issues they had discussed. Kitty noted that Bose 'did not attempt to hide' from her his deep contempt for the Nazis. In the same vein, he cited India's exploitation by British imperialism and explained why he had to do business with the Nazis. 'It is dreadful but it must be done. ...India must gain her independence, cost what it may', he told the couple after a meeting with Hermann Göring. Of Jews, Bose said, 'they are an old and fine race' gifted with 'depth and insight' and felt that they had been 'miserably persecuted' across the centuries.

It was India's interest that mattered to Bose foremost. Nehru's idea about bringing European Jews to poverty-stricken India was airy and unworkable. So long as Nehru and his family ruled India, I told the German, Israel was not allowed to open its embassy in New Delhi. According to an old Indian saying, an elephant has two sets of teeth. One is for the purpose of eating and the other for flaunting.

All nations pursue nothing but their national interests. Explaining this in the summer of 1990 was Nelson Mandela. In the New York City neighbourhood of Harlem, Mandela was interacting for the first time with American people in a meeting anchored by journalist Ted Koppel. Mandela was bombarded with questions about his dealing with world leaders not approved by America.

Diplomat and political writer Kenneth Adelman commented that 'those of us who share your struggle for human rights against apartheid have been somewhat disappointed by the models of human rights that you have held up since being released from jail'. Then he put this query. 'You've met over the past six months three times with Yasser Arafat, whom you have praised. You have told Gaddafi that you share the view and applaud him on his record of human rights in his drive for freedom and peace around the world; and you have praised Fidel Castro as a leader of human rights and said that Cuba was one of the countries that's head and shoulders above all other countries in human rights, in spite of the fact that documents of the United Nations and elsewhere show that Cuba's one of the worst. I was just wondering, are these your models of leaders of human rights, and if so would you want a Gaddafi or an Arafat or a Castro to be a future president of South Africa?'

In response, Mandela asserted the following amid standing ovation from the audience:

> One of the mistakes which some political analysts make is to think their enemies should be our enemies. Our attitude towards any country is determined by the attitude of that country to our struggle. Yasser Arafat, Colonel Gaddafi [and] Fidel Castro support our struggle to the hilt. There is no reason whatsoever why we should have any hesitation about hailing their commitment to human rights as they're being demanded in South Africa... They do not support [the anti-apartheid struggle] only in rhetoric; they are placing resources at our disposal for us to win the struggle. That is the position.

No country places her interests after those of the rest of the mankind. In fact, in the pursuit of national interest, nations and leaders would go to the extent of shaking hands even with the devil. It is for the reason of larger national interests that the United States, the land of free, is friends not only with regressive Saudi Arabia, but also Pakistan, which harboured its enemy No 1, Osama Bin Laden.

It was this very reason Subhas Chandra shook hands with Adolf Hitler and, if you please, Indira Gandhi with Saddam Hussein.

While the Western nations regarded him a devil at par with Hitler, for India Saddam was a friend. Iraq did not denounce but support India's right to possess nuclear bombs during the Vajpayee days. Over the Jammu & Kashmir issue, Iraq did not support Pakistan but stood by India. The world's greatest democracy, a long-standing ally of the country whose citizens cried publicly the day Bin Laden was killed, did not come around to appreciating India's position till the horrific 9/11 attacks.

For all his evil deeds and the Holocaust, Hitler was not responsible for the deaths of any Indians. I personally am pro-West in my outlook and would never ever contemplate placing the UK or the US in the same league as Nazi Germany. But it is a plain fact of history that Great Britain, for all her goodness, was not willing to free India even as she and the United States waged war against Hitler in the name of liberty.

It was not Hitler but the British Prime Minister Winston Churchill, I am sorry to write, who hated Indians from every pore on his skin. It was Churchill, not Hitler, who made racist, offensive comments about Indians that made even his fellow Britons wince in disgust.

In his outstanding book, *Britain, America and the Politics of Secret Service,* noted British historian Richard Aldrich writes that despite the full backing of the Indian troops in the Allied efforts against Nazi Germany, the British PM did not trust the Indian Army. He thought of it as an 'army that might shoot us in the back' and therefore a 'huge security problem'. Leo Amery, the Secretary of State for India and Burma, noted that Churchill had a 'curious hatred of India'. Churchill's own private secretary recorded that 'the Hindus were a foul race' who were 'protected by their mere pullation from the doom that is their due'. He wished that the head of British bomber command could 'send some of his surplus bombers to destroy them'.

In recent years, considerable data has emerged from the British archives to show Churchill was responsible for millions of deaths in the 1943 Bengal famine. Madhusree Mukerjee, physicist and former editor of *Scientific American*, after years of research, wrote *Churchill's Secret War: The British Empire And The Ravaging Of India During World War II*. In an interview with the *Outlook* Magazine in September 2010, Mukerjee summarised her findings. She held Churchill responsible for 'deliberately deciding to let Indians starve'. 'Churchill contributed to the famine by removing the shipping from the Indian Ocean area in January 1943', as Japanese threatened the Empire. 'At that point, it was just callousness (on Churchill's part). It was basically preserving Britain at all cost, even at the cost of Indian lives', she underlined.

A counter-argument to this would be that Hitler was directly responsible for the ghastly gassing of millions of innocent Jews. Yes he was, but when Bose met Hitler, those gas chambers had not gone into operation. The Holocaust began after Bose had reached Japan, and he had no clue about it. The world discovered the horrors of Holocaust only after the war ended.

Actually, according to a news item published in the leading Israeli daily *Haaretz*, Prime Minister Benjamin Netanyahu after visiting Auschwitz (former Nazi death camp in Poland) remarked the following on 13 June 2013: 'The Allied leaders knew about the Holocaust as it was happening. They understood perfectly what was taking place in the death camps. They were asked to act, they could have acted, and they did not.'

Subhas Chandra Bose's reaching out to Germany was in continuation of the long-standing connection between Germany and Indian patriots in the national interests of their respective countries. Girija Mookerjee, who was with Netaji in Germany in between 1941-43, would explain later that 'even Imperial Germany during the World War I had taken up the cause of Indian independence and the German Foreign Office had, therefore, a precedent to go by'.

> Men who weighed this question at the German Foreign Office were men of career, who were neither National Socialists nor did they belong to the inner coteries of Hitler. They were German civil servants who performed their duties as good German citizens during the war. These men, guided by the desire to advance German national interests in India, thought it advisable for political reasons to support the movement sponsored by Netaji in Germany.

Many of the stalwarts who backed Gandhi against Bose in the late 1930s weren't the peaceniks they pretended to be. When they and their followers were running India years later, brute state force and streaming inputs from the Intelligence Bureau and not hallowed Gandhian principles saw India through. Goa was not liberated through satyagraha. Rebellious Mizos weren't sent emissaries from Gandhidham; they got pounded from the Indian Air Force fighter planes. 'We attach great value to individual freedom,' reads a Nehru quote on a web portal launched by the Ministry of Culture in November 2014. The words seems hollow as we look at secret as well as declassified records concerning spying on those linked to Bose. On 26 November 1957, the so-called champion of democracy sought

Document obtained in public interest

to find out surreptitiously what a nephew of Netaji was up to during his visit to Japan.

I dare any Indian worth his name, still wanting to raise an accusatory finger at Netaji for his reaching out to Hitler, to apply their holier-than-thou outlook on free India's conduct and come up with similar snap judgments.

- Since 1947, New Delhi has extended a friendly hand to all sorts of dictators and tyrants. The list includes Libyan leader Muammar Gaddafi and Robert Mugabe of Zimbabwe, the latter ranked # 1 in the Forbes' list of world's top dictators in 2011.

- It is not Aung San Suu Kyi, the winner of the Nobel Peace Prize and the Jawaharlal Nehru Award, but the Burmese junta that has received most support from the land of Gandhi.

- Ignoring street protests of scores of average Indians and prominent leaders, India actively backed and even assisted militarily the Mahinda Rajapaksa regime as it was being accused of carrying out war crimes against the Tamils.

- Pervez Musharraf, directly responsible for the deaths of so many Indians, including the soldiers we lost during the Kargil war, was given a ceremonial Guard of Honour by the Indian armed forces upon his arrival in India in 2001 for a start. If this was a triumph of Indian diplomacy, how come Bose's reaching out to Hitler, who had not caused even a single Indian death, became a cause to beat one's chest in the name of morality?

This listing is merely illustrative; one can go on and on. If at all India's intelligence agencies were subjected to scrutiny, it would emerge that most of what they have been doing (in national interest in my personal staunch belief) is in direct contravention of what the Father of Nation preached.

To get back to the points raised by Justice Katju, unknown to him and all those who share his outdated opinion, there is considerable data on record by way of statements of those who mattered, official records and sworn testimonies to prove that all his assumptions about Bose and his benefactor Japan were not correct. Here are the posers as Katju would put them, and their answers:

What was the nature of Japan-Bose relations?

In 1972, Bose's military secretary Colonel Mahboob Ahmed, then a senior Ministry of External Affairs official, in his deposition before the Khosla Commission stated the following:

> There was a great deal of respect for Netaji for his personality, for his person, amongst the Japanese that we came across and his relation with the Japanese government was that of the two interests at that stage coinciding. That is to get the British out of India.

Was Bose a Japanese stooge?

The National Archive in Melbourne, Australia, has a file on Bose made up of formerly secret German-Japanese diplomatic communication intercepted by the Australian Navy. On 30 July 1943, Japanese Ambassador Hiroshi Oshima sent this account of his telling Adolf Hitler about Bose:

> The Japanese government too, has absolute faith in him and is giving him carte blanche where India is concerned.

```
      Speaking of Bose, I said: 'It was good of you to
think of sending Bose to East Asia.  We thank you very
much.  As you have already read in the newspapers, after
reaching Japan he went to Singapore where he is re-
organising an Indian Army of Liberation.  He is working
hard on plans to bring India into line.  The Japanese
Government too, has absolute faith in him and is giving
him carte blanche where India is concerned.'
      Hitler answered: 'Yes, I am very satisfied with
what Bose is doing.'
      I told him that the submarine the Germans had given
us had already reached one of our bases in the South
Seas, and expressed great gratitude.  I then went on to
say: 'The Japanese Navy just wired my Naval Attache that
those new bullets you ordered not long ago will reach you
by the earliest convenience and plenty of them at that.
As for the new warship you wanted, the Japanese Navy has
informed Naval Attache Wenneker that it has been especially
arranged to let you have it.  We are not going to let the
Italians or anybody else know about that.  I just wanted
you to know about it.'
      Hitler answered: 'Thank you very much for that
kindness.  In this war we also want to co-operate in those
technical matters.  I do not mean to say that my army's
equipment is inferior to your, we do not need to compare
them, but if there is any service we can do for you in
this respect, please let me know.'
      I answered: 'Thank you very much.'"
```

TOP   SECRET

Carte blanche is a French word meaning 'complete freedom to do something'. And what it meant at the ground level was explained in a reported titled 'INA's role in Imphal battle' filed in *The Hindu* on 10 December 1945. During the Red Fort trials of the INA men and their Japanese benefactors, General Tadasu Katakura, Chief of the Japanese staff of Burma Area Army, testified that 'though INA troops had come [to be under] overall Japanese command, they…had their own operational assignment'.

Was Japan interested in conquering India?

In a paper on Bose, eminent historian TR Sareen, who otherwise supports the air crash theory, observed after studying the British records that it was just a myth propagated by the colonial British to enlist support of the Indian political parties during the war. 'Interrogation of Japanese high officials confirmed that they had never contemplated the conquest of India.' Late Barun Sengupta, eminent journalist and a fighter for democracy during the Emergency, had a point when he said that if the Japanese had no respect for Bose, why was he tailed by their senior generals? 'How often during the liberation war of Bangladesh, our Lt Gen JS Arora was moving about with the acting president of Bangladesh…or their prime minister?' he asked.

In the Red Fort trial, the defence counsel called five Japanese witnesses who had been closely involved with the INA. Ota Saburo of the Japanese Foreign Ministry produced documentary evidence that Japan recognised the free and independent status of Netaji's government. Mastumoto Shun'ichi, Vice-Minister of Foreign Affairs and chief of the Treaty Bureau during the war, testified that the Japanese Government had helped Bose and the INA for two reasons: to promote Japan's own war aims and also to help India achieve independence, which was one of Japan's war aims. Lieutenant General Tadasu Katakura testified that that the Japanese Army never used the INA soldiers as labourers.

Lt General Iwaichi Fujiwara, co-founder of the INA, told the Khosla Commission on oath in 1972 that 'Netaji was highly respected by Japanese people'. In 1956 when Shah Nawaz committee went to Japan, it was noted that 'Netaji's name was still a household word in Japan, and a great deal of interest was taken about him both by the public and the Press.' Japan had a terrible record with the Koreans, the Chinese and others during the World War II, but not with the Indians—especially after Netaji's arrival in South East Asia. That's why many in Japanese establishment think of their wartime association with the INA as a bright spot. Even the Ministry of External Affairs in New Delhi came to hold the view that 'India as the country of origin of Buddhism and Netaji and INA's association with Japan during the war also invoke friendly feelings among a section of the Japanese society'.

This factor is one of the reasons for the current bonding between Japan and India. In September 2014, Saichiro Misumi, a war veteran, Indologist and former executive director of Japan-India Association, became symbol of that bonhomie. A picture of his with Prime Minister Narendra Modi kneeling down to listen to the old man

became viral after it was tweeted by MEA spokesperson Syed Akbaruddin.

On 30 March 2015, Misumi (99) was conferred the Padma Bhushan at the Rashtrapati Bhawan 'in recognition of his contribution to India-Japan relations for almost seven decades', according to a release from the Indian Embassy in Tokyo.

I clearly remember there was a story in the media that Netaji 'wanted ruthless dictatorship in India for 20 years'!

It was in *The Times of India* on 19 April 2015. It appeared soon after the spying scandal came to light. Interestingly, the story was tweeted by @withCongress and further retweeted/favourited by official Twitter handles of Maharashtra Pradesh Congress Committee, Chhattisgarh Pradesh Congress Committee, Secretary

Assam Pradesh Youth Congress Committee and the Rahul Gandhi Mission.

Taken out of context, anything can be made to look suspicious. If the writer of the story had dug deeper, he would have found out that Bose had also used this term for Gandhi, many a time. He wrote in his book *The Indian Struggle* that Gandhi wanted him to be 'a puppet President'. And, Gandhiji had used the term dictator for himself during the Khilafat days—because unquestionable obedience to one was a prerequisite to taking on a powerful enemy. All the Congress leaders fell in line.

Anyhow, what concerned me more was the manner in which a free thinking journalist should have dismissed as mere 'allegations' the snooping revelations based on proper, legally tenable, verifiable documentation available at the national archives in New Delhi and London.

These 'allegations', the writer went on to hallucinate in his report, were being used by 'conspiracy theorists and spin doctors... to push their agenda—

that Netaji was a greater patriot than Pandit Nehru'. Then an attempt was made by him to demonstrate that Nehru, being an anti-Nazi, was actually a greater patriot than Bose who was pro-Nazi. 'Bose's admirers conveniently ignore his Faustian treaty with Nazi Germany and the Empire of Japan', we were reminded.

But isn't it true that the Japanese during the WWII showed barbarity against Indians? There have even been reports of their cannibalizing Indian POWs.

In a series of articles written in 2014-15, the same *The Times of India* correspondent glorified as 'fallen heroes' and 'martyrs' the Indian mercenaries because of whose betrayal the British Empire thrived in India for so long. An outrageous story in the series was titled 'Japanese ate Indian PoWs, used them as live targets in WWII' (TOI, 11 August 2014).

It opened with a reference to an April 1946 story from a *Reuters* correspondent in Melbourne, Australia, alleging that in the ongoing war crimes trial one Japanese lieutenant had been 'found guilty of the murder of 14 Indian soldiers and of cannibalism at Wewak (New Guinea) in 1944'.

Then the *TOI* correspondent felt compelled to reject what he thought was 'the nationalist narrative' which 'has long projected the Second World War as a clash between the patriots of the Indian National Army (INA), supported by the Japanese Empire, and the evil British Empire'. He referred to 'the refusal of many [British Indian Army soldiers] who were taken prisoner to renege on their oaths of loyalty in the face of extreme torture also showed remarkable bravery'.

The article went on to cite several graphic illustrations of war crimes committed against the Indian POWs by the Japanese forces. 'The most spine-chilling of all Japanese atrocities was their practice of cannibalism,' the article said. 'One of the first to level charges of cannibalism against the Japanese was Jemadar Abdul Latif of 4/9 Jat Regiment of the Indian Army, Latif's charges were buttressed by Captain RU Pirzai and Subedar Dr Gurcharan Singh.'

For source of information were cited WWII era reports published in the *Times of India*, which in those days ran British propaganda on account of its foreign ownership, statementsof Indian soldiers loyal to the colonial British and supporting statements of an Australian and a UK-based Indian historian, and that of a Japanese historian who had dug out records in Australia giving the Allied point of view regarding the charges of war crimes by his country in the WWII.

Essentially what was done in the article was to take a selective look at the issue of war crimes. Only those allegedly perpetrated by the Japanese were highlighted and the mercenaries of British Indian army painted as victims and heroes, which they were not from Indian point of view.

The issue of war crimes is a rather complex one. Approached selectively, one could use the available data to show any country that went to war in a poor light. For instance, the first in the following picture combo was published in the American *Life* Magazine on 22 May 1944. It shows a girl gazing at a skull of a Japanese soldier sent to her from New Guinea by her boyfriend serving in the Pacific. The other image shows a Japanese soldier's severed head hung on a tree branch. Americans were outraged when they came to know about such details.

There is no civilised way to go to war unfortunately. War crimes, excesses, torture, violation of human rights are reported in all wars and conflicts. Even in our enlightened times we saw what some among the world's most professional armed forces did in Iraq. Remember those shocking images from Abu Ghraib? But the conduct of some Americans in Iraq in no way meant that the entire American army had carried out or backed these brutal acts. Those were instances of deviations by a few. Indians do not blame all English men for what few colonial rulers did in India. I personally do not even think that majority of them were evil; I think that the British rule in India had several positive points and there were innumerable heroes among the British who came to India.

But if one is going to treat as gospel reports published in war time and claims of those who have reasons to be biased, I am afraid the same approach can be employed to portray just about any country negatively. Countless motivated reports in world and Indian media about the so-called human rights abuses allegedly carried out by the Indian security forces in J&K and elsewhere in our times. There are people in India who would disregard the 27 December 2013 statement issued by the Indian Army (with which I fully agree) that 'more than 90 percent of the allegations of human rights violation complaints filed against it in J&K and the northeastern States have been found to be false'.

Such allegations have been made with regard to past events as well. In an interview carried on the *TOI* edit page on 27 December 2013, Sarmila

Bose, a senior research fellow at Oxford University and writer of a book on the 1971 Bangladesh war, refused to hail the Indian intervention as heroic. 'What constitutes a "just war" can be a contested issue. India acted in its own strategic interests. The public discourse is a continuation of wartime partisan propaganda and nationalist myth-making by all sides', the paper quoted her as saying. Sarmila Bose is the daughter of late Sisir Bose and a die-hard supporter of the air crash theory of Netaji's death.

Both the nationalist as well as official narrative since in 1947 in India has cast Japanese in a bad light, so the *TOI* story's claim about either being pro-INA is not accurate. INA men were not considered to be patriots in free India and were therefore kept out of the Indian Army. And all those who served the British Empire with distinction and defended it were retained in the armed forces and awarded. This is the official view till date.

As reported in the *Hindu* on 30 November 2013, President Pranab Mukherjee, Supreme Commander of the Armed Force, after visiting the Kohima War Memorial, honouring the British soldiers and their Indian lackeys who fought the INA-Japanese army soldiers, said that he 'was honoured' to have visited the cemetery 'built on the very site where hundreds of gallant British and Indian soldiers fought and achieved martyrdom'. According to a *Times* report, he wrote this in the visitor's book: 'There is no mistaking the meaning, significance and enormity of this hallowed site where lie the mortal remains of those who distinguished themselves through their acts of conspicuous gallantry and intrepidity at the risk of life above and beyond the call of duty.'

On 16 March 2015, Prime Minister Modi visited an exhibition commemorating World War I and said that he was touched to meet the descendants of some of the decorated soldiers. He went on to tweet: 'We salute the sacrifice of each and every Indian soldier martyred in the war.'

No President, Prime Minister or even Army chief has ever visited the INA War Memorial in Moirang, leave alone made such heartfelt tributes to the INA and their Japanese comrades.

While I do not have information about Jemadar Abdul Latif and others referred to the in the *TOI* article, I do have some about others of his ilk. These details demonstrate that the claims of such votaries of the British Raj were unreliable. In the first place, it must be asked what Latif and other Indian mercenary soldiers were doing in SE Asia in mid-1940s? Were they part of some UN peace keeping force, or were they doing some work to make India free?

As Gandhiji himself agreed, the very *raison d'être* of British Indian Army was 'to hold India in subjugation'. 'It has been completely segregated from the general population who can in no sense regard it as their own,' he pressed. 'Every Indian child knows that that British Army is there, including the Indian Army, for the defence of British interests.'

The mercenaries of British Indian Army, including my own grandfather, clashed with the Japanese not for their duty towards India but to protect the British Raj, for which they were handsomely paid. If the Japanese killed some of them, I'd say, in the context of Indian freedom struggle, that it served them well. I'd rather shed tears on those patriots who died while fighting for the nation and those thousands of Japanese who died fighting on their side. Never forget that General Dyer only gave an order, it were the men of Indian Army who fired upon their own people at Jallianwalla Bagh.

After the Second World War got over, many British Indian Army men, including those who had joined INA, supplied 'evidence' against the INA men and the Japanese for their alleged 'war crimes'. I don't deny that the war crimes did not happen. I simply refuse to believe that every such claim, as the one reported in the *Times* story, was gospel, or that only the Japanese indulged in war crimes.

And what about the crimes perpetrated against the INA men? *The Journal of the United Service Institution* (Vol. CXXXIV) in April-June 2004 carried an interview of Pratap Singh, an INA veteran, with Lieutenant Commander Neeraj Malhotra. In his 80s, penniless and frustrated, Singh recalled his harsh experiences. How in 1945 they were brought to Delhi and how those compatriots of his accused of serious charges were 'segregated'— 'never heard or seen again'. He recalled that a 'team' was used to 'pull out such soldiers and take them to Red Fort—from where no one returned'.

On walking distance from *The Times of India* office in New Delhi is the historic Red Fort. Linked to the fort by two arched bridges are the ruins of the Salimgarh fortress. It was used as a prison by the Mughals and the British. Anyone who has grown up in Delhi as I have would know that it was here that the INA men were incarcerated and, in some instances, tortured.

Recalling his experience in his 1998 memoirs *From my bones* was INA veteran and Red Fort Trials hero Colonel Gurbaksh Singh Dhillon. He referred to the fate of Major Maghar Singh and Major Ajmer Singh of the INA secret service. 'When they felt that they might not be able to keep the secret under daily torture, they planned to snatch a guard's rifle one night and committed suicide.'

It is a matter of common belief in Delhi that the ghosts of forgotten INA martyrs continue to wander in the Salimgarh prison cells. I distinctly remember having read it for the first time in the *Indian Express*. Guards posted at Salimgarh report hearing groans and rustlings of iron shackles at night.

Since no one in free India bothered to carry out elaborate research into such charges, they were never documented the way Japanese excesses were. Otherwise, contemporary newspaper reports, like the following published in Indian-owned, nationalist *Hindustan Times* in late 1945, were littered with many such allegations:

On the other hand, the National Archives in New Delhi has several war-era records wherein one can see how trumped-up charges of war crimes against the INA men were sought to be established, by the testimonies of the votaries of the colonial rulers.

MANY I.N.A. MEN ALREADY EXECUTED

MYSTERY OF 1,900 I.N.A. MEN'S FATE

A pre-1947 Ministry of Defence file shows that top INA men were branded 'war criminals' on the basis of shady testimonies of the loyalists.

WAR CRIMINALS.

Those responsible for , condoned or took part in atrocities against Indian Ps.O.W.

	I.A. Rank.	Name.	Unit.	Category.	Witnesses.
	Captain	MOHAN SINGH	1/14 Punjab	I.N.A.	)
	Lieut.	MOHD ZAMAN KIANI	"	"	)
(a)	Major	AZIZ AHMED	Kapurthala S.F.	Ex-I.N.A.	) Any loyal K.C.I.O. or I.C.O.
	Major	PRAKASH CHAND	R.I.A.S.C.	"	)
	Lt-Col	A.C. CHATTERJEE	40 I.G.H., I.M.S.	"	)
		S.C. ALAGAPPAN	12 I.G.H., I.M.S.	"	)
	Capt.	B.M. PATTANAYAK	att 2/1 G.R., I.M.S.		)
	Naik	SURJA SINGH	I.A.O.C.	Changi Guard.	) Capt H.C. BADHWAR (3 Cav)
	Lieut	ABDUL RASHID	1/14 Punjab	I.N.A.	) Any loyal K.C.I.O. or I.C.O.
(a)	Sub	SHANGARA SINGH	5/14 Punjab	I.N.A.	) Lt-Col P.C. DUTTA (40 Fd Amb, I.M.S.)
(a)	Jem	FATEH KHAN	5/14 Punjab	I.N.A.	) Hav Maj NUR KHAN (4/22 Mtn Regt)

Mohan Singh was the INA founder, Mohammed Zaman Kiani was the INA head after Bose, AC Chatterjee [Chatterji] and SC Alagppan were Azad Hind Government ministers. The list even counted as 'war criminals' GS Dhillon and Mahboob Ahmed, Bose's military secretary and later a senior MEA official; 'plus complete staffs of all INA concentration camps'.

In more than one case, the 'witness' to 'war crimes' was certain Capt HC Badhwar, a Military Intelligence mole whose activities have been described in the previous chapter. In free India, this mole led a comfortable, respectable life as a general.

For what Japan did for India, I'd rather go with the words of patriots. Dhillon praised the British and the Australians where it was due and truthfully recorded how the Japanese were mistreated in India.

> Yet another episode occurred after midnight when four Japanese POWs were brought and pushed into a cell next to my cell. On arrival they were beaten and cursed.... Whenever the Japanese movements got slack, they were beaten and cursed in filthiest words. Their tortured continued throughout the

night. The Japanese conducted themselves with dignity and bore up under each blow so bravely that neither a worn nor a moan ever escaped their being.

'I remain under a debt of gratitude to them forever,' he said of the Japanese.

Captain SS Yadav, general secretary of now defunct INA veterans' association, provided an explanation in a letter which now appears as an inscription in Tokyo's Yasukini Shrine for Japan's war dead:

> We India National Army soldiers express our deepest respect to the Japan empire army soldiers who fought together with us and sacrificed their lives in the battle field of Kohima to liberate India. We people of India, perpetually for generations to come, will never forget our gratitude to the brave Japanese soldiers who sacrificed their lives for the great cause of liberating India. We console the spirits of these valiant warriors and wish their happiness in Heaven.

Eminent lawyer PN Lekhi in his message for the shrine stated that 'Indian people will never forget the debt of gratitude towards Japanese'.

Seventeen

Of all the national leaders, Subramanian Swamy is the only one to have been consistently espousing the cause of Subhas Chandra Bose. Much before he exposed the telecom scam, Swamy flagged before the nation the mystery surrounding the missing INA treasure. Then, through a letter to Prime Minister Morarji Desai, Swamy sought a probe into the matter in view of information available to him that Jawaharlal Nehru had something to do with the missing war chest of Subhas Bose.

This was in 1978—much before this writer was able to access classified documents con-cerning the loot of the INA treasure and discuss the matter threadbare in *India's Biggest Cover-up* (2012).

After the declassification issue raised by Mission Netaji picked up steam, Swamy lost no time in articulating his views. He backed

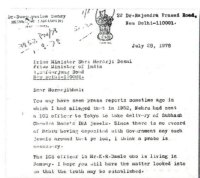

the demand and as I understood after speaking with him, he raised it with Prime Minister Narendra Modi as well.

In that respect, I hold Swamy in high esteem and welcome his intervention, which is in national interest. All the same, in view of the evidence on record, I am constrained to disagree with Swamy's repeated statements that Netaji was killed in Soviet Russia, on Russian dictator Joseph Stalin's orders, issued at the behest of Jawaharlal Nehru.

God forbid it should be true! But, considering Swamy's eminence and popularity, these allegations have been turning into media headlines and creating quite a flutter on the social media. I am often asked to reflect on the same.

Addressing media in Kolkata on 10 January 2015, Swamy repeated the killing charge. According to a report published on the online version of *The Times of India*, Swamy 'admitted that disclosing the secret files might jeopardise India's relation with Britain and Russia'.

> According to the papers that exist with us, Bose had faked his death and escaped to Manchuria in China which was under Russian occupation, hoping Russia would look after him. But Stalin put him in a jail in Siberia. Somewhere around 1953, he hanged or suffocated Bose to death.

'The mystery of Bose's disappearance must be solved and the files must be declassified. Because it was Bose's heroics that played a catalytic role in the British leaving India despite winning the World War', he remarked for good measure.

Addressing a gathering of RSS workers in Gurgaon the next day, Swamy said that he'd make some important disclosure in Meerut on 23rd January, Netaji's 118th birth anniversary.

In Meerut, Swamy dropped what he considered a bombshell. Citing his 'own research' in the matter, he said that 'Stalin wrote a letter to Nehru in December 1945 that Bose was in his custody and asked Nehru what he should do with Bose. Nehru, after receiving the letter, immediately summoned his stenographer Sham Lal Jain [of Meerut] on December 26, 1945 and dictated a letter meant for the then British PM'.

Swamy said that 'Jain had stated these facts before the Khosla Commission, set up in 1970 to investigate the mystery behind Bose's death'.

The Times of India further reported:

> Swamy said as per Jain's version, Nehru had told the British PM that he had received information that Bose was in a jail in Soviet Union. 'In my opinion, soon after that British officials reached the Soviet Union and ensured Bose was put to death.'

As he made known his views about the Russian angle in the Bose mystery, Swamy rubbished the Bhagwanji angle out of hand. He said it was a mere red herring planted by the Intelligence Bureau.

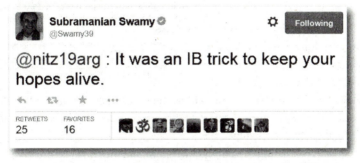

To a sophisticated mind, Swamy's charge about Stalin killing Netaji, coupled with the Home Ministry's assertion in 2006 that disclosure of certain Top Secret records relating to Netaji's fate would 'lead to a serious law and order problem in the country, especially in West Bengal' would seem plausible. In such an earth-shattering scenario, it would be absolutely valid to fear anoutbreak of violence across India, especially in Bengal, where admirers of Joseph Stalin, Jawaharlal Nehru and Mahatma Gandhi outnumber those of Subhas Bose.

It may seem incredible to people residing in other parts of the country, but there are ardent admirers of Pandit Nehru and Gandhiji in Netaji's family also. When the snooping saga became a national rage, the wife and son of late Sisir Bose, one of the subjects under surveillance of IB, sprang to the defence of Nehru. Krishna Bose wrote an article in the *Anandabazar Patrika,* giving Nehru a clean chit, ignoring the facts. Her son Sugata made statements on the same line.

Earlier, in his book *His Majesty's Opponent* Sugata had proudly enclosed his picture with the nation's first Prime Minister. One wonders if it is 'Nehru

Research Bureau' that this section of the Bose family is actually running! Sugata Bose got elected to Lok Sabha using to the hilt his blood relation with Netaji, but in Parliament he has thus far asked not one question relating to Bose. In fact, in very second question he expressed apprehensions about the condition of the Mahatma Gandhi papers kept at the National Archives, even though it is well known fact that the Government of India throws public money around to perpetuate the Gandhian myth.

In July 2012, for instance, India stopped an auction at Sotheby's in London and bought for an unimaginable price a collection of letters between Gandhi and a friend, allegedly containing a whiff of scandal.

All the same, for all his genuine admiration for Netaji and the long-standing desire to know the truth, Swamy has got it all wrong. In fact the very premise he cites in favour of his charge does not back it actually. So much so, that it can be used to turn his theory on its head and instead, use it to support the Bhagwanji angle.

Indian government spends £700,000 to buy letters which 'prove national hero Gandhi was gay'

- Letters between Mahatma Gandhi and Hermann Kallenbach are said to shed light on their 'loving relationship'
- They are among archive of documents which cover Gandhi's time in South Africa, his return to India and his contentious relationship with his family

Swamy is missing a vital point. Stalin did not like Nehru and had therefore no reason to order the 'killing' of Bose who had evidently sought an asylum in Russia. Returning to India in 2000 from Russia, researchers from the Asiatic Society recounted the opportunity they had had in Moscow to study hitherto unseen Soviet files. 'Among the papers was one where Joseph Stalin reportedly described Jawaharlal Nehru as a "political prostitute". It was felt that the papers would embarrass the Left in India and the pro-Left Asiatic Society authorities', *The Statesman* quoted them saying on 21 August 2000 in a story titled 'Slur on Nehru ensures Stalinian end to study'.

Juxtapose this to the contents of the letter Russian scholar Victor Touradjev traced in the KGB archive in the early the 1990s. The letter had been written by Bose on 20 November 1944 to Yakov Malik, the Soviet Ambassador in Tokyo.

Bose began without any frills: 'I am seeking help of the Soviet Government through you to fulfill the task of our freedom struggle to free India.'

The second para was an explanation of his position in the Axis bloc, and the fact that he did so for Indian freedom. He stressed that his INA waged war against the Allies but not the USSR:

'The German Government has also understood and appreciated the fact that we are not interested to go against Soviet Russia. Certainly, the activities of my organisations in Europe have generated an exclusive impression that we are only against the Anglo-American bloc and not against the Soviet Russia. This was the understanding of cooperation between the Axis power and our organisation in Europe.'

Fourth para of the letter contained a much needed dash of emotion: 'I have always been encouraged by the fact that Lenin in his time always, from the core of his heart, extended support to the countries which were struggling against colonial rule. So far I understand, the Soviet attitude to the problems of the oppressed nations like India has not been changed after his death.'

Bose also stressed that his pro-USSR outlook was not new: 'As to my party—Forward Bloc, I can say that when the Soviet Foreign policy had been condemned by almost all the political parties of India in 1939-1940, ours was the only party which had openly supported the Soviet Foreign policy in relation to Germany and Finland.'

For every one person that Stalin dispatched to their end, there were several he did not harm. There was a method to his madness. There was nothing he stood to gain by having a friendly asylum-seeker killed to please someone he simply abhorred.

The mantelpiece of Swamy's evidence, that is the charge made by Sham Lal Jain, has been widely known and believed by many for decades. If a daily of the standing of *Hindustan Times* could report them favourably in the year 2000, one can imagine how indelibly itched they would be on the minds of a large section of people.

Jain's story was that in 1946 he was serving as a steno to Asaf Ali, secretary of the INA Defence Committee fighting to secure the release of the INA prisoners. He claimed that in December that year, he was summoned to Ali's residence by Pandit Nehru. The rest of the account, as reported in the *Hindustan Times* in 2000, is:

> Jain alleged that Pandit Nehru had asked him [to] make typed copies of a handwritten note that said Bose had reached Russia via Diren [in Manchuria]. He also alleged that Pandit Nehru asked him to type a letter to British Prime Minister Clement Attlee that 'Bose, your war criminal, has been allowed to enter Russian territory by Stalin. This is a clear treachery and betrayal of faith by the Russians, as Russia has been an ally of the British-Americas. Please take note of it and do what you consider proper and fit.

Having gone through the nearly 100-page long testimony of Sham Lal Jain as it appears in the record of the oral proceedings of Khosla Commission, I do not think that on its own this testimony is worthy of much credence.

The reason why Jain's account has became so well known is that Samar Guha, in his 1978 book *Netaji: Dead or Alive* carried a short edited portion of it. The excerpts from the book have been available on the Internet for years. Guha himself believed that Bhagwanji was Bose and all his efforts were motivated by a desire to tell the people of India what he knew.

That little detail aside, Jain's version as it really was and as it has been amplified by Swamy has a missing chunk. Not only did Jain not support the theory that Bose was killed in Soviet Russia, he actually believed that he was alive at the time Jain deposed before the Khosla Commission on 4 January 1971. The focus of Jain's testimony was that Bose was alive and in India. The following image shows a part from the record of his deposition before GD Khosla:

```
Chairman:  Did you have any further contact with Netaji after
           this, or have you heard anything more about him?
Witness:   No, Sir, I heard nothing.  But my belief is that he
           is alive.
Chairman:  Last time that he visited was 7-10-67.
```

In other words, Swamy's assertion is based on his erroneous reading of Jain's statement.

Swamy has a further argument to make. He stated on *NewsX*, in my presence, that he became convinced of Jain's statement after he came across some official records supporting it during the short-lived Chandrashekar government, in which he was a Cabinet Minister.

In fact, Swamy had dwelt into this aspect earlier in 2006 by way of a press release, whose relevant portion reads:

> When Chandrashekhar's Janata government was in office, the Cabinet Committee on Political Affairs [of which I was member as Minister], had considered the Japanese request to send the ashes back to India but after reviewing the files we decided to reject it. This was because the Cabinet papers contained a record of a deposition by a stenographer of Prime Minister Nehru stating that in December 1946 long after the alleged crash of Netaji's plane, he had taken down a letter dictated by Nehru addressed to Britain's Prime Minister Attlee complaining that Joseph Stalin was keeping Netaji in a camp in eastern USSR, and that Britain had to do something since Netaji 'is your war criminal'. This stenographer had deposed before the Khosla Commission but Justice Khosla ignored the evidence.

Insofar as the role of Chandrashekhar's government is concerned, since it survived on support of the Congress party, the very question of it doing anything positive with regard to the Netaji mystery did not arise. Documents from that time, sent to the National Archives by the Manmohan Singh government following the efforts made by Mission Netaji, tell their own tale.

On 5 September 1990, NK Sinha, Joint Secretary to PM, wrote to Home Secretary Naresh Chandra that in view of dispute concerning Netaji's fate, Prime Minister VP Singh was desirous of brining the matter before the Cabinet Committee on Political Affairs (CCPA) for a decision.

National Archives, New Delhi

This was complied with, and the CCPA discussed this matter on 21 February 1991, when Chandra Shekhar was the PM.

National Archives, New Delhi

The deliberation at the CCPA were focused around a proposal presented by the Home Secretary with the approval of Home Minister (Prime Minister Chandra Shekhar himself) outlining the Netaji mystery matter in a most superficial and biased manner. The CCPA approved this proposal.

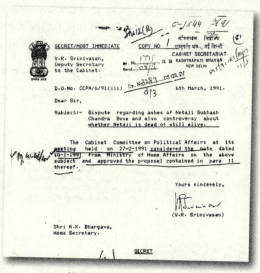

National Archives, New Delhi

Contrary to what Swamy thought, the view of the Chandra Shekhar government was that since 'it has already been accepted that Netaji Subhas Chandra Bose died in the air crash… no useful purpose would be served by bringing the ashes back to India at present as this might create unnecessary tensions'.

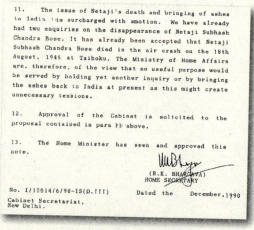

National Archives, New Delhi

In conclusion, there is nothing on record to back Swamy's claim that CCPA's rejection of the Japanese request to send the ashes back to India was prompted by Sham Lal Jain's allegation. There was no way a lame duck Prime Minister such as Chandra Shekhar could have summoned the courage that even Narendra Modi hasn't displayed so far.

Likewise, Swamy's theory that Bhagwanji was planted by the Intelligence Bureau has nothing to stand on. The very question of IB keeping our hopes alive by planting Bhagwanji does not arise as the Faizabad holy man's case came to light only in late 1985 after he was reported dead. By that time, the Bose mystery had ceased to be of any consequence. At that time, the Congress party commanded the largest ever majority in Parliament in the history of India. So, for the IB to plant such a story at that time made no sense. Why would the Rajiv Gandhi government want to revive a dead issue?

In fact, the records of the UP government and possibly of the Central government blame the BJP and the Janata Party for fanning public outcry in late 1986. Swamy was leading the Janata Party till recently, when he decided to merge it with the BJP.

Copy of No. BS-543/85-CX-2   Dated 3/12/85 U/C
From- Home UP Lucknow To- D.M.,Faizabad.
....   (24)

Janta Party B J P Leaders of Faizabad are reported to have been trying to arouse public feelings regarding identity of one Gumnami Babu who died on 16 th September 85(.)
Please furnish a detailed report in the matter in triplicate atonce for transmission to Government of India(.)

....

MOST URGENT

OFFICE OF THE DISTRICT MAGISTRATE,FAIZABAD
....

NO. J.A./Gumnami Baba   Dated 4-12-85

Copy forwarded td S.S.P.,Faizabad for immediate in quadruplicate (4 copies) please.

For District Magistrate
Faizabad.

A claim has been made in private talks by Purabi Roy that Bhagwanji's handwriting samples were planted by the government authorities .

Again, this is absurd. It was beyond the capacity of the Intelligence Bureau to pull through a forensic fraud of that scale.

Yes, documents can be fabricated, but only in a small number. A case in point pertains to the so-called five Black diaries of Irish revolutionary Roger Casement, purportedly containing accounts of his homosexual liaisons with young men. They came into the possession of the Scotland Yard after Casement's capture in 1916. They were then used to publicise Casement's 'sexual degeneracy' before he was hanged. Since the 1930s, a controversy raged about the authenticity of the diaries. It was repeatedly claimed that the British authorities had forged the diaries in order to discredit Casement. In 2002, tests carried out by Audrey Giles, an internationally respected figure in the field of document forensics, established that the handwriting appearing in the diaries as indeed that of Casement's.

Commenting on the issue in 2009 in his authorised history of the British Security Service, Christopher Andrew, the world's top most expert on the history of intelligence services, wrote that it was never possible for any British intelligence services to fake so many handwriting specimens. 'Even the KGB, whose disinformation department Service A made far more use of forgery than any Western intelligence agency, never fabricated a handwritten document of comparable length', wrote Prof Andrew in *The Defence of the Realm: The Authorized History of MI5.*

Hundreds of handwriting specimen, written by Bhagwanji across a span of three decades, couldn't have been fabricated even if all the world's intelligence agencies were to attempt such a feat in 1985 or earlier. It is scientifically impossible for a man to write in someone else's handwriting in two different languages, English and Bangla, for decades.

Roy has also continued to harp on her belief that Netaji was killed in Russia—all on the basis of unsubstantiated heresy. It sounds credible to some people because of her credentials as a professor, fluency in English language and tendency to refer to important, foreign names. All of which add up to conjure up a believable scenario.

Roy flagged the Netaji issue before the nation in the 1990s. She fought when others lacked courage to utter a single word. She came up with innumerable insights, inspired so many, including myself to an extent. But, I have to write, nothing in her 2011 book *The Search for Netaji: New Findings* or any of the records furnished by her before the Mukherjee Commission, or the record of the cross-examination of Russian witnesses she helped bring before the Commission qualify as evidence for Netaji's presence in Russia after 1945—forget the liquidation matter altogether. The portion from the record of Russian witness A Raikov's testimony before Justice Mukherjee speaks for itself:

> As a journalist and researcher not guided merely by the Indian Evidence Act, I believe that that basic thrust of Roy's finding that Netaji was in Soviet Russia after 1945 is right and sincere. She has made a most valuable

Q.8: Did you have any interactions with Dr. Roy about the alleged disappearance of Netaji Subhas Chandra Bose in 1945?

Yes, had some talks but not serious talk.

Q.9: Dr. Roy has stated on oath before the Commission that you right from the beginning was appointed by the Soviet Government to deal with matter concerning Subhas Chandra Bose. Is it a fact?

No.

Q.10: Dr. Roy has also stated that you had access to all the classified documents lying in the archives of Federal Security Bureau and in the archives of Military Armed Forces of Russian Federation. Is it a fact?

It is absolutely Absurd.

Q.12 : Dr. Roy also has stated on oath that you suggested her that the materials would be available in the archives of Omsk? Did you go through the archival documents of Omsk?

It is not correct. It is absurd.

contribution in the advancement of our understanding of this matter. But, being a man of law, Justice Mukherjee was constrained to write in his report that Roy's assertion 'regarding Netaji's presence in Russia after August 18, 1945 cannot be acted upon'.

He explained: 'Roy had produced quite a number of Russian documents during her testimony and, according to her, those were relevant for the purpose of the inquiry. The Commission got them translated into English only to find, on scrutiny, that none of those documents were relevant to any of the terms of reference of this Commission.'

'No notice can be taken of the evidence' of Roy in the respect of 'her testimony that some Russian scholars had told her about Netaji's presence' in the USSR, the judge also stated.

Another claim, which has been often made, has it that Netaji had been imprisoned in Yakutsk Prison in Siberia and possibly killed there. This has made it to headlines in the 31 August 2015 edition of *The Sunday Standard*.

The claim stems from adventurer and former MEA official Satyanarayan Sinha, who first recounted it in his 1965 book *Netaji Mystery* and then repeated it before GD Khosla in 1970. Sinha sourced this information to the son of Abani Mukherji, a revolutionary and co-founder of the Communist Party of India. Sinha claimed that in Moscow in 1960 he met Abani's son 'Goga', from whom he gathered the following information:

> He was the first one to communicate to me the statement of the rehabilitated Comintern functionary Mazut, that he had seen Subhas Babu at Yakutsk in 1950-51. According to Mazut, Subhas Babu was locked up in Cell No 45 and Abani Babu in No 57 of the Central Prison of Yakutsk.

Today, it is an established fact that Mukherji had fallen victim to the Great Purge in the late 1930s. He was executed in October 1937. His soldier son Gora Guar Mukherji also died during the Second World War.

Lastly, several members of the Bose family have refuted the Bhagwanji angle on the basis of their 'belief' that he couldn't have been Netaji. There is a world of difference in what one believes in and what is a matter of fact. The views of Rajiv Gandhi's family members about the conspiracy behind his tragic assassination are inconsequential in getting at the truth. Of course, there have been Netaji family members whose beliefs and statements are most relevant. Tallest among them was Sarat Bose, who clearly held the view that in 1949 his brother was in China, a line of thinking which one can connect only to the Bhagwanji angle. Suresh Bose stated on oath before the Khosla Commission that his brother was alive in 1971. Further evidence shows that he regarded Bhagwanji as his brother.

Netaji's siblings are now no more. So we are getting to hear from his nephews, nieces and their children. When Netaji's nephew DN Bose told me at a gathering a few years ago that he agreed with the report of the DNA test on Bhagwanji's teeth conducted in the CFSL Kolkata, I asked how would he react if the Renkoji remains were brought to India and tested at the same lab. I reminded him that the lab operated under the Ministry of Home Affairs, which had been indicted in the Mukherjee Commission report for not fully cooperating with it. Bose's response was that he did not trust the government on this matter. He did not appreciate it when I told him that we were of the same mind after all.

More recently, another nephew made the following comment on a Facebook post of mine:

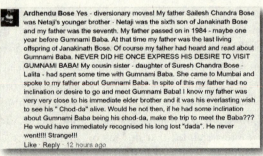

Ardhendu Bose Yes - diversionary moves! My father Sailesh Chandra Bose was Netaji's younger brother - Netaji was the sixth son of Janakinath Bose and my father was the seventh. My father passed on in 1984 - maybe one year before Gumnami Baba. At that time my father was the last living offspring of Janakinath Bose. Of course my father had heard and read about Gumnami Baba. NEVER DID HE ONCE EXPRESS HIS DESIRE TO VISIT GUMNAMI BABA! My cousin sister - daughter of Suresh Chandra Bose - Lalita - had spent some time with Gumnami Baba. She came to Mumbai and spoke to my father about Gumnami Baba. In spite of this my father had no inclination or desire to go and meet Gumnami Baba! I know my father was very very close to his immediate elder brother and it was his everlasting wish to see his " Chod-da" alive. Would he not then, if he had some inclination about Gumnami Baba being his chod-da, make the trip to meet the Baba??? He would have immediately recognised his long lost "dada". He never went!!!! Strange!!!
Like · Reply · 12 hours ago

My fair response to Ardhendu Bose was:

The only thing right about your comment is this: 'My father Sailesh Chandra Bose was Netaji's younger brother—Netaji was the sixth son of Janakinath Bose and my father was the seventh. My father passed on in 1984—maybe one year before Gumnami Baba. At that time my father was the last living offspring of Janakinath Bose.' The rest that you have written is essentially a conjuncture based on a very poor and blinkered understanding of a complex matter.

The explanation is that hardly anyone had a clue about Bhagwanji's existence in 1984, when according to Ardhendu's claim Lalita Bose came to Mumbai and discussed the Bhagwanji matter with his father. Actually, there was no way Shailesh Bose would have known about Bhagwanji, unless Shailesh himself was secretly in touch with him, like many others. Lalita Bose did not come in the picture until after Bhagwanji was reported dead in September 1985, so there was no way for her to know either and report to her uncle Shailesh in 1984. Importantly, all those who knew Bhagwanji before 1985 knew him as such only. The term 'Gumnami Baba' was coined by local media and it became well known only after September 1985.

Like other members of his family, Ardhendu Bose, otherwise well-meaning and supportive of the declassification demand, merely indulged in making assumptions that are clearly incorrect. To those who are sticking to the 'Netaji was killed in Russia theory', I say this: There is not even a shred of evidence in support of it. On other hand, the Bhagwanji angle, howsoever unbelievable it may be, has a lot going for it.

When the chips are down, I expect many retired government officials to speak out in national interest. One has done that already. Backing the Bhagwanji angle to the hilt is Vikram Singh, former Director General of the UP Police, and the most decorated IPS officer according to the Limca Book of Records.

'Gumnami Baba was Netaji, let me tell you as a police officer!' Singh asserted in his lecture at the IIT, Kanpur on 23 January 2014. He repeated his assertion when I met him personally at the NOIDA University, where he is the Vice Chancellor. 'What more circumstantial evidence do you require to show that Gumnami Baba was Subhas Chandra Bose?' he asked, having enumerated some of the evidence that came to light in 1985.

As to what really constitutes evidence should be left to the judges. Both Justice MK Mukherjee, seen here in a recent picture, and the Allahabad High Court have already spoken.

If Subhas Chandra Bose died in Siberia or Taipei city, no power on Earth can bring him back from the dead and put him in Faizabad. And if indeed Netaji was in Faizabad, no clinching evidence whatsoever of his death will ever emerge from either Russia or Taiwan.

Eighteen

The question which acquires outmost priority at the moment is: Why isn't the Narendra Modi government willing to release the Netaji files? What prevents the BJP from fulfilling their pre-poll promise when everyone agrees that the party will gain at the cost of the Congress, its main political rival, if the truth is exposed?

In one line, the truth isn't as simple and easy as Subramanian Swamy and others think. If declassification of secret files is going to establish that Subhas Chandra Bose was killed in Russia at Jawaharlal Nehru's behest, then it becomes an open and shut case against the Congress party. The Modi government then would have no problem in disclosure of files. Such a move will go a long way in realising the BJP's dream of a *Congress-mukt Bharat*, Congress-free India. And if Bose was actually killed in Taipei, the government's declassifying the files will harm no one. It would only bring laurels to Modi.

But as things stand today, Prime Minister Narendra Modi is not walking the pre-poll BJP talk on declassification, despite his personal commitment to unravel the mystery. For every good gesture, there are two acts demonstrating that the new BJP government is not deviating from the

Congress line. The reason for that must be rooted in a scenario far different from what Swamy is rooting for. So what it could really be the reason?

In my assessment, four problem areas make up the BJP's Catch 22 situation:

1. The official files contain canard against Netaji. As a result, disclosure of files would give birth to myriad controversies, adversely impacting the political windfall accruing for the BJP government in case of its ordering declassification.

2. Telling the complete truth might reflect poorly on not only Jawaharlal Nehru but a host of other leaders, including President Pranab Mukherjee. In the ensuing letting of bad blood, the legacies of Sardar Patel and perhaps even Mahatma Gandhi may come under assault.

3. Top government officials, both of bygone and present era, will be shown in unflattering light for their collaboration with the politicians in depriving the people of India the truth.

4. The truth about Netaji lies in Faizabad and stating this as such may outrage Indians, and this is likely to have severe repercussions.

Before anything else, it must be kept in mind that the secret information being sought to be disclosed was largely created by different Congress regimes. Would the leaders of a party, which single-handedly lorded over the country for so long, be so naïve as to put down the unadulterated truth as perceived by Swamy and others in the official files and keep those files in the government record rooms? Wouldn't they be, in such a case, providing their political opponents with a loaded *Brahmastra*, ready to be fired against them once the opponents have come to power?

So, the first and the biggest stumbling block in the way of the Modi government is that the Netaji files have been *Congressified*. Put another way, many of the classified records are full of distortions as they were produced by those who either thought nothing of Netaji, or plainly disliked him.

'The more I think of Congress politics', wrote Subhas Chandra Bose in 1940 to his elder brother Sarat, 'the more convinced I feel that in future we should devote more energy and time to fighting the High Command. If power goes into the hands of such mean, vindictive and unscrupulous persons when Swaraj is won, what will happen to the country?'

If he was indeed alive seven years later, which I think was the case, Netaji must have felt devastated to see his words ring true. Only a year earlier, the Congress leaders were rallying around the Indian National Army (INA) soldiers, raising cries of *Lal Quile se aayee awaz, Sehgal, Dhillon, Shah Nawaz. Inqlab Zindabad*. 'The war cry comes from the Red Fort. Sehgal, Dhillon, Shah Nawaz. Long live revolution.'

After having attained independence, largely due to the sacrifices of INA men and women, the Congress leaders had little time or use for them—and their 'dead' leader. The start was ominous: Nehru's stirring 'Tryst with destiny' speech on 15 August 1947 had not a word about the man, but for whom the day would not have come. Exultant Congress supporters raised the slogan of 'Mountbatten ki Jai' and Nehru's toast for that day was 'for King George'. By this time he had discovered a new friend in Mountbatten.

In the words of Mountbatten, this was how this friendship was forged in March 1946 in Singapore: 'One of the things in his programme was to lay a wreath on the memorial of the Indian National Army which had fought against the Allies', wrote Mountbatten in the Forward to *The Scope of Happiness* (1979), the memoirs of Nehru's sister, Vijaya Lakshmi Pandit. And I was able to persuade him not to lay the wreath on the pro-Japanese Indian National Army. In fact, his whole nine-day visit went extremely well, and this was the beginning of a deep friendship between Jawaharlal Nehru and Edwina and me.'

Filling in a most hideous detail was lawmaker Sasankasekhar Sanyal. He alleged that Nehru was actually asked a pointed question by Mountbatten. Who will be the Prime Minister 'if Subhas comes back to India?' This Sanyal said in the Lok Sabha on 3 August 1977.

In the three decades of the Congress party rule after 1947 the real liberator of India was relegated to the periphery of the national discourse about freedom struggle. Since the people who created classified files about Netaji during this period and afterwards were largely hostile towards him, some extant files are reported to be containing British Raj-era propaganda against him. In fact, Bose has been given a negative image in the secret files.

In case you find this observation too crude to be true, please take a careful look at the relevant portion from an affidavit shown here. It was filed by a person no less than Home Secretary (later Cabinet Secretary) Kamal Pande in 2001, before the Mukherjee Commission. Explaining why certain secret documents regarding Bose could not be given to the commission, Pande claimed that the disclosure would 'hurt the sentiments of the people at large and may evoke widespread reactions as these documents if disclosed may lower the image of Netaji Subhas Chandra Bose'.

9   I have carefully examined the documents contained in Annexures-II, III, IV, V & VI and I am bonafide satisfied that the disclosure of the documents would cause injury to the public interest and the public interest would suffer thereby. I believe that disclosure of the nature and the contents of these documents would also hurt the sentiments of the people at large and may evoke wide-spread reactions as these documents if disclosed may lower the image of Netaji Subhas Chandra Bose. Diplomatic relations with friendly countries may also be adversely affected if the said documents are disclosed.

10   In the circumstances, I withhold permission to produce the said records or to disclose their contents or to give any evidence derived therefrom, and claim privilege under Sections 123 and 124 of the Evidence Act.

11.   However, I submit that I have no objection to the records in respect of which privilege has been claimed being produced for perusal by the Hon'ble Commission for satisfying itself about the bonafides and genuineness of the plea of privilege.

(KAMAL PANDE)
DEPONENT
(KAMAL PANDE)
Home Secretary

'Lower Netaji's image?' How? In a story titled 'Sleeping bomb lies in Netaji vault', *The Telegraph* on 25 March 2001 provided an insight that the government possessed 'seven to eight Cabinet notes, prepared on the basis of information provided by British intelligence'. These notes contained 'personal' remarks against Bose.

What I found out on my part was that among the records Pande referred to, some actually peddled an outrageous theory coming from a Russian scholar in 1993. Wrongly interpreting some still-classified KGB records, the scholar deduced that 'Bose was an MI-6 (British) agent...[because] one of his close associates was a KGB agent'.

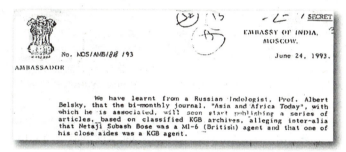

This implied calumny in the government records was the reason Pande made the blood-curdling averment about Netaji's image. And by claiming this in a duly-sworn affidavit, the Home Ministry under LK Advani actually hurt my sentiments at least. Because I fail to see the logic behind the government's acquiescing to the Russian scholar's stand, that since Bhagat Ram Talwar (one of the many persons who helped Bose in his great escape in 1940) had turned out to be a 'collaborator of the Soviet intelligence service and simultaneously a highly secret agent of the British Secret Intelligence Service', it somehow dented Netaji's credentials.

If you accepted this logic, someone might say that since we know now— thanks to unassailable declassified CIA and State Department records—that during the 1971 war someone from Indira Gandhi's Cabinet betrayed India's war plans to the hostile Richard Nixon administration, Prime Minister Gandhi's image stands tarnished as well.

No, it doesn't. The CIA informant in the Indian cabinet betrayed Prime

Minister Gandhi's trust and committed high treason. Bhagat Ram Talwar was not Subhas Bose's childhood pal. He was one small operative of communist orientation, and Netaji came in touch with innumerable people like him. The Bose-MI6 agent theory was laughable. For Government of India to bring it in the official records, as if it were a serious matter, betrayed its jaundiced view of Netaji.

While it has not dared to maintain any records about the amorous adventures of other national leaders, the government has taken due care in keeping a meticulous record of information whose revelation could be misused to scandalise Netaji's personal life. These records would provide fodder to a long-standing belief among a section of society that Bose's marriage with his one-time secretary, Emilie Schenkl was, to use Nirad Chaudhury's words, 'a well-cultivated myth'. Of course, the Bose family members that I know have utter contempt for such thoughts. 'Nehru and Patel were spreading calumny about Netaji', Madhuri Bose, Sarat Bose's granddaughter, told the *Outlook* magazine in February 2014.

Sarat, incidentally, had come to know about the secret marriage of his brother in August 1947 from Nehru and Patel, who had been informed by a source in Vienna in June that year. 'Nehru and Patel did not communicate the information to Sarat Bose until August 1947, on the eve of India's independence day. Understandably, Sarat was displeased', Madhuri Bose wrote in *Outlook*.

With a view to ascertaining facts, Sarat wrote to Emilie in April 1948. The later was laced with suspicion and bitterness. 'It is difficult these days to trust many people here. Most of the eminent Congress leaders were political enemies of my brother and tried their best to run him down. Their attitude does not seem to have changed much, even after all that has happened since 1941.... I would, therefore, prefer to correspond directly with you.' In the autumn of 1948 Sarat, his wife and three of their children travelled to Vienna for 'an emotional family meeting', wrote Madhuri Bose.

It is intriguing that according to Sardar Patel, Sarat had a negative view towards Bose's daughter Anita. 'Sarat Bose has refused to have anything to do with her', Patel wrote to Nehru in July 1948, according to the text of his letter reproduced in Volume 13 of the *Collected Works of Sardar Vallabhbhai Patel* complied by veteran historian PN Chopra. Earlier, in a 1946 letter to Sarat Bose, Emilie had stated that Subhas and she had 'married according to Hindu fashion in January 1942'.

On the other hand, Bhagwanji of Faizabad denied ever getting into matrimony. Was he trying to keep his family out of harm's way, or was he being truthful?! All of Bhagwanji's followers cannot imagine him saying anything which was not true. According to *Oi MahamanabAasey:*

> Could a man who is going to jump into fire even think of getting married? And if a woman tells him that she wants to enter into a relationship, the natural thing for him to say would be—'let me first get out of this dangerous situation and then I will think about it'. He went away leaving behind a newly married woman and newborn baby? And the woman also agreed?! [Translated from Bangla]

Adding to the confusion is the fact that both, the Ministry of Home Affairs and the Intelligence Bureau, 'have no record pertaining to Netaji's reported marriage...or birth of a female child by that marriage'.

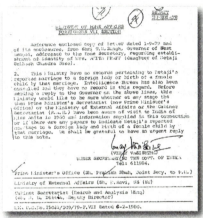

Mission Netaji's attempts to get clarity from the government did not bear fruits. Despite Chandrachur Ghose's repeated attempts, the Prime Minister's Office refused to provide copies of classified files concerning Emilie Schenkl and Anita Pfaff.

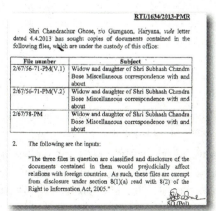

The Manmohan PMO's line was carried forward by the Modi PMO in July 2014. On behalf of Chandrachur, I argued before Chief Information Commissioner Rajiv Mathur that non-disclosure was not in keeping with the RTI spirit and that no proper reason was given for not disclosing the files. I also pointed out that not releasing these files would give further currency to certain conspiracy theories about Netaji's marriage. I made these submissions knowing well that these secret files contained explosive notes, such as the one seen in the picture.

> MHA U.O. No.25022/109/79-F.VII dated 6.2.1980 (with enclosures)from Shri Vinay Vasishtha , Under Secretary , Ministry of Home Affairs to Sh. Prakash Shah ,Joint Secretary , PMO regarding establishment of the identity of Ms. Anita Pfaff, daughter of Netaji Subhash Chandra Bose.

However, the PMO reiterated that the release would 'prejudicially affect relations with foreign countries'. Mathur, a former IB chief, agreed with this assessment. The PMO refused to budge even after Chandrachur filed another RTI application, in which he cited recently declassified MI5 papers in which uncharitable reference to Bose and Schenkl were made during and just after the Second World War.

The fear that the disclosure of ultra secret/records—apart from those referred to by Pande or those dealing with Bose's personal life—would somehow be detrimental to Netaji's image came in the way of the Atal Bihari Vajpayee government telling the nation the truth. Vajpayee was, after all, personally interested in the matter for decades. After the Calcutta High Court issued the order for a new inquiry, his government even toyed with the idea of releasing a white paper on the controversy before it was shelved. The dilemma was articulated to a stumped *The Pioneer* journalist, Deepak Sharma—who rose to be the editor of *Aaj Tak*—by a Secretary to the Government in these grim words:

> Whatever is relevant will be shown to the Commission. But beyond a point, the files cannot be made public. It is too explosive.

The problem was that the BJP leaders saw the world from the eyes of bureaucrats. Normally, it is the right thing to do, but Subhas Bose must be one exception to the rule. The notes prepared in Vajpayee's time merely put forward the skewed facts and arguments cited in records created during previous regimes, with the first prototype going all the way back to the days of Nehru.

Today, most of the classified files relating to Netaji available with several ministries do not contain gospel. They merely outline government's partisan views and cover-ups, in response to unceasing public yearning for truth. Take, for instance, the following 1990 note by the then Home Secretary, RK Bhargava. The note had the approval of Prime Minister Chandra Shekhar, also holding the Home portfolio.

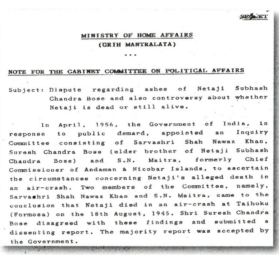

MINISTRY OF HOME AFFAIRS
(GRIH MANTRALAYA)
. . .

NOTE FOR THE CABINET COMMITTEE ON POLITICAL AFFAIRS

Subject: Dispute regarding ashes of Netaji Subhash Chandra Bose and also controversy about whether Netaji is dead or still alive.

In April, 1956, the Government of India, in response to public demand, appointed an Inquiry Committee consisting of Sarvashri Shah Nawaz Khan, Suresh Chandra Bose (elder brother of Netaji Subhash Chandra Bose) and S.N. Maitra, formerly Chief Commissioner of Andaman & Nicobar Islands, to ascertain the circumstances concerning Netaji's alleged death in an air-crash. Two members of the Committee, namely, Sarvashri Shah Nawaz Khan and S.N. Maitra, came to the conclusion that Netaji died in an air-crash at Taihoku (Formosa) on the 18th August, 1945. Shri Suresh Chandra Bose disagreed with these findings and submitted a dissenting report. The majority report was accepted by the Government.

Similar formulations are seen in all such notes issued since the 1950s. Using the cut and paste technique, the Secretaries have mostly been simply repeating the narrative originally set in the Nehruvian era. Every few years, they merely add some new details without impairing in any way the basic structure, which seeks to find no fault with Government of India's deceitful handling of the Netaji matter. Any interested minister or bureaucrat who would get to read the notes produced by such biased minds can never understand the true state of affairs.

Bhargava's glowing description of the Khosla Commission and its works is an illustration. Not a whiff of GD Khosla's dubious acts of omissions and commissions is seen in it:

> In response to a demand for fresh inquiry by a number of Members of Parliament belonging to different political parties, the Government decided to appoint a Commission of Inquiry to go into the entire matter in July, 1970. Shri GD Khosla, retired Chief Justice of Punjab High Court, was appointed as a one-man Commission to 'inquire into all the facts and circumstances relating to the disappearance of Netaji Subhash Chandra Bose in 1945 and

the subsequent developments connected therewith and make a report to the Central Government'. The Commission visited Japan, Burma, Thailand, Singapore, Malaysia, South Vietnam and Formosa (Taiwan) and examined 224 witnesses including 100 examined abroad. A large number of files and documents were produced and cited in evidence. The Commission arrived at the same conclusion that was reached by the Shah Nawaz Khan Committee in 1956, that Netaji died in an air-crash at Taihoku on the 18th August, 1945.

Further, Home Secretary Bhargava confounds the matter by writing the following in his note:

> Forty five years have passed since the reports of death of Netaji and during the intervening period there have been moves to have these ashes brought back to India with all the reverence—as befitting a man of the stature of Subhas Chandra Bose. Proponents of this line of action include organisations like the All India Freedom Fighters Organisation led by ex-MP Shri Sheel Bhadra Yaji as well as individuals such as Shri L Joychandra Singh of Manipur. The most recent voices added to this group for the return of Netaji's ashes and who accepted the ashes as being genuine are the members of the INA and colleagues of Netaji, viz. Col PK Sehgal who is Chairman of the Netaji Research Bureau in Calcutta and his wife Col Laxmi Sehgal. In addition, there are also some family members of Netaji who reportedly accept these views and moves.

Nowhere does the note mention the Congress links of 'some family members of Netaji' supporting the air crash theory in return for pecuniary and other gains. Colonel Laxmi Sehgal was to disgrace herself by committing perjury before the Mukherjee Commission, lying on oath that she believed in Bose's death in Taiwan whereas she actually believed that he was in Soviet Russia after 1945. Sheel Bhadra Yaji is seen in many pictures greeting his latter-day revered leaders Jawaharlal Nehru, Indira Gandhi and Rajiv Gandhi.

Joychandra Singh was an interesting character. In December 1996, he appeared from nowhere to tell the media that there was nothing more to the Bose mystery other than the Taipei crash. He harped on his '12-year-old research' on the issue, which had incidentally been inspired by a communication from the Indira Gandhi government urging him to propagate the Taipei death story. He claimed that Russia too upheld this theory. This he claimed on the misreading of a response he had received from the Russian Defence Ministry archives.

Quite remarkable that a private citizen like Singh should have been able to elicit a direct response from the Russians, who hardly ever entertained such requests, even when they were from eminent citizens like former Congress party president and Karnataka Chief Minister S Nijalingappa, who was supportive of Samar Guha's long-standing efforts.

Even more remarkable was the fact that the same Joychandra Singh was able to obtain a fake certificate of Bose's death, manufactured by Dr Yoshimi in 1988.

Prime Minister Narendra Modi, by now, must have seen many such official notes, and be confronting the same predicament as Vajpayee did. The bureaucrats, whose basic instinct in this matter would be to avoid complications and save the skins of their friends and predecessors, must have fed him a twisted, *Congressified* view of Netaji and the controversy surrounding his death. The only way the PM can come around this charade is by including unbiased non-government experts in the declassification process. The matter is far too sensitive to be left in the hands of those brainwashed by a state, which has over the decades engaged in a blatant cover-up.

Fake certificate: Mukherjee Commission exhibit No 112

As and when PM Modi decides to order declassification, he will have to worry, for a start, about its effect on our President at the time of writing. Because it would be exposed that Pranab Mukherjee, a staunch Congress party loyalist all his life, went out of his way to prove Netaji's death in Taiwan even though he had good reasons not to.

On 21 October 1994, the following Top Secret letter was sent by Joint Secretary (Internal Security), Ministry of Home Affairs to Joint Secretary (Asia Pacific region) in the Ministry of External Affairs. He sought 'a copy of the Japanese govern-ment report on the death of Netaji, which is stated to be available in MEA'.

In response, the MEA sent MHA the copy of a Japanese communication claiming that a cremation permit issued for Ichiro Okura was 'believed to be' for Bose. On its receipt, the confused MHA Joint Secretary telephoned the MEA to say that his Ministry 'would like to have a confirmation that the Japanese government had indeed confirmed' Netaji's death.

The MEA obviously did not share the Japanese government's belief that the Okura record pertained to Bose. On November 10, the JS (AP) stated in a Top Secret note that

> for us to state on this basis that the Japanese government had indeed confirmed the death of Netaji Subhas Chandra Bose, would be going beyond the scope of the Japanese government letter and have major internal ramifications for us.

```
4.      As instructed by FS, on receipt of MHA letter,
a copy of letter from our Ambassador in Tokyo, along
with its enclosres was forwarded to MHA. · Subsequently,
Shri C. Phunsog, Joint Secretary(IS(I) rang up to
say that they would like to have confirmation from
MEA that the Japanese Government had indeed confirmed
that Netaji Subhash Chandra Bose had died 'in the
air crash in 1945. As will be seen from the enclosures
attached with the Ambassador's letter at S.No.20,
(Flag 'Z')the response of the Japanese Government
is contained at para 2.  [For us to state on this
basis that the Japanese Government had indeed confirmed
the death of Netaji Subhash Chandra Bose would be
going beyond the scope of the Japanese Government
letter and  have major internal ramifications for
us.] It is, therefore, submitted that while replying
```

Document obtained in public interest

Despite these and other facts on record, the following unfolded.

On page 17 of PMO Top Secret file No G-16(3)/95 NGO is a letter written on 28 October 1995 by the then External Affairs Minister himself. It outlines Pranab Mukherjee's hush-hush tour of Japan and Germany in his quest to bring to India the ashes of Ichiro Okura and fob them off on Indians as Netaji's ashes.

In Germany on October 21, Pranab Mukherjee had sat down with Emilie Schenkl for an important meeting. Also in attendance was her daughter, Anita Pfaff, Anita's husband, Martin Pfaff and India's ambassador to Germany, SK Lambah.

Mukherjee, the master strategist, started building the whole thing up by telling Emilie that Indian government was keen to 'bring back Netaji's ashes' to India at a suitable time, provided the controversial issues were resolved. Ambassador Lambah stated that the Japanese had reacted negatively to the proposal of transferring the ashes to Germany. The only option left was to take them to India.

Emilie was put off by the suggestion. She reacted angrily to Mukherjee's proposal that she should sign on a paper, approving Netaji's death in Taiwan. According to a duly-sworn affidavit, filed subsequently before the Mukherjee

Commission by her Germany-based grandnephew Surya Kumar Bose, 'she did not believe that Netaji had died in a plane crash...and that those "ashes"...had nothing to do with Subhas, because she was of the opinion that "Netaji was in the Soviet Union after 1945"'.

II. Minister of External Affairs, Government of India, Mr Pranab Mukherjee's visit to Augsburg on 21 October 1995

1. On 20 October 1995 Auntie rang me after 10:30 pm from her daughter Anita Pfaff's home in Augsburg. She was quite agitated. She told me that Mr Pranab Mukherjee was coming to Augsburg on 21st October 1995 to convince her and Anita to give their approval for bringing the so-called "ashes" of Netaji to India. Mr Mukherjee also wanted her to sign a document which he would take back to India as proof of her approval. She again emphasised to me that she had never believed in the plane crash story and would neither sign any document nor agree in any way to bringing the "ashes" to India or to anywhere else.

Never the one to give up easily, Pranab Mukherjee tried to convince Emilie that Netaji was never in Russia. According to his letter in the Top Secret PMO file, he furnished an official communication from the Russian government, purporting to claim that Moscow had no record of Netaji's presence in the Soviet Union during or after 1945. The English translation of that communication in Russian, also kept on file, is seen here.

What Pranab Mukherjee—someone most familiar with the

(rough translation)

Ministry of Foreign Affairs
Russian Federation

No. 2/YuA

The Ministry of Foreign Affairs of the Russian Federation presents its compliments to the Embassy of Republic of India and with reference to the Embassy's Note dated 16 September 1991, has the honour to inform that according to the data in the Central and Republican Archives, no information whatsoever is available on the stay of the former President of Indian National Congress, Netaji Subhash Chandra Bose, in the Soviet Union in 1945 and thereafter.

The Ministry avails itself of this opportunity to renew to the Embassy the assurances of its highest consideration.

Moscow
8 January 1992

Embassy of the
Republic of India
Moscow

warts and woofs of diplomacy—did not tell the Bose family was that this response from the Russian side was hardly convincing. The assertion made in it was based on the records in open archives, not those related to security and intelligence. Therefore, it fell in the same category as the misleading responses the Soviets had sent to the Swedes in the Raoul Wallenberg case.

Subsequent Ministry of External Affairs records (see page 81) demonstrate that the ministry's January 1996 proposal to seek a Russian response by way of issuing a 'suitable démarche to the Russian authorities', seeking a search for relevant records in the formerly KGB archives was not approved by Mukherjee.

Emilie saw through it all. She refused to go by Pranab's persuasive words. After she made it clear that she could not even tolerate his presence there, Anita and Martin Pfaff took Mukherjee out to thrash out the matter over lunch.

Surya called his grandaunt after a few days, when an Indian daily carried a newsitem quoting Pranab Mukherjee as saying that Emilie 'had given her approval to the Government of India's plans for bringing the "ashes" to India, and that he (Mukherjee) had a document to prove it'. Emilie turned furious as she

> reiterated that she had signed no such document and had approved of nothing. Mr Pranab Mukherjee was propagating an untruth for reasons best known to him and the Government of India.

She passed away in March 1996, believing that Renkoji ashes were not of Bose. This was the reason why, as long as she lived, she neither visited Renkoji temple and nor did she allow the ashes to be brought over to India. The following, 1990 classified document from a PMO file is one of the many reiterating her position.

But despite Emilie's categorical 'No', Pranab Mukherjee twisted facts in his 28 October 1995 letter kept in the PMO Top Secret file. He wrote that both Emilie and Anita had, 'agreed to bringing the ashes of Netaji to India'.

For reasons only she can explain, Anita agreed to Mukherjee's preposition against the wishes of her family members, excluding those linked to the Congress party. In February 1998, she wrote a letter to Prime Minister IK Gujaral. It is now lying in the PMO Top Secret file number G-12(3)/98-NGO.

In this letter Anita requests Gujaral to transfer Ichiro Okura's ashes to India—something that many of her cousins, like her dead mother, thought was an 'an act of sacrilege'. Then she goes on to give a less-than-truthful account of her family's view about Netaji's fate.

While it is an open secret that Nehru did little for Bose's legacy, Anita went on to tell *The Times of India* in February 2000 that she 'dismissed the popular perception that Jawaharlal Nehru looked upon Netaji as a rival and that Nehru and Indira Gandhi had ensured that Netaji's role was "ignored"'. She even said, 'It is unfair to paint Panditji as a villain'.

As Indians world over rooted for declassification of secret files about Netaji, Anita's initial response, I have the mortification to write, was undaughterly. Everyone wanted to see the veil go off on official secrecy, but Netaji's daughter remained silent. Worse, during a panel discussion on *Times Now* she appeared miffed with this writer for highlighting the demand that she came around to reluctantly supporting only in September 2015.

Anita's move to get Ichiro Okura's ashes to India in late 1990s was thwarted by the ruling of the Calcutta High Court, leading to the formation of the Mukherjee Commission. At no point in time during the inquiry of the commission did Anita make no attempt to assist it or meet Justice MK Mukherjee. She kept on reiterating her support for the air crash theory.

In March 2006, something scandalous happened. At this time, Justice Mukherjee's report negating the air crash theory was yet to be made public by the Congress-led government, of which Pranab Mukherjee was a prominent part. Like a scene from a James Bond flick, Sugata Bose flew to Japan on a secret mission, whose full details are yet to emerge. There he met a friend of his, who also happened to be the scion of the Murti family, accused of having misappropriated the INA treasure. From him, Sugata collected certain human remains, put them in his suitcase and brought them over to Kolkata surreptitiously. Other than Sugata's immediate kin and Anita, no other Bose family members were told anything. The story Sugata Bose later on tried to dish out to unsuspecting people of India was that with the approval of the Prime Minister of India, a portion of Renkoji temple remains kept with the Murtis was brought to India.

But the story fell flat as in two back-to-back RTI responses to Chandra chur the Prime Minister's Office denied outright having any knowledge about the secretive transfer of ashes and the Ministry of External Affairs refuted that there were any 'ashes of Netaji in the custody of Shri Ramamurti or his family'.

If a man of the stature of Pranab Mukherjee could falsify facts in an official record, one can well imagine what else would have been resorted to by the minions of Congress party in government services. Now all of this has added up, posing problems for the Modi government.

Another area of concern for the Prime Minister would be the likely affect of the revelation of truth on the image of both Sardar Patel and Mahatma Gandhi. If it emerges that Netaji was alive after 1945, the role of these icons would be seen with suspicions by many. The Congress party is already aware of this dimension. Recall the April 2015 unraveling of the Netaji family spying scandal, and the Congress response to it. The party spokesperson lost no time in dragging Patel into the matter.

'Between 1948 and 1968, India had seven Home Ministers—Sardar Patel, C Rajagopalachari, Kailash Nath Katju, Govind Ballabh Pant, Lal Bahadur Shastri, Gulzarilal Nanda and Yashwantrao Chavan.

'Why is the BJP trying to malign the great Home Ministers and veteran freedom fighters like Patel, Rajagopalachari, Govind Ballabh Pant, Shastri and others?' said a Congress statement, released by party spokesperson Abhishek Manu Singhvi.

Put the other way, the Congress party reminded the BJP that Nehru alone wouldn't take the hit if the truth about Bose emerged.

While I hope that declassification would reveal something positive in this context, on available historical evidence Patel's equations with Bose do not appear rosy. And nor does Patel appear to have played a very positive role over the mystery of Netaji's disappearance and subsequent developments.

Like Gandhi, Vallabhbhai Patel never got along well with the much younger Subhas Bose. A time came when it seemed that the Congress was at war with Bose, not the colonial rulers. In fact, Bose himself accused the Congress high command of undertaking 'repeated pilgrimages to the Viceroy's House and lick[ing] the feet that kick you'. This very high command, Bose continued, refrained from making 'any demonstration of toleration, goodwill and generosity' towards him as it continued 'with full wrath and ferocity a policy of vendetta' against him.

With Gandhi, Bose at least maintained a semblance of good relations, but he could not do so with Patel. The bitterness between the two came to the fore over the Sardar's elder brother's affection and admiration for Bose. In the 1930s, Vithalbhai Patel (picture) and Subhas Bose had opened a front against Gandhi after his unilateral, shocking decision to wind up the Civil Disobedience Movement, citing a stray incident of violence in Chauri Chaura.

'A political warfare based on the principle of maximum suffering for ourselves and minimum suffering for our opponents cannot possible lead to success. It is futile to expect that we can ever bring about a change of heart in our rulers merely through our own suffering or by trying to love them', read the Bose-Patel statement issued in May 1939 from Vienna. 'We are clearly of the opinion that as a political leader, Mahatma Gandhi has failed', it added.

Vithalbhai later bequeathed a part of his fortune for Subhas, so that the same could be utilised 'for the political uplift of India and preferably for publicity work on behalf of India's cause, in other countries'.

'Where can you find such a man', wrote Vithalbhai about Subhas in his will. 'It is for this reason that all my hopes are centred on him.'

When he was sick in Europe, Vithalbhai had been taken care of by Subhas, himself convalescing there. In his 1933 tribute to Patel senior, Gandhi recorded his 'deep appreciation of Mr Subhas Chandra Bose's magnificent and devoted nursing of Vithalbhai at much risk to his own health'.

There is nothing, however, to show that Vallabhbhai ever expressed any gratitude to Subhas. In fact, even before Vithalbhai's body was brought to India, he complained to Gandhi about the bequest of money to Subhas and raised certain 'doubts' about it. He went to court to deny Subhas Vithalbhai's bequest. Later, the Bombay High Court decided that the amount should go to Vithalbhai's legatees. Gandhiji persuaded Sardar Patel to give it to the Congress for national service. Subhas Bose was so much hurt by the episode that he never ever talked about it to anyone.

With regard to Bose's role in making in India free, Patel, like Gandhi and Nehru, thought of him as a 'misguided' patriot. The Naval Mutiny of 1946, an important milestone in our freedom struggle, was suppressed by the joint efforts of the British and the Gandhi-Patel-Nehru trio. In October 1946, when he was interim Home Member, Patel stated that the Government of India (which was the same entity before and after August 1947) was not in a position 'to make any authoritative statement' on whether or not Bose was still alive.

But after some time, on the basis of information one would not call very reliable, Patel, like Nehru changed his stand so say that Bose had died in Taiwan. This was when Patel as Home Minister had access to intelligence reports which suggested Bose could have been in Soviet Russia after his reported death in August 1945 in a plane crash we now know never took place.

Therefore, if it is proven that Bose was left out in the cold in Soviet Russia, the blame would lie not on just Nehru but unfortunately also on Deputy Prime Minister Patel.

As regards Gandhiji, there is sufficient information on record to show that he knew that Bose was alive after his reported death in August 1945. The following has been excerpted from a declassified 1946 intelligence report, now available at the National Archives in New Delhi:

> Gandhi stated publicly at the beginning of January that he believed that Bose was alive and in hiding. He has not afforded any satisfactory reason for the belief he says he possesses, ascribing it to an inner voice. Congress circles have elaborated in some case Some reports declare that Congressmen believe that Gandhi's inner voice is secret information which he as received. Communists

The question is what did Gandhi do with this and other pieces of information coming his way regarding Bose's disappearance. For a start, he did make public statements expressing his belief in Bose's remaining alive. A little thereafter, he too started supporting the air crash theory. Writing in April 1946, he appealed to 'everyone to forget what I have said and…reconcile themselves to the fact that Netaji has left us'. But privately, the Apostle of non-violence and truth expressed similar fears as the British intelligence officers were having. Lying in a secret PMO file is the copy of a letter written in July 1946 to American journalist and Gandhi's biographer Louis Fischer at Gandhi's behest by his secretary Khurshed Naoroji. A reading of this letter suggests that Gandhi believed that Bose was in Russia, but not a prisoner.

> The Indian Army is no longer of the same temper as it was in the First World War. Besides the disaffection among the Indian officers and the rank and file, a revolutionary group has been working among them and they are pro-Russian. At heart, the Indian Army is sympathetic to the Indian National Army. If Bose comes with the help of Russia, neither Gandhiji nor the Congress will be able to reason with the country….

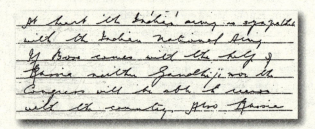

Post-independence, Gandhiji was put on a pedestal higher than that of God almighty. Gandhi is the reigning deity of the temple called India. It is sacrilegious to point a finger at him. He stays in that exalted place, no matter which dispensation is in power. In our collective memory, his visage is etched alongside that of his main protégé, Nehru. Hence, in the event of the revelation of the truth about Netaji, Gandhiji is going to be judged with a very different yardstick if it turns out that Nehru was complicit in suppressing the truth.

I know what you are thinking. That I am seeing only one side of the story, ignoring the fact that despite their differences Gandhi and Bose had mutual respect for each other. It was Netaji who called Gandhiji 'The Father of the Nation'!

Actually, I have factored that aspect in. That's why I dismiss a horrendous conspiracy theory which holds that Gandhiji and others had agreed with the British demand to hand over Bose to them in case he resurfaced. This theory was brought on record before the Khosla Commission by one Usman Patel, who claimed to be a bodyguard of Bose.

But what I cannot ignore is that there is evidence suggesting that the colonial British directly 'helped Gandhi by sharing with him intelligence information' against Bose. In a series of insightful articles on *Daily O*, Saswati Sarkar, a professor in the University of Pennsylvania, has dissected several issues related to India's independence movement. The outcome invariably is not what we have been made to believe thus far by the court historians in India who cannot see beyond Gandhiji and Panditji.

According to an article jointly penned by Sarkar and others, 'JB Kripalani, one of Gandhi's men' had informed Bose's biographer, Leonard Gordon in an interview in New Delhi on 10 September 1976 that 'Gandhi knew a lot more about Bose's connections to men of violence and to plans for potential violence than he ever let on in public'. ...'His source, very likely, was the British intelligence, as would become evident from a letter by KM Munshi: "The Government of India knew my (Munshi's) relations with Gandhi and Sardar and often saw to it that confidential information reached Gandhiji through me. On one such occasion, I was shown certain Secret Service reports that Netaji had contacted the German Consul in Calcutta and had come to some arrangement with him, which would enable Germany to rely upon him in case there was a war. I conveyed this information to Gandhiji, who naturally felt surprised.'"

'This intelligence sharing', the article further reads, 'had happened during 1938, when Bose was the president of Indian National Congress. Note that Gandhi did not raise a public hue and cry on why the British were snooping on the president of the Congress, but he was contented receiving this information. Also, note that the first citation shows that this was not a one time exchange—confidential information that British acquired often reached Gandhi and Vallabhbhai Patel through the intermediary KM Munshi. It has now emerged that this tradition continued post-independence, during Nehru's and subsequent regimes as Bose's family was snooped upon and the information thus acquired was shared with British intelligence'.

I think that too much has been made of the pleasantries and courtesies extended by Bose and Gandhi to each other, even after they clashed bitterly. In his last letter to Gandhi on 10 January 1941, Bose took exception to Gandhi's writing to him that 'till one of us is converted to other's view, we must sail in different boats, though their destination may appear but only appear to be the same'.

'Does this mean that in your view our political goals are different? How could that be? Kindly tell me what exactly you mean', Bose wrote back. There was no answer from Gandhi.

The most-quoted words of Netaji about Gandhiji are the ones he aired from Azad Hind Radio in Rangoon on 4 June 1944. 'Father of our Nation, in this holy war for India's liberation, we ask for your blessings and good wishes'. The fact is that the show of courtesy and personal admiration never did overshadow the political differences. If they did, Subhas wouldn't have been thrown out of the Congress and wouldn't have been forced to leave the country. None of them forgot their fundamental political differences. That's the reason why Bose wrote to Rash Behari Bose in 1941 from Germany that 'there is no room for cooperation with Gandhi'. For some reasons, Bhagwanji of Faizabad wanted a copy of this letter delivered to him after it became available at the German archives:

> Every show of strength and defiance that Gandhi puts up is always followed by an attempt at a compromise. Hence we now see that Gandhi is again working for a compromise with the British government. It would be a fatal mistake now to lionise Gandhi or praise him too much. ...To expect that Gandhi will come over to our point of view is only an idle dream. Consequently, to strengthen Gandhi's position by praising him too much, amounts to weakening our own following and committing political suicide. You may occasionally pay compliment to Gandhi as a political manoeuvre, but you should always remember that Gandhi will never come over to your side.

```
policy. To expect that Gandhi will come over to our point of
view is only an idle dream. Consequently, to strengthen
Gandhi's position by praising him too much, amounts to weaken-
ing our own following and committing political suicide. You
may occasionally pay a compliment to Gandhi as a political
manoeuvre, but you should always remember that Gandhi will
never come over to your side.
```

German Foreign Office, Records No 350084-85

At first, this might appear to be a hypocritical attitude, typically associated with political leaders. But in reality, it was only a pragmatic piece of advice; obvious but critical. What was the point of organising armies, if they had a deep admiration for Gandhian ways and if they had to keep chanting his name? The programme of armed uprising could not be allowed to be swallowed by respect and courtesy.

Apart from the possibility that declassification of secret Netaji files might impact, one way or the other, legacies and good names of several top political icons of ours, the Modi government would also have to face the prospects of harming the image of top government officials. Exposed to public, the secret papers would bring into question the roles played by several high-profile public servants, including the deceased and the living. Some of them would face the charge of either obstructing justice or having prolonged the controversy by not applying their brilliant minds to the matter, probably in dereference to the views of their political bosses.

In this context, I am in complete agreement with a statement Subramanian Swamy made in September 2014 while discussing obstacles in the way of declassification of the Bose files. 'There will be a great tussle within the bureaucracy. The supporters of the Nehru dynasty are sitting in different places and they will get a bad name [if the truth comes out]', he said.

Some random examples would illustrate the point.

Tucked away in a secret file is the following 1966 letter, written by the then Director, East Asia Division in the Ministry of External Affairs. KR Narayanan (later President of India) came up with a novel solution to the problem created in the wake of the Renkoji temple priest's insistence that the ashes must be taken back to India.

```
intended to show that he is no more. Far from agreeing
to the ashes being brought to India and exhibited in
the museum, the relatives, family as well as politikou
might raise an agitation against the Government for
trying to assert that Netaji is dead. Therefore,
unless the family gives its consent, it would not
be appropriate to try to bring the ashes to India now
It seems to me that the only thing we can do at
present is to give some financial assistance to the
Priest who is now looking after the ashes in the
Tokyo temple. I shall be grateful if F.S. will see
this and give his advice.

                              (K.R. Narayanan)
  157-                        Director(East Asia)
                              21/11/66
```

As far as the Government is concerned, they have accepted the findings of the Shaw [sic] Nawaz Khan Committee and have no difficulty in treating the ashes as those of Netaji. It is, however, a different matter for the family of Netaji who still believe that he is alive. ...It seems to me that the only thing we can do at present is to give financial assistance to the priest who is now looking after the ashes in the temple.

In a stupendous testimony to the Indian official secrecy, no one in the country, no newspaper whatsoever, ever heard a whisper about India paying a yearly tribute to the temple authorities from 1967 onwards.

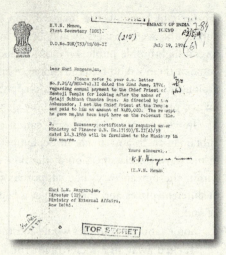

The following 1995 Top Secret note for the Union Cabinet, prepared by then Home Secretary K Padmanabhaiah with the approval of Home Minister SB Chavan, gives away the bureaucracy's closed mind on the issue. The Committee of Secretaries (CoS) comprising Cabinet, Home, Foreign, Defence, Finance Secretaries, all servants of their political lords, averred with a clear bias that

> there seems to be no scope for doubt that he died in the air crash of 18th August, 1945 at Taihoku. Government of India has already accepted this position. There is no evidence whatsoever to the contrary. If a few individuals/organisations have a different view, they seem to be guided more by sentimentality rather than by any rational consideration.

```
Consideration of the Committee  of Secretaries

9.      In view of what has been mentioned in foregoing
para 6, a decision will have to be taken soon.  There
seems to be no scope for doubt that he died in the air
crash of 18th August, 1945 at Taihoku.  Government of
India has already accepted this position.  There is no
evidence whatsoever to the contrary.  If a few
individuals/organisations have a different view, they
seem to be guided more by sentimentality rather than by
any rational consideration.  The belief of these people
that Netaji was alive and out of contact with any Indian,
but would appear when found necessary, has also lost

F.No.I/12014/27/93-IS(D.III)
Ministry of Home Affairs
```

Document obtained in public interest

On 5 August 1992, Shyam Saran, then a Joint Secretary in the Prime Minister's Office, dealt with demands raised in a letter from Samar Guha to the PM.

Guha's seeking 'high-level investigative enquiry to be instituted to go into the question of the so-called disappearance of Netaji Subhas Chandra Bose' had the backing of the then Opposition leader LK Advani. Guha had particularly drawn attention to fresh material which could be available in the former KGB archives, 'which may now be accessible due to changes that have taken place in Russia'. He had also referred to possible documents 'available in other countries such as the UK, USA, Japan and Taiwan'.

But Shyam Saran, an exceptionally sharp and wise person, unreasonably trashed Guha's pleas. He wrote that the Shah Nawaz Committee and Khosla Commission 'had undertaken very extensive investigations and had finally come to conclusion that Netaji had died'.

'If the matter is re-opened once again, there is unlikely to be any fresh light thrown on this matter', he prophesied and added: 'The evidence of Netaji's death is compelling and examination of archival materials in Russia and other countries is unlikely to throw up any different conclusion.'

This is to say that without knowing what the Russians possessed in their secret archives, Saran had formed an opinion that whatever two distinguished persons (Shah Nawaz and Khosla) linked to the first family of India had concluded was gospel truth. And whatever Morarji Desai had stated in Parliament in 1978 was of no consequence, probably because Desai did not belong to that illustrious family.

Saran's boss and then Foreign Secretary JN Dixit held similar views. 'I personally do not see any useful purpose being served in re-opening the enquiry into the question of whether Netaji Subhas Chandra Bose is dead or alive', he commented in a secret note.

I wonder how these high officials reacted to the Calcutta High Court ordering a fresh enquiry in 1998, not on the basis of sentimentality, rather by rational consideration. In February 2005, a month after the sudden demise of Dixit, the National Security Advisor in the Manmohan Singh government, this (picture) news about the crach came from Taiwan.

Shyam Saran would have understood its implications better as he was the Foreign Secretary at that time. He was the man who had dismissively noted in 1992 that 'no further action need to be taken on this case' as the revelations 'of any fresh archival material on this subject from Russian or other sources may merely serve to keep alive this controversy'. What an incredible way to empathise with the fate of India's liberator!

Finally, the truth about Netaji as I have found, takes us to Faizabad. Exposing it officially will cause havoc for some time in India. Netaji's admirers would be outraged, to say the least. They will undoubtedly hold those who were in power for so long responsible for the tragic situation. But those opposed to Netaji would declare him a 'coward' for going into hiding. This situation would not have a pleasant outcome. The Congress party supporters would leave no stone unturned to save the reputation of the Nehru-Gandhi family. As anyone who witnessed what had happened in November 1984 would know better, they are hardly the practitioners of non-violence.

A threat has already been dangled in the form of the response the Home Ministry came up with when Mission Netaji sought release of certain papers in 2006. In case you did not note, to say that disclosure of certain Netaji-related records 'may lead to a serious law and order problem across the country' is actually an euphemism for violence.

Bhagwanji himself was aware of this possibility and counted it as an impediment to his surfacing, as he did not want people to suffer because of him. Asked in 1977 about any possibility of his coming out, he responded in the negative, saying that if he did that 'many innocents would die'.

Nineteen

Everything that I have come to know, deduce and conclude in the last fifteen years inexorably lead me to the mysterious Bhagwanji. The more I dwell into the most incredible angle of the Netaji mystery, the closer I get to believing that the final act of India's longest-running controversy was not played out in the salubrious surroundings of Taipei's Shongshan airport or the snowy expanse of Siberia, but in the dusty Faizabad town.

Making me hurtle even more nearer to this unimaginable realisation are inputs coming from sources I reckon credible—all pointing to the fact that the Government of India too knew of Bhagwanji's real identity and maintained continuous connection with him from 1970 or so, till 1985.

Emissaries, including UP state and Central ministers and intelligence operatives would be sent to him to pay courtesies, seek his advice on various matters and keep an eye on him. On his part, Bhagwanji was always careful. An otherwise devoted and trustworthy follower was once asked to fetch some medicine. When he returned with it, he was asked to taste it there and then. Bhagwanji even carried something which was *fully sufficient to bring eternal sleep within six seconds*. Cyanide.

I am not aware of any occasion when the powers that be were overtly threatened by the prospects of Bhagwanji's emerging. The decision to remain in hiding in national interest was Bhagwanji's own. A victim of adverse circumstances, aggravated by his political opponents who had long departed from the scene, the old man came to terms with the situation he was in.

A holy man, who had met Bhagwanji once or probably twice, pestered him to come out. When it did not work out, he made a futile attempt to compel him to emerge. Today, many of Jai Gurudev's young followers carry the misconception that he himself was Subhas Bose. Jai Gurdev died in 2012, leaving his disciples squabbling over his multi-million rupee estate. A bigger controversy happened in 1975, when Jai Gurudev announced that he'd produce Netaji at a public rally at Kanpur. Since Bhagwanji had no intention of obliging Jai Gurudev, he remained where he was. In the sprawling Phool Bagh area, standing before a swelling crowd of several thousand chanting *Netaji-Netaji* Jai Gurudev did not know what to say. He mumbled something which sounded to others as if he was claiming that he, (Jai Gurudev) himself, was Subhas Bose. Bhagwanji said Jai Gurudev was Indira's man.

The chants turned to jeers and disorderliness gave way to incidences of stone pelting. Targeted with shoes and fists, Jai Gurudev had to make a hasty retreat to safety. The farce dashed the dream-like hopes of some Rashtrapati Bhavan staffers in the crowd. They had been sent to Kanpur, just in case Netaji really showed up.

This factoid came to me only recently from one of the staffers, who had informed a person of standing in the political arena. A few years after the Kanpur incident even more remarkable things happened in full public view in New Delhi. Thirty years ago, President Neelam Sanjiva Reddy released Samar Guha's *Netaji: Dead or Alive* in March 1978 knowing well that the book carried the claim that Bose was alive at that time. On 23 January 1979, he and Prime Minister Morarji Desai unveiled Netaji's portrait in Parliament House, fulfilling the demand first made in 1947. As the choir sang *Jana Gana Mmana, Vande Maataram, and Oi Mahamanaba Asey*, Reddy looked at the portrait and said: 'Let us see him (Bose) even for one day.'

In 1983, a better-informed Morarji Desai made a rare public appearance since bidding public life goodbye in 1979 to release Samar Guha's book in Mumbai. The former Prime Minister, who surely was in the know of a thing a two, strayed a little during his speech and, according to a report in the *Indian Express*, alluded to the 'story that he (Bose) was alive and had taken *sanyas*'.

'Morarji knows that I am here', Bhagwanji had remarked once. Every word that left his lips had a ring of extraordinariness about it. Take it as you would an entry from *Ripley's Believe or not*, three Bhagwanji followers I have known for years and trusted, told me to my utter astonishment that one of the government emissaries they saw going to Bhagwanji with his head bowed down was none other than Pranab Mukherjee.

Bhagwanji praised Mukherjee for possessing a sharp memory. An elaboration of sort came on 13 August 2014, with Prime Minister Modi remarking that 'a half-an-hour talk with Mukherjee is like reading a good book'. *IBNlive.com* further reported:

> Praising the President, who pops out with dates and time of historical events and detailed information, Modi wondered 'what software his brain was made of'.

My misfortune is that the only time I had the pleasure of seeing Pranab Mukherjee in person, this veritable human computer appeared to be malfunctioning. As witness No 50 before the Justice MK Mukherjee Commission of Inquiry, I saw Witness No 48 Pranab Mukherjee fumbling on basic facts concerning the Netaji mystery.

JUSTICE M.K. MUKHERJEE COMMISSION OF INQUIRY

Proceedings dated 15th October 2001 (Eleventh – D 1)
Held at Committee Room "C" of Vigyan Bhavan Annexe,
New Delhi

October 15, 2001   Of the seven witnesses summoned for examination today, three are present. They are – Sri Pranab Mukherjee (CW 48), Sri Shali Ittaman (CW 49) and Sri Anuj Dhar (CW 50). While Sri Pranab Mukherjee has been discharged after examination and cross-

---

He entered New Delhi's Vigyan Bhawan on 15 October 2001 with nervousness writ large on his face. Why would such an eminent person of such exalted stature, unmatched experience and boundless wisdom be so anxious at such a low-key occasion no media was interested in covering?

From barely 2 meters away, I observed Pranab Mukherjee closely as the commission examined him. He answered Justice Mukherjee's questions with his face flushed, and his fingers twitching.

What Pranab Mukherjee told the commission on oath would cast a new light on what has been described in the previous chapter.

PROCEEDINGS 01

Justice Mukherjee Commission of Inquiry For inquiry into the alleged disappearance of Netaji Subhas Chandra Bose held in Committee Room "C", Vigyan Bhavan, Annexe, New Delhi.

on this the   15th   day of   October   2001

Witness No. 48

Deposition on oath/affirmation of Sri/Smt   Pranab Mukherjee
son/wife/daughter of Late Kamada Kinkar Mukherjee
residing at   13, Talkatora Road, New Delhi
                                                and
aged about   56   years

Question No. 1   : Mr. Mukherjee, please tell the Commission your full name, your father's name, your age, your address and your occupation.

Ans.   : My name is Pronab Mukherjee, father's name is late Kamada kinkar Mukherjee, my age is

'Mr Mukherjee, in 1995 you were the Minister in charge, External Affairs, Government of India?' Justice Manoj Mukherjee asked him.

'Yes', Pranab Mukherjee answered.

'In that capacity, did you deal with the issue of bringing the alleged ashes of Netaji Subhas Chandra Bose kept in the Renkoji temple to India?' the judge further asked.

On getting an affirmative response, the judge put the next query:

'Does not that necessarily mean that you were in firm conviction that Netaji was dead?'

'No', Pranab Mukherjee replied instantaneously.

It meant that it was not Pranab Mukherjee's personal conviction that Netaji had died in 1945.

Pausing a little, he elucidated this:

'At that time, the position of the Government of India was that the ashes were of Netaji.'

Therefore, what Pranab Mukherjee tried to do in 1995 was in deference to the Government of India's stand, which he, as a minister, was duty bound to follow.

More telling was his dodging of the last question put to him by Justice Mukherjee.

'Is there any documentary or other evidence within your knowledge, which are relevant to the terms of reference [assigned to this commission]?'

'Except the earlier two reports of the committee and commission as stated earlier, I have no other material.'

Considering the deep reverence he has for Netaji—evident from his bowing before his picture in 2014 as the President of India—it is inconceivable that Pranab Mukherjee's insight about Netaji's fate should be restricted to merely possessing two reports any college student can easily find in numerous public libraries.

Ergo, in my estimate, should Prime Minister Narendra Modi decides to tell the truth about Netaji, our President, being the man who knows too much, will have the choice to either act as a catalyst in bringing a closure to the Netaji mystery, or be a stumbling block. He has reached such a stage in his life that he must consider what legacy he would like to leave behind. The facts about the Bose mystery, as they have trickled out as of now, have the potential to scar Pranab Mukherjee's own name and legacy, unless he does something about it. In time.

Does all of this imply that Prime Minister Modi would also have access to official information to the effect that Bhagwanji was indeed Bose?

I think, yes.

But how can one think that way when nothing revealed by the government has touched upon the Bhagwanji angle? Not one of the known 41 files in the Prime Minister's Office is about him! In fact, all the files, in one form or the other, talk of the government's faith in the air crash theory.

It is not uncommon for official files to keep on harping on the official, rather than the true version, if the latter is an extremely secret matter. And if the truth lies within the remit of the intelligence agencies or the head of the government, it is not something that would be easily revealed in files accessible to many.

But then, it can be well argued, there are dozens of intelligence reports where Shaulmari Sadhu has been discussed, but not once has Bhagwanji been mentioned. Not even in passing!!

The best way to keep something totally secret is to pretend it doesn't even exit—I would say for an answer.

But if the authorities don't even admit to the very existence of something, how can one prove it is there?

Anything that has been kept absolutely secret by a government cannot be proven by direct evidence. One can only demonstrate the proof of its existence by circumstantial evidence and the acts of omissions.

For instance, every time a completely baseless and absurd claim was made that Netaji was in India in the guise of a holy man, the Intelligence Bureau lost no time in cross-checking it.

```
                    INTELLIGENCE BUREAU
                   (Ministry of Home Affairs)
                            ...

        Our enquiries reveal that the original name of
Sant Tulsi, who has issued pamphlets in the name of
'Veer Subhash Seva Sangh', is Ram Sunder Tiwari, xxxxxx
at present working as an Assistant Engineer in Asthapana
Khand, Okhala, New Delhi on a UP Government project.
He has recently formed 'Veer Subhash Seva Sangh' in
Allahabad, which has no following. He believes that
Nemai Chand Goswami of Varanasi is Subhash Chandra Bose.
Tiwari is known to to be a fadist and nobody takes him
seriously. Similarly, Amarnath Sharma, who has asserted
that Subhash Chandra Bose is alive, is a whimsical man
and people do not pay attention to his claims.

                                    (A. V. Karnik)
                                   Assistant Director
```

National Archives, New Delhi

And how does that square with the fact that despite there being so much going for the Bhagwanji angle, not a single record about it is forthcoming from the IB's side?!

Long before Sir Humphrey Appleby employed Beacon's truism, 'he who hath to keep it secret must keep it a secret that he hath a secret to keep' to explain the official secrecy scenario in the United Kingdom, our own Intelligence Bureau had been practicing it in letter and spirit.

Appearing before the Khosla Commission as a witness, Bhola Nath Mullik—a fragile, bespectacled man with avuncular persona—behaved as if he had been living in a cave when the whole of India was discussing the Netaji mystery. It was a curious paradox— for him to have 'Bhola', Hindi for naïve—for his surname, when he was the big daddy of spooks.

As the undisputed czar of the Indian intelligence apparatus for incredible fourteen years when the IB had not been bifurcated to form separate entity of R&AW, Mullik met Prime Minister Nehru virtually each day and was one of his closest confidants. Post-'retirement', Mullik was something of a national security adviser. He finally called it quits in September 1968. And yet, he trotted out one obvious lie after another about the IB's handling of the Netaji mystery matter.

In a brilliant flash of inquisitiveness, the commission's counsel, TR Bhasin, tried to extract from him that the IB must have looked into the gamut of issues linked to the Netaji mystery.

'Now, when you joined as Director of Intelligence Bureau in July 1950, and from there onwards, is it correct that the question of Netaji's alleged death continued to agitate public mind.'

'It did.'

'Did the Intelligence Bureau deal with this aspect?'

'No. During the entire period that I was Director of Intelligence Bureau, we were never asked to make inquiry about this aspect.'

> SHRI T.R. BHASIN: Did the Intelligence Bureau deal with this aspect?
>
> SHRI B.N. MULLICK: No. During the entire period that I was Director of Intelligence Bureau, we were never asked to make enquiry about this aspect.

Document obtained under the Right to Information

He repeated the same line when questions specifically related to the Shaulmari sadhu—who had been set up by Bhagwanji—were put to him.

'We made no inquiries about the Baba of Shaulmari. I am talking about my time', he asserted.

'You were never asked by the Government, by the late Prime Minister Pandit Nehru about Baba of Shaulmari?'

'As far as I remember, I was never asked by the late Pandit Nehru about the Baba of Shaulmari.'

> SHRI B.N. MULLICK: We made no enquiries about the Baba of Sholmari. I am talking about my time.
>
> SHRI T.R. BHASIN: Supposing if there was responsible statement made on the floor of the Parliament that Director of Intelligence has submitted report, that would be incorrect.
>
> SHRI B.N.MULLICK: In my time, it would be incorrect.

Document obtained under the Right to Information

Mullik remained stuck to his assertion, even when Forward Bloc's counsel AP Chakravarty rephrased the same question.

'And the Shaulmari ashram situation had created such a thing in Bengal and Uttar Pradesh and in other parts of India, here also, everything and did you not receive any report in these circumstances?'

'I do not remember to have received any report about the Shaulmari ashram.'

The sum and substance of Mullik's sworn testimony was that 'anything concerning the security of India would bring the Intelligence Bureau into picture'. Since neither the Bose mystery nor the Shaulmari episode had anything to do with national security, they were not looked into by the IB.

But previously Top Secret records obtained under the Right to Information by the Mission Netaji give a lie to Mullik's statements.

K Ram, Principal Private Secretary to Prime Minister Nehru, wrote a letter to Mullik on 23 May 1963. 'Please see the enclosed letter which has been addressed to the Prime Minister by Shri Ramani Ranjan Das, Secretary, Shaulmari Ashram. I should be grateful if you will kindly have suitable inquiries

made into this matter and let me have a report for the Prime Minister's information.' On 12 June 1963, Mullik sent Ram his reply, marked Top Secret. He enclosed an investigation report received from the Bengal CID, on one miscreant who had attempted to kill Saradanand.

On 7 September 1963, K Ram wrote to Mullik again. Through a Top Secret letter, he asked Mullik to throw light on the Shaulmari case, simple and straight.

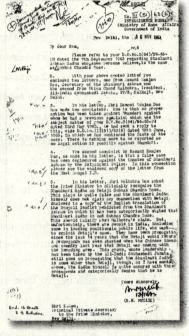

In his Top Secret response, Mullik left no room for any doubt that the IB not only inquired about Shaulmari Sadhu but also kept a tab on the Bose case, no matter what he said on oath before Khosla. Wasn't it Mullik, who had written in his 1971 book *The Chinese Betrayal* that 'the DIB should never have anything to explain. He must ever stand self-explained'?

Now, what was the need to mark this innocuous correspondence 'Top Secret'? If the Bose mystery or its offshoots like the Shaulmari affair were so irrelevant that Mullik did not feel the need to discuss them after 1950, as per his sworn statement before the commission, why make use of the highest level of security grading?

That's because, contrary to what Mullik gave out, the Bose mystery indeed was, and is, a highly volatile and hence a Top Secret issue—details about which could not be given out to anyone, courts of law and commissions included. If Mullik had told the Khosla Commission that the IB was indeed trailing Bose after his death, it would have nullified the official stand on Bose's death in 1945.

Mullik's successor in 1972, the handsome and swashbuckling Atma Jayaram, too appeared before the Khosla Commission to give a fine illustration of the principle which would dawn on Sir Appleby in 1983.

All those who want to master the art of waffling would find Jayaram's response to a basic question most useful.

'Has your department been dealing with the subject of Netaji Subhas Chandra Bose?' he was asked.

Jayaram's answer should have been an empathic 'No', as Bose was officially dead since 1945 and since the matter did not concern national security, the IB had no reason to deal with it.

But this is what this Director, Intelligence Bureau responded:

> As director of intelligence branch I can only say that the intelligence department has wide possibility and whatever the government wishes to know, we will do it but it is difficult for me to say what we do or what we do not.

```
        Shri A. Jayaram, Director of Intelligence Bureau
                took the oath.
                .....
SHRI T.R.BHASIN:  What are you now ?
SHRI JAYARAM:  I am now the Director of Intelligence Bureau.
Q:  Since when ?
A:  Since 12th November 1971.
Q:  Who was your predecessor ?
A:  Mr. M.M.L. Hooja.
Q:  Has your Department been dealing with the subject of
    Netaji Subhas Chandra Bose ?
A:  As Director of Intelligence Branch I can obly say that
                                         res
    the Intelligence Department has a wide/ponsibility and
    whatever the Government wishes to know, we will do it
    but it is difficult for me to say what we do or what
    we do not.
```

Document obtained under the Right to Information

Jayaram was merely trying not to say 'yes'.

Would anyone believe that the all-pervasive Intelligence Bureau looked the other way when even the Foreign Broadcast Information Service (FBIS)—an open source intelligence gathering component of the CIA which is now called Open Source Center—had not failed to take a small note of the claims that Bhagwanji was Bose?

The Near East South Asia report No JPRS-NEA-86-040 of FBIS made note of a February 1986 story appearing in a New Delhi newspaper that mercurial politician Raj Narain 'firmly believes that one Gumnami Baba who died at Faizabad was none other than Netaji Subhas Chandra Bose', and that he has 'sufficient proof of this fact'.

```
Mr Narain firmly believes that one Gumnami Baba who died at Faizabad was
none other than Netaji Subhas Chandra Bose, and according to a local
eveninger, the erstwhile "Hanuman" has sufficient proof of this fact. The
sad demise of the Baba, the report quoting the leader says, has "shell-
shocked" Mr Raj Narain to the extent that he had to be hospitalised.
However, the report fails to shed some light on the delayed shell-shocking
as the death of Gumnami Baba occurred in September last which has affected
Mr Narain now, some six months later. Meanwhile, Miss Lalita Bose, the niéce
```

To get into the side issue of the credibility of Raj Narian would be to
sidestep the real issue. R&AW deputy director SR Mirchandani, a former IB
official, during his examination before the Khosla Commission on 24 July
1972, brazenly accepted that the 'main job' of the Intelligence Bureau in
those days, as in the days of the British Raj, concerned 'political activities of
various parties' and 'the individual of political importance'.

```
Q:  Mr. Mirchandani, I want to understand a little about
    this Intelligence Bureau under the Ministry of Home
    Affairs as you have said.  What is the main job of
    this department which is called Intelligence Bureau?
A:  About political activities of various parties.
Q:  And about the individuals of political importance also?
A:  They would also come.  They have been included in
    the political parties.
```

Document obtained under the Right to Information

The world's oldest intelligence agency, the Intelligence Bureau, has had
such a deep penetration and wide reach across India that it is inconceivable
that blips related to Bhagwanji escaped their radar. More than one journalist
in Faizabad and around told me that the spooks snooped around in the area
after September 1985.

Virendra Mishra, a senior journalist in Ayodhya, recounted his
astounding experience, which has come on record before the Allahabad
High Court. Intrigued by the strange holy man, in 1979 Mishra wrote to
Faizabad Superintendent of Police (SP) in his gopniya (secret) letter, that
there was 'something suspicious about Gurudev Swami' [Bhagwanji]. 'Some
people say Babaji is a CIA agent. He has a transmitter and he sends messages'
he wrote, adding that others are of the view that 'Babaji is Subhas Chandra
Bose and wants to remain in hiding'.

Gyaneshwar Jha, the then SP, took some men along and his jeep arrived
at Bhagwanji's place in Ayodhya. He stomped inside with the usual cop-like
swagger. When he emerged after a while, he looked panicky and was on the
verge of breaking down. Quietly he gestured his men to pull out. The next
day his transfer orders were on his table.

Beat constables are usually the best source of information about an area.
Mohammed Mobin, a beat constable at Basti, told me how men with certain
air of importance about them would emerge from their cars and under cover
of darkness, walk towards the dilapidated house where Bhagwanji lived in
the late 1960s and early '70s.

VN Arora, part of the NIP team that investigate the matter in 1985-86, narrated how his only chance to meet the living Bhagwanji was thwarted by an IB officer. 'You are an educated person; why are you wasting time over that baba?' the officer told him. Arora rues till date for believing him.

The Faizabad police inquiry report of 1985 about Bhagwanji states that when he 'was in Basti, he had become a matter of inquiry and it is reported that some central intelligence agency had conducted a thorough enquiry about him'.

So where are the reports of the enquiry by this central intelligence agency (IB)?

The reports must be there, but their very existence is denied for the simple reason that acceptance would lead to the removal of the pall of secrecy from India's best kept secret.

Do I have any proof, even indirect, to substantiate my claim about the existence of such ultra secret information about Subhas Bose with our government?

To paraphrase former US Defense Secretary Donald Rumsfeld, information concerning Netaji available with the Government of India can be divided into three broad categories. The first is of 'known knowns'. There are records we know exist for sure. The records in the National Archives fall into this category.

We also know that there are records falling into the 'known unknown' category. For instance, we know that there 29 classified files with the Ministry of External Affairs regarding Netaji, but we know not what are their contents.

The last and most important of such category of records is that of 'unknown unknowns'—the ones whose every existence is unknown to us.

But just because we do not know of something doesn't mean it's not there. Every day, thousands of reports land up at the desk of Director, IB. Not one of them become known to even the best reporters in the city. So do we take it that those reports aren't there? The absence of evidence is not the evidence of absence, so goes a legal phrase.

An input available to me, if proven true in the course of time, would end the Bose mystery as most people understand it. The input is: That available with the government (in the days of Atal Bihari Vajpayee) was a minute of discussion between Prime Minister Indira Gandhi and Subhas Chandra Bose.

But how can that be possible, you will say. How can a government in a democracy, where the rule of law is supreme, keep such a earth-shattering piece of information secret?

Records are nothing, governments can even deny the existence of projects, departments and even massive organisations. In Britain, the home of democracy, the formal acceptance that MI6 actually existed came more than eight decades after it was formed. Our government did not accept that an entity such as R&AW existed quite some time after it was formed. On 18 October 2013, *The Guardian* reported the discovery of a secret archive at a high-security government communications centre in Buckinghamshire, north of London. 'Foreign Office has unlawfully hoarded more than a million files of historic documents that should have been declassified and handed over to the National Archives', the paper said.

If disclosure of something is not going to serve the interest of a nation—democratic or otherwise—its rulers will never disclose or accept it. Unless there's some sort of pressure working on them to make a revelation.

As reported by the BBC, Japan revealed in March 2010 that for forty years, it had kept a lid on the very 'existence of a secret Cold War deal, allowing the transit of nuclear-armed US vessels through its ports'. The hi-voltage disclosure—Japan is the only nation to have suffered a nuclear Holocaust—came after decades of downright denials by officials.

Not that such things don't happen in the land of Gandhi and Nehru. Let us digress a little and go back to the days, when we are told, that Indians were morally far more superior then they are today. In 1963, US President John F Kennedy revealed to Sudhir Ghose, an eminent Gandhian and ambassador-at-large for Indian interests since pre-independence days, that the Chinese attack of the previous year had made Prime Minister Nehru beseech the US for military support. Two years later, on 15 March 1965, Ghose stated during his speech in the Rajya Sabha that 'the father of nonalignment asked for American air protection' and the US President 'did respond and order one of the American aircraft carriers to proceed to the Bay of Bengal'.

Though it was aimed at reminding the nation that Nehru gave precedence to national interest over the principles he talked about, Ghose's statement created a furor. Loyal Congress MPs mauled Ghose for making such an outrageous allegation to sully the memory of the late Prime Minister. Backed by the Left MPs, they sought clarification from the Prime Minister. Lal Bahadur Shastri summoned Ghose to his chamber. In the presence of Home Minister Gulzari Lal Nanda and Foreign Secretary C S Jha, Shastri told Ghose that there was nothing on record to suggest that Nehru had ever made such a request to Kennedy.

Since Ghose had heard it straight from Kennedy, he stood his ground and requested Shastriji to ascertain the facts from the US Ambassador in

New Delhi before making a statement in Parliament. He said if he was proven wrong, he would apologise publicly. A day before the PM was to make a statement in Parliament, Ghose learnt from his American sources that Jha had been told by the embassy that the US Government did have the letters from Nehru and the same could be produced if the Government of India desired it.

Thereafter, Ghose marched into the PM's office to see Shastri. Now the PM was unwilling to meet him, because he had by then discovered that the copies of Nehru's letters were indeed available with the government somewhere.

The PM went on to state in Parliament that Nehru did not ask for an American aircraft carrier. Shastri was playing with words and Ghose was not willing to play ball. Having lost face, he shot off a personal letter to Shastri, telling him that his clarification made no difference to the substance of his statement that India had sought military support from the US. Ghose repeated that Nehru's letter to Kennedy, personally delivered by Ambassador BK Nehru, had sought '16 squadrons of fighting aircraft', which was much more than a carrier.

In his reply, Shastri—whose name is a byword for honesty in present-day India—asked Ghose to let the matter rest. Ghose would have perhaps let that be, but he was publicly humiliated when the US State Department backed Prime Minister Shastri's statement that Nehru did not ask for an American aircraft carrier, leaving out the other vital details. Ghosh then used his formidable connections and goodwill with the US lawmakers, and managed to corner Secretary of State Dean Rusk during a public hearing in the Senate in 1966. Rusk was evasive at first and then said it was not proper for him to discuss correspondences between the two heads of governments.

Ghosh averred in his 1967 book, *Gandhi's Emissary,* that Rusk's cross-examination in the US Senate 'clearly established that India did ask for air protection and the US did respond to the request'.

It was not until recently—long after Ghose's death—that his version finally prevailed. On 15 November 2010, the *Indian Express* ran a story titled, 'JN to JFK, "Eyes Only"' by veteran journalist Inder Malhotra, laying bare the contents of Nehru's letter upon their declassification by the US government.

Nehru had asked for a 'minimum of 12 squadrons of supersonic all-weather fighters' and a 'modern radar cover' and also support of US air force personnel 'to man these fighters and radar installations while our personnel are being trained'. The letters had indeed been secretly and personally delivered by the Indian Ambassador in Washington to President Kennedy.

RK Nehru, the ambassador and the Prime Minister's cousin, never discussed
their contents with anyone but told Inder Malhotra, a reputed biographer of
Indira Gandhi who counted for friends luminaries as Rameshwar Nath Kao,
that he had 'locked them up in a safe that only the ambassador could open'.

Within governments the world over, including India, information of
grave sensitivity is secured separately from the other Top Secret records. In
America, conspiracy theorists think of this class of information as falling in
the 'Above Top Secret' category. In the Central Intelligence Agency the term
used is Sensitive Compartmented Information (SCI)—information which is
so sensitive that it requires special, separate handling than other Top Secret
material.

In India, such information is usually entrusted to the Officers on Special
Duty, kept under the personal custody of ministers and other top officials,
placed in secretive 'T branch' or handed over to intelligence agencies for
safekeeping. The advantage with the intelligence agencies is that they can
work beyond the periphery of law. IB's own secret archive, located outside
New Delhi, is said to be holding a fabulous collection, a veritable Aladdin's
Cave for researchers like me. Every time former IB chief and National
Security Advisor MK Narayanan teased people with his "I have a file on
you" jibe, he was unknowingly paying a compliment to the richness of the
documentation in the possession of India's spy agencies.

The most secret records of all are held directly by the Prime Minister,
who is not answerable to any court of law as a person. The records produced
before a court or commission usually come from the Prime Minister's Office
in South Block, which has something like 30,000 classified files. Only the
PM himself knows what is there in his personal safe at his residence, etc.
National interest necessitates this sort of secrecy because there have been
instances when even the minister's and top officials have betrayed India's
secrets to other nations.

So, are there any Netaji-related records with the Prime Minister of
India falling into the Sensitive Compartmented Information or the so-called
Above Top Secret category?

In November 2014, the Prime Minister's Office turned down my request
made in July that year to place my RTI query regarding Bose's fate before
Prime Minister Narendra Modi. 'There is no provision under the [RTI] act
to place the application before the Hon'ble Prime Minister', was the blank
answer I received.

More pertinently, I wanted to know whether or not there is 'any
information available to the Prime Minister showing that Subhas Chandra

Bose was alive or was possibly alive long after his reported death in August 1945'. I also requested the PMO to 'confirm whether or not there are matters so secret that they are known only to the Prime Minister of India. And if yes, within the ambit of such ultra-secret matters and records/information related to them, is there any information concerning the survival of Subhas Bose long after his reported death?'

The PMO responded: 'As per records, no such information is available.'

The PMO told me a lie. The phrase 'matters so secret that they are known only to the Prime Minister' used by me in my RTI application had originated from an official 2004 speech of Prime Minister Atal Bihari Vajpayee. According to Prime Minister Vajpayee, there indeed

By Speed Post A.D.
Right to Information

PRIME MINISTER'S OFFICE

South Block
New Delhi - 110 011
No. RTI/4039/2014-PMR   Dated: 25 November-2014

To

Shri Anuj Dhar,

New Delhi – 110 01

Subject: Application under the Right to Information Act, 2005

Sir,

In continuation of this office's letter of even no. dated 13.8.2014, in response to your application 11.7.2014, on the subject mentioned above, it is stated that office has informed in respect of point nos. 1&2 that "as per records, no such information is available". As regards point no. 3, the information sought is exempted under section 8(1)(a). read with 8(2) of the RTI Act, 2005 as disclosure of the class of information may be prejudicially affect relation with foreign State and also there does not seem any larger public interest in the matter. In respect of point no. 4, it is stated that two files, i.e. Nos. 23(11)/56-57-PM-NGO and T-2(64)/78-PM-NGO, have been declassified and sent to NAI. Also, there is no provision under Act to place the application before Hon'ble Prime Minister.

2. For the purpose of Section 19 of the Right to Information Act, 2005, Shri Krishan Kumar, Director is the appellate authority in respect of this office.

Yours faithfully,

(P.K. Sharma)
Under Secretary and
Central Public Information Officer
☎ : 2338 6447

are matters so secret that they are known only to the Prime Minister of our country. It is his duty, when he hands charge to his successor, to inform the latter of these matters ...Matters that spell life or death for India.

On 25 December 2004, Vajpayee, no longer Prime Minister, gave another illustration. A report in *The Telegraph*, and in other newspapers, quoted him crediting PV Narasimha Rao as the 'true father' of India's nuclear programme.

An emotional Vajpayee said when he assumed the Prime Minister's office in 1996 (the 13-day stint), he received a paper from his predecessor urging him to continue the country's nuclear programme. 'Rao had asked me not to make it public; but today when he is dead and gone, I wish to set records straight'. In typical Vajpayee fashion, the former Prime Minister went on: 'Rao told me that the bomb is ready. I exploded it. I did not miss the opportunity.'

The holy grail of India's longest running controversy lies within the remit of the Indian version of Above Top Secret information, held or controlled by our Prime Minister. It is for this reason why successive prime ministers have tried not to wade into the Netaji mystery, even though their office holds so many files about it, and many of the incumbents themselves claimed to be Netaji's admirers. Making the Ministry of Home Affairs the nodal ministry in the Subhas Chandra Bose disappearance was a stratagem. Mission Netaji has endeavoured to establish the centrality of the Prime Minister over this matter.

All said, if Bhagwanji was Netaji and the official files record that fact, why can't Modi go public with it? What would he have to lose even if all that the previous chapter says is true? On the contrary, he and BJP would only gain for ending, so to speak, the mystery that has gnawed at the conscious of the nation for decades!

I agree. But things are complicated nevertheless. Recall the *Congressification* of files argument in the previous chapter. It is my understanding that while the 'Above Top Secret' files accept that Bhagwanji was Bose, perhaps they also accept that he had served the nation behind the screen. But, at the same time, since the story has been told from the government (read Congress party's) point of view, it has been tweaked to give Bhagwanji a bad name.

Key problem area in the official narrative, in my understanding, is the branding of Bhagwanji a traitor. The records accuse him of having a hand in the Chinese assault on India in 1962.

While I obviously can't show you anything from such Above Top Secret records in support of this charge, I can make a point, using a document from the time of Nehru, when the government's approach towards Netaji was set.

A relevant portion from BN Mullik's November 1963 Top Secret report, discussed on page no 270, is zoomed here for your perusal.

```
unfortunately, there are people in India, including
some in leading positions in public life, who want
to exploit Netaji's name. They have been propagatir
since the last 14 years that the Netaji would return
A propaganda was even started when the Chinese invad
our country last year that Netaji was coming with
the invading army. This group, whose leadership
```

As any junior-level intelligence officer can tell, the IB Director's personally signed notes like this one are distilled from heaps of material. So, for this one document, there must be several reports detailing each and every aspect mentioned in it. The IB must have several reports regarding the 'propaganda' during the Chinese attack that 'Netaji was coming with the invading army'.

While Bhagwanji himself claimed that he covertly operated alongside the Soviets, and through them with the Chinese over matters of international concern, nothing done by him brought any harm to India. Bhagwanji said he always kept Indian interests on top of his priorities. His scale of time concerning the good of India spanned not just the time he lived in, but also that was to come.

Bhagwanji did discuss China a lot. His perspective and approach was hundred per cent pro-India. He vehemently denied a conspiracy theory propounded in the booklet *Liu Po-Cheng or Netaji* (1956) by Shiv Prasad Nag that Subhas Chandra Bose was in the guise of Chinese marshal Liu Bocheng. *I never led in those thrice-cursed infernal Han lands!!! It is blasphemous—even to dream that.*

Bhagwanji's take on the 1962 war at that very time was not much different to what security experts came to hold much later on. In fact, his analysis carried so much of foresight and incisiveness, which even BN Mullik might not have managed back then:

> *Take it from me, this aggression is the greatest blessing Mother India could invoke for her children. …war has some purpose that is beyond the ambit of human reason, despite palpable unreasonableness as a way of settling human issues. That purpose may be corrective to greater evil, as a cleansing of the spirit of a people and an age from corruption. Errors in the domestic sphere can be condoned and remedied. There is room for trial and error in home politics. But in external sphere costly mistakes cannot be tolerated.*

What Modi governments needs to do is, factor in Bhagwanji's side of the story, not merely go by records created during regimes that where deeply hostile towards him. The disclosure of the truth is going to serve the national interest, and that of the BJP and the Sangh Parivar. Because in his 'second' life, Bhagwanji had embraced a world view which was quite close to the RSS. For all their admiration for Gandhiji and Sardar Patel, the Sangh Parivar hasn't ditched Guru Golwalkar, whose link to Bhagwanji is a stark reality. KS Sudarshan, the recently-deceased fifth Sarsanghachalak, personally vouched that the handwriting on the letter discovered at Bhagwanji's residence was indeed of Golwalkar's. He did his own inquiry and made repeated public statements that he was convinced that Bhagwanji was Netaji.

Bhagwanji's claims about the 1971 war, if true, would take the wind out of the sails of Congress party's biggest triumph on the external affairs front—the creation of Bangladesh.

To cite the fear of hurting relations with foreign nations is an excuse for not telling the truth about Netaji. It is an artifice devised to keep the courts of law from making an intervention. That's because, in ordinary circumstances, the judges are not going to arrogate to themselves the power to overrule government's decisions concerning the foreign affairs of India.

Foreign relations with no country are going to get harmed even if all that Bhagwanji said was true in view of period of time that has lapsed. For instance, nothing that happened during the Vietnam war era has a bearing on India's robust ties with the US at the moment. We live in a different world. The only sensitivity now left in the Netaji matter is on the home front.

On the flip side, the Sangh Parivar, including the BJP, must understand that the Modi government's not revealing the truth about Subhas Chandra Bose would severely undermine their 'nationalistic' credentials. You cannot talk of the need for settling the truth about Netaji or Syama Prasad Mukherjee before elections, and forget about it when you are in power. I did not vote for Modi to see him chant Gandhiji's name all the time. If I wanted that Congress party was doing a fantastic job. Come to think of it, *swachchata* [cleanliness] was *not* one of Gandhi's famous Eleven Vows. *Satya* or truth surely was. And truth, Gandhiji would say, was above God.

When the next General Elections come around, I would vote for Modi even if the BJP is going to renege on its promise about Netaji. But that vote would be for all the other good things Modi is doing for India. No more would I be swayed by the talk of nationalism by the Sangh Parivar.

I hope it doesn't come to that. I do hope that the feeler Prime Minister Modi and BJP president Amit Shah are giving out in private meetings that 'we shall do it at the right time' will turn true in the near future.

And with that Mission Netaji would stand accomplished.

#DeclassifyNetajiFiles